An Easy Course in Using the HP 17BII

by Chris Coffin
and Dan Coffin
Illustrations by Robert L. Bloch

Grapevine Publications, Inc.
P.O. Box 2449
Corvallis, Oregon   97339-2449

Acknowledgments

We extend our thanks once again to Hewlett-Packard for their top-quality products and documentation.

Printed in the United States of America
ISBN 0-931011-20-5

First Printing – March, 1993

CONTENTS

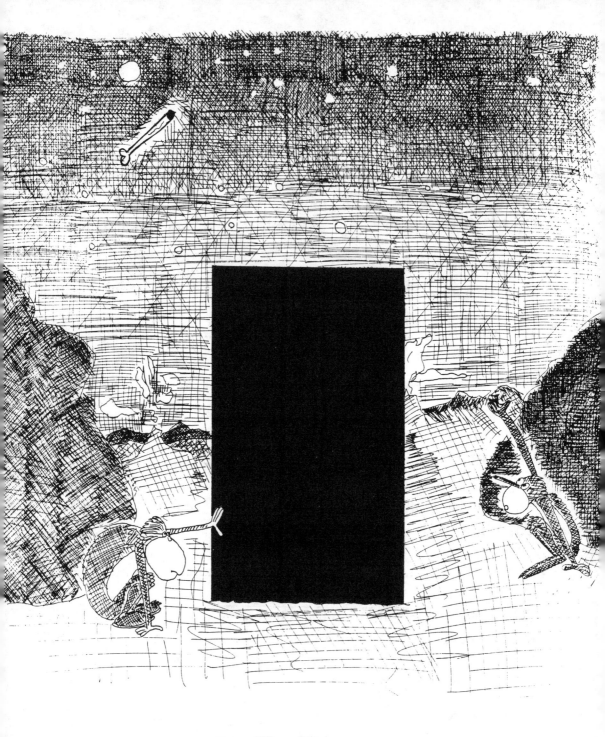

0. TO BEGIN

Read This First!

Time is an investment. If you spend it wisely, it will give you
Enormous returns.

Invest your time in this book.

It covers exactly what you need to know to use your HP 17BII effectively
—and quickly. If you have time to use this machine, you have time to
learn it first (it doesn't take that long). And you've already finished the
toughest part of this Course—getting started—so just keep going.

In this book, you'll see many applications in financial analysis. But as
you read, keep in mind that the goal here is not just to memorize a set
of keystrokes and formulas. You're also going to get an understanding
of the fundamental *principles,* so that whenever you encounter a new
problem, you'll be able to analyze it and solve it confidently. That skill
is the most valuable asset of all.

1. Looking Under the Hood

What's In This Machine?

Your HP 17Bɪɪ is a loyal and friendly calculator engine—congratulations on a great choice! It represents a new generation of calculators, with more power and flexibility than ever before. It can do all sorts of things for you, from analyzing investments to remembering appointments to customizing formulas.

You simply need to tell it what to do.... And that brings up the next question....

What's Not In This Machine?

As sophisticated as technology is nowadays, it still hasn't progressed to the point where the machine can speak to you in your own language. For now, you must "speak" *its* "language," translating your everyday calculation problems into forms it can understand.

Of course, this means you must define each problem correctly for yourself first (often the hardest part). Don't overlook that very important step. But once you've set a problem up so that *you* understand it clearly, it's quite simple to translate it for your HP 17Bɪɪ. In fact, learning to operate it is a lot like learning to drive a car: It all seems strange at first, but after some training and practice, you'll be doing things quite automatically—without even thinking much about them.

That training and practice is what this book is going to give you.

What's In This Book?

This book is indeed your Drivers' School for the HP 17Bɪɪ. After learning about your machine's controls and buttons, you'll take it through the Course for extensive "road training." There you'll encounter lots of explanations, diagrams, quizzes and answers. Once you complete those, you'll be ready to drive anywhere your vehicle can go (and that's a lot of places).

What makes the Course Easy is the fact that you can choose your own speed and route. So don't worry about how fast you're moving. It's not a race; you can go over the same stretch of road again and again until you're comfortable with it. You'll also get some rest areas to stop and review where you've been, and some alternate "routes," in case you already know certain things and don't need to practice them.

What's Not In This Book?

You won't find equal time given to everything, because some things just don't need as much explanation. Anyway, if you want a complete description of everything, you already have it right there in your Owner's Manual. That's what it's there for—as a reference manual to let you conveniently look up keys, functions, and quick examples.

But this book is *not* a reference manual. It's an entirely different approach, a tutorial approach meant to be taken as presented. So start here and "stay on the road!" Then, when you finish, a good reference source like the Owner's Manual will be much clearer and more useful to you.

A Few Words about the Example Problems

You may be more interested in, say, real estate lending than in leasing, or in securities rather than personal finance. Well, there are example problems in each of these areas in this Course. But do yourself a favor: Don't skip over the ones that aren't in your favorite area.

"Why not?"

Because you're going to find that most financial problem-solving boils down to the same basic concepts—just expressed in different words. There are often far more differences in the *terminology* of the various financial disciplines than in their underlying calculations.

So don't skip over the problems that don't seem exactly fitted to your most immediate everyday work. That would be cheating yourself out of part of your investment. Every financial problem has something to teach you about the Time Value of Money, and the more practice you get with it, the more fluent you'll become in its language, and the more skilled you'll soon be in every area of financial problem-solving.

2. IN THE DRIVER'S SEAT

Turning the Key

You probably know how powerful the HP 17BⅡ is, so here's the first question that you probably want to ask.

Question: "Is it complicated to use?"   Answer: Not at all.

The [ON] Button

Turn the machine on. The [ON] button (also marked [CLR]) is at the lower left of the keyboard.

The [OFF] Button

Now turn it off, by pressing ▇[OFF]. That is, press the gold ▇ key, then the [ON]/[CLR] key.

The gold ▇ key is the "shift" key, which, like a shift key on a typewriter, you must press first in order to perform any of the functions printed (in gold) *above* the other keys. The only difference between the ▇ key and a standard typewriter shift key is that you don't need to hold down the ▇ key while you then press another key.

(If you're already familiar with the keyboard and the display, you can skip ahead now to page 21.)

A Good First Setting

At this point, there's no telling what might be in the display. So to be sure you're starting from the same point as this Course, you're going to do a few preparatory keystrokes.

Don't worry if you don't understand these yet—you will soon. But you can't very well learn until you get the machine ready to learn with. So turn your machine on, and...

Do This: Press the gold ■ key, then the [EXIT] key. Now press ■, then the [INPUT] key.

Next, press the [DSP] key, then *the upper-left* ⌃ *key* (just under the display), then [2] and [INPUT].

Finally, press ■, then the [÷] key.

If you've done everything right, the machine will probably beep, and then you'll see this:

(If this doesn't work the first time, just try it all again.)

The Display

Even when things are going wrong, the display usually tries to tell you what's going on. When in doubt, look at the display for clues.

(If you already know all about the display, what it's telling you and how to adjust it, then skip ahead now to page 19).

The Viewing Angle

Can you see and read the display comfortably? It's hard to read if it's aimed at the wrong angle, but you can adjust that angle.

Try It: With the machine on, press *and hold down* the ON/CLR key. Then press and hold the + or the − key and watch how the viewing angle varies. Play around with it until you find a comfortable angle.

Messages and How to Clear Them

The ERROR: ÷0 is a good example of a *message*—usually telling you of an error or asking you for something. A message just temporarily covers part of the display. To get rid of it, simply press the ◄ key.

Do that now (◄).

The Calculator Line

Now your display should look like this:

The display has two full lines. For numbers (and messages), it usually uses the upper line.

Try This: Key in a number—say, 123.45. Press $\boxed{1}\boxed{2}\boxed{3}\boxed{\cdot}\boxed{4}\boxed{5}\boxed{\text{INPUT}}$. See how the number keys work? When you're doing calculations, the upper line is shows the arithmetic, so it's called the *Calculator Line*.

The Menu Line

The lower line is the *Menu Line*. Each of the selections on the Menu Line is associated with the ⌃ key directly beneath it. Whenever you want to make a menu selection, you simply press its ⌃ key.

The Menu Line is the best way to tell "where" your calculator is. For example, the menu you're seeing this right now (above) is the *MAIN Menu*, the "home base" starting point. (After all, it only makes sense to start a "Driver's Course" from home.)

The Keyboard

Now look at the keys (if you already know the basics of the keyboards, go ahead and jump now to page 21).

The Arithmetic Keys

Look first at the lower five rows of keys on the keyboard. This is where you'll find the keys for your arithmetic and other number-oriented operations. The digit and math keys are here, as are (ON)/(CLR) and (◄), which you've seen already.

The Other Keys

Look next at the upper two rows of keys. These keys are mostly for moving and selecting the numbers and operations in your HP 17Bɪɪ. Also, as you'll soon see, you can use them to spell out words and names, very much like a typewriter.

And of course, you've already learned that many keys have second ("shifted") meanings too—again, just like a typewriter.

Take a closer look now at the "shift" key....

The ■ Key

As you know, the gold key on the keyboard is the shift key (shown here as ■). It's no coincidence that each key's "shifted" meaning is printed in <u>gold</u> right above it.

Try This: Press the ■ (shift) key. What happens? The ⤴ *annunciator* appears (a little signal up there in the *Annunciator Area*), telling you that the next key you press will produce its *gold* operation.

Press ■ again. The ⤴ disappears. ■ is a *toggle* key, because it alternates its meaning.

Keep these things in mind about the shift key:

Unlike a typewriter, you don't hold it down while pressing the key you're "shifting." Just press and release the ■ key, then press the key you want. The ⤴ will always tell you when the ■ is in effect.

But the ⤴ is cancelled *after every use;* you need to re-press the ■ for every gold character you want. That is, ■ is *not* a "Caps Lock" key.

Pop Quiz

This is just a quick little stop-and-check point. Things move pretty slowly here at the beginning, but that doesn't last very long. Be sure you know these things before you go on.

The answers are on the next page, but don't look until you need to. Along with those answers, you'll find page numbers for re-reading, just in case. Take your time—who cares if you re-read? It's *your* Course.

1.   What's a toggle key? Name one such key.

2.   How many lines does the display have? How are they used?

3.   What's an annunciator?

4.   What's a message? How do you get rid of it?

5.   What will happen to your calculator if you forget to turn it off before leaving for Nepal?

Pop Answers

1. A toggle key is like a light switch: hit it once to turn something on; hit it again to turn it off. ■ is one such key (see page 20 for review).

2. The display has two lines. The upper line is called the Calculator Line, because it shows you numbers (and messages, sometimes). The lower line is the Menu Line, which tells you your current calculation choices (to review all this, see pages 17-18).

3. An annunciator is a little signal, a status indicator that appears in the Annunciator area, above the Calculator Line, to keep you informed of the current "doings" of the machine.

   You generally can't and shouldn't do anything about it—just understand what it means. For example, the shift annunciator, ⭢, means that any key with a gold operation written above it will now produce that operation if pressed (page 20).

4. A message is a phrase or question that appears temporarily *in front of* the Calculator Line, to notify you of an error or ask you to do something. When you want a message to go away, just press ⬅ (page 17).

5. After about 10 minutes, it will turn itself off. Then, when you come back and turn it on, its display (and memory) will be the same as when you left—so don't lose any sleep over it.

3. LEARNING TO DRIVE

Warming Up the Arithmetic Engine

Basics first:

Arithmetic truly is the "engine" of any calculator. No matter how else you use your HP 17Bii, it should certainly be able to add 2+2.

(At this point, if you're already very comfortable with doing arithmetic—including percentages, negative numbers, and display settings on your HP 17Bii—then feel free to jump to page 46.)

Ready to "crunch" a few numbers, then?

As you know, most arithmetic happens on the Calculator Line (the upper display line). So turn your machine on (if it's not on already) and look at that line....

Clear For Departure?

You're starting with some numbers already in the display. Do you need to clear anything before starting a new calculation?

Try It: Press ②⑤ ■ √x̄ and see the result: **5.00**
That **123.45** didn't mess up anything, did it?

Again: What if you now want to find $\sqrt{495,616}$? Do you need to clear away that **5.00** first?

Nope: Full speed ahead: ④⑨⑤⑥①⑥ ■ √x̄, (ans.: **704.00**). The **5.00** was just "bumped" out of your way.

Anytime you finish a calculation, the machine knows it. And it will automatically "bump" that result up out of your way when you begin the next calculation. You don't need to clear anything!

You don't need to clear the display if you've just <u>completed</u> a calculation.

OK ?

OK, But: What if you decide to scrap a calculation midway—when it's *not* complete?

Suppose you're trying to find $\sqrt{495,616}$, as you did on the previous page, but you mistakenly key in 496561... and right then you discover your goof. How do you fix it?

Two Ways:

#1: To back the wrong digits out, just use the ⬅ key. It's a simple backspace key, so...

First, back out the wrong digits: ⬅⬅⬅⬅.

Now key them in correctly: ⑤⑥①⑥...
...and finish the problem: ■√x̄

Or, #2: To simply start over, you can clear the entire Calculator Line in one "swell foop:" Press CLR (lower left corner).

Now that you know how to clear things if necessary, you're ready to start "driving around...."

How Many Digits Do You Have?

As you begin, notice that the display is showing exactly two digits past the decimal point on every number. Since the HP 17Bɪɪ is a financially-oriented calculator, this simply makes good "cents."

But is this the best precision you can get?

Not by a long shot.

In fact, every number has 12 digits, *no matter how many you can see at the moment*. For example, that 704.00 you just computed is really

704.000000000.

(Count 'em—there should be a total of 12 digits.)

You just aren't allowed to see beyond those first two zeros right now.

Ah, but...

Notice This: Key in ②①⓪·⑨⑧⑦⑥⑤④③②①, then press (INPUT) (the (INPUT) key simply tells the machine that you've finished keying in a number).

Here's what you'll see: **210.99**

"What gives? Why did the number change?"

It didn't change. The calculator merely changed its *presentation* to you.

The entire 210.987654321 is still in the machine, but the display has been instructed to show you only the first 2 decimal places, rounded like this, to represent the number as accurately as possible.

Therefore the display rounds the number 210.987... *up* to 210.99. But if the 7 had been a 4 or smaller, the number would have been rounded *down* to 210.98.

Again, the point of all this is: It's the display doing the editing—for your eyes only. *Your machine will always do all your arithmetic with 12 digits in each number.*

How Many Digits Do You See?

Here's how your display probably looks right now:

```
210.99
FIN  BUS  SUM  TIME SOLVE
```

Now, how do you tell the display to *change* its "editing policy?" What if you want to see 4 decimal places rather than 2?

Say the Word: Press the [DSP] key. Here's what you'll see:

```
SELECT DISPLAY FORMAT
FIX  ALL   .    ,
```

When in doubt, look at the display for clues as to what to do: You want to FIX the number of decimal places at four. So press the [⌃] key under  **FIX**,

Now you get another set of directions:

```
TYPE #DIGITS (0-11);
PRESS [INPUT]
```

You want 4 digits past the decimal point, so press [4][INPUT].... Voilá.

Your display now shows this:

```
210.9877
FIN   BUS   SUM  TIME SOLVE
```

Just For Laughs: Set your display to show you ALL the decimal places that aren't merely trailing zeros.

Solution: Press (DSP), then ▓ALL▓. Here's the result:

```
210.987654321
FIN   BUS   SUM  TIME SOLVE
```

Now you see ALL decimal places except any unnecessary trailing zeroes. The 210.9877 reveals its true identity.

(Now go back to dollars and cents format, by FIXing 2 decimal places. You know how, right?)

Simple Arithmetic: A Matter of Choice

At this point, you have a choice to make. As you probably know, the HP 17BII offers you two different ways to do arithmetic.

Do This: Press ■(MODES). Among other menu items, you'll see these two choices: **ALG** and **RPN**.

Try each one: First, press **ALG** (notice how your display then echoes your choice: ALGEBRAIC MODE).

ALGebraic arithmetic uses the (=) key. For example, to add 2 and 3, you would press (2)(+)(3)(=) (do it now).... As you can see, this method imitates the way in which you might *say* the problem to yourself: "Two plus three equals..."

Now try the other method: Press ■(MODES)(RPN) (your display now echoes this choice: RPN MODE).

RPN stands for Reverse Polish Notation, so-named for the Polish mathematician who developed the efficient logic it uses. In this "reverse" method of arithmetic, you give the operation *last,* thus eliminating the need for an (=) key.

To add 2 and 3, for example, press (2)(ENTER)(3)(+) (in RPN mode, the (=) key acts as the (ENTER) key).

So, why the choice—and which way is best for you?

Long ago, HP calculators adopted the less conventional RPN style of calculation, because it's simply more efficient (for series of calculations it requires fewer keystrokes than the ALGebraic method—and no parentheses). So most users who took the time to learn RPN soon "swore by it" and became loyal to HP calculators as a result.

However, many other persons prefer to do arithmetic in the "left-to-right" ALGebraic method. And since, for a long time, HP built only RPN calculators, these persons missed out on the many other great features of HP machines.

Then, when HP *did* build some ALGebraic machines (as part of its new generation of calculators), the situation became reversed: RPN users began to wish that *they* could enjoy the latest technology and features —but without having to switch from their beloved RPN.

Well, you know the rest of the story: HP is now offering a choice within the same machine—so you don't have to "un-learn" the method of arithmetic you're now using. It's that simple.

So choose the way that's easiest for you (press ▇ MODES), then either ALG or RPN)....

‒ ‒ ‒ ‒ ‒ ‒ ‒ ‒ ‒ ‒ ‒ ‒ ‒ ‒ ‒

...And then, once you've made your choice:

If you chose RPN , go now to page 40; otherwise, just turn the page....

Arithmetic with the ⬛ Key (ALGebraic Mode)

This method of arithmetic doesn't take much practice to learn. The basic rule of thumb is: "saying it = doing it."

Here's a good set of examples (and remember that you can use the ⬅ or [CLR] keys to back out or clear any mistakes):

Example: Calculate $342 - 173 + 13$

Solution: Press ③④②⊖①⑦③⊕①③⊜   Answer: 182.00

See? You just press the keys just as you would say the problem to yourself—left to right. And as you proceed, you automatically get intermediate results (do the problem again and watch what happens after you press the ⊕ key). Then the ⊜ key gives your final result.

Example: Find $101.00 - 47.50 \times 2$

Solution: Press ①⓪①⊖④⑦・⑤⊗②⊜   Answer: 107.00

This left-to-right rule works even when you *mix* multiplication (and/or division) with addition (and/or subtraction)! And notice that you don't need to key in any trailing zeroes (i.e. 101.00 is just 101).

Example: What's $342 - (173 + 13)$?

Solution: Press ③④②⊟⟮⟮①⑦③⊞①③⟯⟯⊜ Answer: 156.00

If parentheses appear in the written problem, you use them in your calculator, too. And notice how ⟨173+13 changes to 186.00 when you close the parentheses.

Example: Calculate $\dfrac{101.00 - (47.50 \times 2)}{64 - \left(25 \times \frac{3}{4}\right)}$

Solution: ①⓪①⊟⟮⟮④⑦•⑤⊠②⟯⊟
⟮⟮⑥④⊟⟮⟮②⑤⊠⟮⟮③⊟④⊜

Answer: 0.13 (Reminder: This is just the first two decimal places, with the second digit rounded. To see more digits, you know how to adjust the display, right?)

Notice that the keystrokes include an extra set of parentheses (around the entire denominator of the problem). After all, that's what is meant by that big horizontal line between the numerator and denominator.

Notice also that at the very end, you don't actually need to close a parenthetical expression with the right parenthesis. The ⊜ key says that you're finished, so the calculator closes all the open parentheses for you.

Changing the Sign of a Number

Try This: Find 34 × (–19)

Solution: Press ③④⊗⊖①⑨⊜   <u>Answer:</u> `-646.00`

This is the simplest way to key in a negative number. And again, you do it just as you say it: "34 times negative 19 equals..." (the parentheses in the problem statement are simply for clarification—they're optional).

But there's another way to do it, also.

Like This: Suppose now that you want to change that `-646.00` into `646.00`.

Solution: Press the ⊞⁄⊟ key.

That's the "change sign" key. It changes the sign of the number you're working on. Notice that this ⊞⁄⊟ key is a *toggle* key—with alternating meanings.

So there are *two* ways to make a number negative in ALGebraic mode, the ⊟ key and the ⊞⁄⊟ key.

Playing the Percentages

Do you realize how easy it is to do percentage calculations on the HP 17Bɪɪ? Yes, even these—everybody's *least* favorite math problems—are a breeze.

Watch: What's 25% more than 134?

Solution: ⊡③④⊞②⑤%⊜   <u>Answer</u>: 167.50

Whenever you want to increase or decrease a number by some known percentage, you just add or subtract that percentage—again, just as you would say it.

And how do you find an unknown percentage of any given number?

Example: What's 40% of $21.95?

Piece of Cake: Press ②①·⑨⑤✕④⓪%⊜   <u>Answer</u>: 8.78

To increase or decrease by a known percentage, you add or subtract. To simply take a percentage of a number, you multiply. What could be easier? Try a few more problems on your own....

Notice in all cases that the machine evaluates the percentage as soon as it can—just as it does with parentheses.

The History Stack

By now, you're probably wondering something: When you start a new problem, your previous results simply "bump out of the way"—but where do they go?

Do This: Press ⓵⊟⓶⊟⓷⊟⓸⊟. There—you have just "finished" four arithmetic problems, one after another.

Now notice the arrow keys, ▲ and ▼, and also the ■x≷y and ■R↓ keys. You can use these keys to make those four most recent results "roll around" or change sequence. The calculator holds them in its *History Stack*—a "history" of the four most recent results. Try them....

Now rearrange them back to their original order and press ⓹⊟. Can you now roll five results around? Try it.... Nope. The History Stack holds only the last four results. But it truly is a "stack" of your recent calculating History—and regardless whether you can *see* all four of those numbers, they're still there.

So the History Stack will let you see the results of previous calculations.

Stack

Display

3. LEARNING TO DRIVE

Problem: Your gross incomes and total taxes for the last three years were as follows (not really—just suppose):

Gross Income	Total Taxes
$ 81,500.00	$ 28,525.00
96,850.00	39,708.50
103,700.00	38,887.50

In which year were your total taxes highest *in proportion* to your income?

Solution: To find this out, you'll need to do three separate calculations, one for each year:

2 8 5 2 5 ÷ 8 1 5 0 0 =
(Result: 0.35—the fraction you paid three years ago).

Next, press: 3 9 7 0 8 • 5 ÷ 9 6 8 5 0 =
(Result: 0.41—two years ago).

And: 3 8 8 8 7 • 5 ÷ 1 0 3 7 0 0 =
(Result: 0.38—last year).

Just by looking through the History Stack (using ▲ and ▼), you can see that you paid the biggest fraction two years ago, right?

Skip now to page 46.

Arithmetic with the [ENTER] Key (RPN Mode)

This method of arithmetic takes a little practice to learn—but the rewards are *definitely* worth the trouble.

Here's a good set of examples (and remember that you can use the [◄] or [CLR] keys to back out or clear any mistakes):

Example: Calculate $342 - 173 + 13$

Solution: Press [3][4][2] [ENTER] [1][7][3] [−] [1][3] [+]
Answer: 182.00

Get the idea? When you key in the numbers you're going to combine, you separate them with the [ENTER] key (also known as the [=] key). And the operation comes *last*.

Another: What's $2 \times (101.00 - 47.50)$?

Solution: [1][0][1] [INPUT] [4][7][·][5] [−] [2][×]   Answer: 107.00

Notice that you can use the [INPUT] key as an [ENTER] key also—just for convenience!

And notice also that you don't need to key in any trailing zeroes (i.e. 101.00 is just 101).

But the most important point to notice is this: *You don't need parentheses, because you do the calculations inside the parentheses first.*

One More: Find $\dfrac{101.00 \times (47.50 - 2)}{64 + \left(25 \times \frac{3}{4}\right)}$

Solution:

$\boxed{4}\boxed{7}\boxed{\cdot}\boxed{5}\boxed{\text{INPUT}}\boxed{2}\boxed{-}\boxed{1}\boxed{0}\boxed{1}\boxed{\times}$
$\boxed{3}\boxed{\text{INPUT}}\boxed{4}\boxed{\div}\boxed{2}\boxed{5}\boxed{\times}\boxed{6}\boxed{4}\boxed{+}$
$\boxed{\div}$

<u>Answer</u>: **55.53** (Reminder: This is just the first two decimal places, with the second digit rounded. To see more digits, you can adjust the display, right?)

See how you work from the inner parentheses outward? And notice how—although you couldn't see it—your intermediate result (the numerator) simply "floated up above" in the History Stack until you were ready to use it.

Bear in mind the purpose of $\boxed{\text{ENTER}}$ ($\boxed{\text{INPUT}}$): It allows you to separate numbers that you are keying in "back-to-back" (i.e. without any arithmetic operation between them). But when an operation has been performed between numbers, you must *not* use $\boxed{\text{ENTER}}$ ($\boxed{\text{INPUT}}$). For example, in the above problem, you need $\boxed{\text{ENTER}}$ ($\boxed{\text{INPUT}}$) *only* two places: between the 47.5 and the 2 and between the 3 and the 4.

Changing the Sign of a Number

Try This: Find $34 \times (-19)$

Solution: Press ③④ INPUT ①⑨ +/− ✕   <u>Answer</u>: -646.00

That's how you make a positive number negative—with the +/− key.

But if it's already negative, then...

Hmmm: Suppose you now want to make that -646.00 into a 646.00.

Guess What: Just press the +/− key.

Like the shift key, the +/− ("change sign") key is a *toggle* key—a key with alternating meanings.

Playing the Percentages

Do you realize how easy it is to do percentage calculations on the HP 17Bɪɪ? Yes, even these—everybody's *least* favorite math problems— are a breeze.

Example: What's 40% of $21.95?

Piece of Cake: Press ②①·⑨⑤ INPUT ④⓪ %   Answer: 8.78

The % operation needs two numbers, just like other arithmetic. The first number you key in is the "whole;" the second number is the "part" —the percentage of the "whole" that you want to find.

Watch: What's 25% more than 134?

Solution: ①③④ INPUT ②⑤ % ＋   Answer: 167.50

Notice how the % calculation leaves the "whole" intact afterwards—so that you can conveniently add it to the "part" if you wish. What could be easier?

Try a few more problems on your own.

The RPN Stack

By now, you've probably noticed how your previous and intermediate results simply "bump upwards." What's happening here?

Do This: Press [1][INPUT][2][INPUT][3][INPUT][4]—to pretend that you've just done some arithmetic problems, one after another.

Now notice the arrow keys, [▲] and [▼], and also the [■][x≷y] and [■][R↓] keys (they're the "shifted" parenthesis keys, but since parentheses are not used in RPN mode, you'll get [x≷y] and [R↓] even without pressing the [■] key).

You can use these keys to make the *four most recent results* —the *History Stack*—"roll around" or change sequence. Try them....

Now arrange them back to the way they started and press [5]. Can you now roll five results around? Try it....

Nope. The Stack holds only the last four results. But notice that regardless whether you can *see* all four of those numbers, they're still there.

So the History Stack lets you review *and re-use* the results of previous calculations....

Problem: Your gross incomes and total taxes for the last three years were as follows (not really—just suppose):

Gross Income	Total Taxes
$ 81,500.00	$ 28,525.00
96,850.00	39,708.50
103,700.00	38,887.50

In which year were your total taxes highest in proportion to your income? What was the difference between this highest fraction and the lowest?

Solution: To find this out, you'll need to do three separate calculations, one for each year:

2 8 5 2 5 ENTER 8 1 5 0 0 ÷
(Result: 0.35—the fraction you paid three years ago).

Next, press: 3 9 7 0 8 • 5 ENTER 9 6 8 5 0 ÷
(Result: 0.41—two years ago).

And: 3 8 8 8 7 • 5 ENTER 1 0 3 7 0 0 ÷
(Result: 0.38—last year).

Just by reviewing the History Stack (using ▲ and ▼), you can see that you paid the biggest fraction two years ago and the smallest fraction three years ago, right? To find the difference, rearrange the Stack and subtract: R↓ x≷y −. Result: 0.06   About 6% of your income.

More Math If You Want It

At this point, you may well be satisfied with your level of arithmetic on the HP 17Bɪɪ:

- clearing the display and changing its number formatting;
- addition, subtraction, multiplication and division;
- negative numbers;
- percentages;
- moving around the History Stack a little bit.

If that's enough for you, skip now to the quiz at the end of this chapter (page 50)....

On the other hand, you may be interested to know about some of the other, "higher math" operations this machine offers you. If so, "stick around" and work through the next few pages (the examples will have both ALGebraic and RPN solutions).

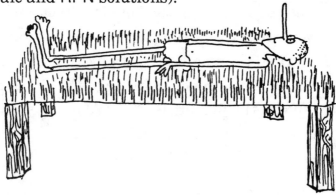

Scientific Notation

Try This: What's $2,000,000 \times 2,000,000$?

Solution: Press [2][0][0][0][0][0][0][×][2][0][0][0][0][0][0][=] (ALG mode)

or [2][0][0][0][0][0][0][INPUT][2][0][0][0][0][0][0][×] (RPN mode)

Answer: 4.00E12

As you may know, this shorthand way of writing very large (or very small numbers) is *scientific notation.* You would read this as "four-point-zero-zero times ten to the twelfth power." The E means "...times ten to the..."

Notice the little gold E above the [+/−] key. It's there so you can also use scientific notation when you *key in* numbers.

Go For It: Find "two million times two million" once again—but this time, you're not allowed to use the [0] key.

Solution: Press [2]█[E][6][×][2]█[E][6][=]   (ALG mode)

or   [2]█[E][6][INPUT][2]█[E][6][×] (RPN mode)

Saves a few [0]'s, doesn't it? Anyway, whether you like this notation or not, just be sure to recognize the E when your calculator uses it.

You might be surprised at the useful things you can do with some other MATH functions in your HP 17Bɪɪ....

Try One: A bank account earns 6% per year, compounded constantly. If you put $100 into this account and let it grow for 6 months, how much would you have then?

Solution: The formula for continuous compounding is

Ending balance = (Beginning balance)(e^{rt}),

where r is the yearly rate (in decimal form) and t is the number of years. The other number, e, is the natural logarithm base. You will also see e^{rt} written as $\exp(rt)$, i.e. the "exponential of rt."

In this problem, $r = .06$ (that's 6%, written as a decimal) and $t = 0.5$ (half a year). So, compute (rt):

⟨·⟩⟨0⟩⟨6⟩⟨×⟩⟨·⟩⟨5⟩⟨=⟩   (the ALGebraic way), or
⟨·⟩⟨0⟩⟨6⟩⟨INPUT⟩⟨·⟩⟨5⟩⟨×⟩   (the RPN way).
Result: 0.03

Now *exponentiate* this: Press ▮(MATH) ▮EXP▮.
This is e^{rt} (or $\exp(rt)$). So now multiply by your beginning balance: ⟨×⟩⟨1⟩⟨0⟩⟨0⟩⟨=⟩ (ALG),   *or*   ⟨1⟩⟨0⟩⟨0⟩⟨×⟩ (RPN)

Answer: 103.05

Did you notice that the ▓▓▓ function doesn't care whether you're using ALGebraic or RPN arithmetic? That's true in general: When you select an operation from a menu like this, it simply operates on your current number—no matter how that number got there.

Try Another: The answer from the previous problem is not *exactly* $103.05. Prove this to yourself—press ■ SHOW ....

See? It's really 103.045453395. Your display is rounding its presentation of the number—"for your eyes only," because you've set a FIX 2 display setting.

By contrast, to round (i.e. actually *change*) the number—to match your current display setting— press ■ RND ....

Nothing much seems to happen, right? Ah, but now SHOW full precision (■ SHOW), and see 103.05.

That's a different number than before: there are no more hidden digits out past the second decimal place.

Again, notice that it doesn't matter which kind of arithmetic you use. The function simply operates on the current number.

Arithmetic Quiz*

Solve these on your HP 17BII. As usual, the solutions are on the next pages, with some page references for review (and you'll see new twists, too). In some problems, it won't matter whether you use ALG or RPN arithmetic—the keystrokes are the same either way. But (as is the case throughout this book) for any problems where the two methods do have different keystrokes, both solutions are given (ALGebraic first).

1. Find $\dfrac{100/75}{(25 \times 64) + (34 \times (-19))}$

   Then find $\dfrac{(25 \times 64) + (34 \times (-19))}{100/75}$ by two different methods.

2. Which is greater: $4/7$ or $\dfrac{6.281}{11}$?

3. 4.00E12 is "4 trillion" (a very large number). How much is 4.00E-12? How would you key this in?

*For more practice with RPN arithmetic specifically, see also Appendices D and E in your HP Owner's Manual.

4. Suppose that this year's income is 35% more than last year's, but next year's will be only 85% of this year's. If last year's was $25,000, what will next year's be?

5. Calculate $(-19) \times (-19)$ by three different methods, two of which don't use the ☒ key.

6. Compute $\sqrt{4096}$ two different ways. Then find $\sqrt[12]{4096}$.

7. Find $\left(\dfrac{1 - 1.1^{-10}}{.1} + 100 \right)\left(1.1^{10}\right)$

Arithmetic Quiz Solutions

1. ⌈1⌉⌈0⌉⌈0⌉÷⌈7⌉⌈5⌉÷((⌈2⌉⌈5⌉×⌈6⌉⌈4⌉)+(⌈3⌉⌈4⌉×−⌈1⌉⌈9⌉))=(ALG),*or*
⌈1⌉⌈0⌉⌈0⌉INPUT⌈7⌉⌈5⌉÷⌈2⌉⌈5⌉INPUT⌈6⌉⌈4⌉×⌈3⌉⌈4⌉INPUT⌈1⌉⌈9⌉+/−×+÷
<u>Answer (to 8 decimal places)</u>: 0.00139762

The easiest way to solve the second part is to "flip" the first
answer with the ▮⌈1/x⌉ key, taking the reciprocal of the current
number. <u>Answer (to 2 decimal places)</u>: 715.50

Of course, the other way is to start from scratch:
⌈2⌉⌈5⌉×⌈6⌉⌈4⌉+(⌈3⌉⌈4⌉×−⌈1⌉⌈9⌉)÷((⌈1⌉⌈0⌉⌈0⌉÷⌈7⌉⌈5⌉)= (ALG), *or*
⌈2⌉⌈5⌉INPUT⌈6⌉⌈4⌉×⌈3⌉⌈4⌉INPUT⌈1⌉⌈9⌉+/−×+ ⌈1⌉⌈0⌉⌈0⌉INPUT⌈7⌉⌈5⌉÷÷

(To review basic arithmetic methods, re-read pages 32-45).

2. To compare, find both answers: ⌈4⌉÷⌈7⌉= (ALG), *or* ⌈4⌉INPUT⌈7⌉÷
and ⌈6⌉·⌈2⌉⌈8⌉⌈1⌉÷⌈1⌉⌈1⌉= (ALG), *or* ⌈6⌉·⌈2⌉⌈8⌉⌈1⌉INPUT⌈1⌉⌈1⌉÷.

If you're looking only at the first two decimal places, they look
identical (0.57). But ask the DISPlay to FIX more than three
decimal places, and you'll see the difference: $\frac{4}{7}$ is greater (see
page 30 to brush up on FIX).

3. This is "four times ten to the negative twelfth power," or "four trillionths."
Written out fully, it would be 0.000000000004. To key this in, you
would press ⌈4⌉▮E−⌈1⌉⌈2⌉.

4. ⟨2⟩⟨5⟩⟨0⟩⟨0⟩⟨0⟩⟨+⟩⟨3⟩⟨5⟩⟨%⟩⟨×⟩⟨8⟩⟨5⟩⟨%⟩⟨=⟩ (ALG), *or*
⟨2⟩⟨5⟩⟨0⟩⟨0⟩⟨0⟩⟨INPUT⟩⟨3⟩⟨5⟩⟨%⟩⟨+⟩⟨8⟩⟨5⟩⟨%⟩   <u>Answer</u>: $28,687.50$
(See page 37 or 43 to review ⟨%⟩ calculations)

5.   **(a)**   ⟨1⟩⟨9⟩⟨+/−⟩⟨×⟩⟨−⟩⟨1⟩⟨9⟩⟨=⟩ (ALG), *or* ⟨1⟩⟨9⟩⟨+/−⟩⟨INPUT⟩⟨×⟩ (RPN)
<u>Answer</u>: 361.00

(b)   ⟨1⟩⟨9⟩⟨+/−⟩■⟨x²⟩. The ■⟨x²⟩ key squares the current number.

(c)   ⟨1⟩⟨9⟩⟨+/−⟩■⟨yˣ⟩⟨2⟩⟨=⟩ (ALG), *or* ⟨1⟩⟨9⟩⟨+/−⟩⟨INPUT⟩⟨2⟩■⟨yˣ⟩ (RPN).
The ■⟨yˣ⟩ key raises a number to a power. $(-19)^2$ is "negative nineteen raised to the second power."

6.   **(a)**   ⟨4⟩⟨0⟩⟨9⟩⟨6⟩■⟨√x̄⟩. The ■⟨√x̄⟩ key operates on the current number. <u>Answer</u>: 64.00

(b)   ⟨4⟩⟨0⟩⟨9⟩⟨6⟩■⟨yˣ⟩⟨•⟩⟨5⟩⟨=⟩ (ALG), *or* ⟨4⟩⟨0⟩⟨9⟩⟨6⟩⟨INPUT⟩⟨•⟩⟨5⟩■⟨yˣ⟩.
The "square root" is the one-half (.5) power.

(c)   ⟨4⟩⟨0⟩⟨9⟩⟨6⟩■⟨yˣ⟩⟨1⟩⟨2⟩■⟨1/x⟩⟨=⟩ (ALG), *or*
⟨4⟩⟨0⟩⟨9⟩⟨6⟩⟨INPUT⟩⟨1⟩⟨2⟩■⟨1/x⟩■⟨yˣ⟩ (RPN).

$\sqrt[12]{4096}$ is the same as $4096^{\frac{1}{12}}$.   <u>Answer</u>: 2.00

7.   ⟨1⟩⟨−⟩⟨(⟩⟨(⟩⟨1⟩⟨•⟩⟨1⟩■⟨yˣ⟩⟨−⟩⟨1⟩⟨0⟩⟨)⟩⟨)⟩⟨÷⟩⟨•⟩⟨1⟩⟨+⟩⟨1⟩⟨0⟩⟨0⟩
⟨×⟩⟨(⟩⟨(⟩⟨1⟩⟨•⟩⟨1⟩■⟨yˣ⟩⟨1⟩⟨0⟩⟨=⟩(ALG), *or*
⟨1⟩⟨INPUT⟩⟨1⟩⟨•⟩⟨1⟩⟨INPUT⟩⟨1⟩⟨0⟩⟨+/−⟩■⟨yˣ⟩⟨−⟩⟨•⟩⟨1⟩⟨÷⟩⟨1⟩⟨0⟩⟨0⟩⟨+⟩
⟨1⟩⟨•⟩⟨1⟩⟨INPUT⟩⟨1⟩⟨0⟩■⟨yˣ⟩⟨×⟩ (RPN)   <u>Answer</u>: 275.31

4. YOUR FIRST BUSINESS TRIP

Road Signs: Menus and Their Keys

So much for arithmetic and math. The good news is: Most of the time, you won't need to do "manual" arithmetic on your HP 17BII, because it has so many built-in formulas. But you do need to know how to use those formulas.*

Up to now, you've just been "driving around the block." That is, the Menu Line has generally looked like this:

`FIN | BUS | SUM | TIME |SOLVE`

This is "home"—the MAIN Menu. But now you're going to leave home and drive off for the road training you've been waiting for.

With the driving analogy, it may seem strange to be talking about maps, roads, and then *menus,* but it does make some sense: On the freeway, those big green signs showing lanes and exits are indeed a kind of menu. And how do you use these freeway menus? You choose the proper lane and exit—and you remember them for your return trip.

So you can think of the MAIN Menu on your HP 17BII as the "freeway," from which you may exit to, say, the **FIN** or **TIME** "highways." From those, you can exit onto still smaller "routes," and so on. Reaching your destination—the formula you want to use—is just a matter of reading the "road signs" in the calculator's Menu Line.

---

*If you already know how to find these formulas and tools by navigating back and forth through the menus, then skip over now to page 61.

A Menu Map

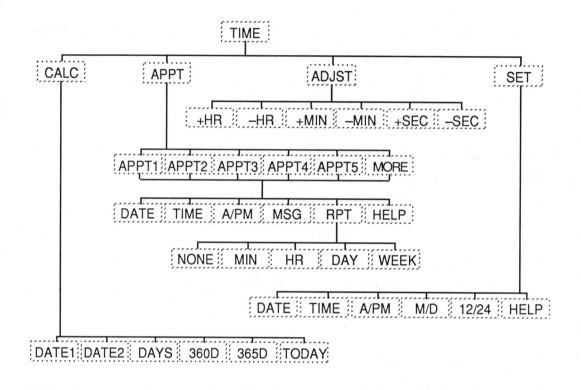

Try This: Look at the map above. This is one "major route" (the TIME Menu)—and its "suburbs." Use this map to guide you on a quick trip to the "place" called `TODAY`—starting from the MAIN Menu.

Solution: Press `TIME` `CALC` `TODAY`. See what happens? `TODAY` is a *calculation* that gives you the date and day of the week.

Notice that some menu selections are merely exits to get you onto a different "road." The selections at the *ends* of the roads are your actual destinations—where the HP 17BII does its calculations.

Next Question: How do you get "home" again?

Next Answer: You can retrace your road route—or you can "fly."

To retrace your route, use the (EXIT) key. Every time you press this key, you retrace your route back to the previous EXIT. Thus, you press (EXIT) to go from

here ⇒

```
┌─────────────────────────────────────────┐
│                                         │
│                                         │
│ DATE1 DATE2 DAYS  360D  365D  TODAY      │
└─────────────────────────────────────────┘
```

to here ⇒

```
┌─────────────────────────────────────────┐
│                                         │
│                                         │
│ CALC  APPT  ADJST  SET                   │
└─────────────────────────────────────────┘
```

and then (EXIT) once more to arrive "home" at the MAIN Menu.

To demonstrate how you can "fly" home, first go out to TODAY again.... Now press ■ (MAIN).

■(MAIN) is the quick way home—the "When-All-Else-Fails-And-You-Can't-Figure-Out-Where-You-Are" key.

So never fear—no matter how lost you think you are, there's always a way to get back to a familiar route.

Pages in a Menu

A word about the "road signs" in the Menu Line: Sometimes there's just not enough room to list all the choices. What then?*

When this happens, the menu becomes more of the restaurant kind, because then it has more than one _page_.

Try This: Look at the menu map on the opposite page. Starting from your MAIN Menu, "move" through this map until your Menu Line looks like this:

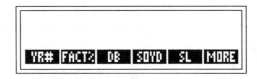

Solution: Press ■ (MAIN) **FIN** , **DEPRC**, then **MORE**.... That **MORE** is an extra item—a "turn-the-page" key—that appears on every page of any multiple-page menu.

---

*Traffic engineers just use smaller writing on their road signs, but your HP 17Bɪɪ can't do that.

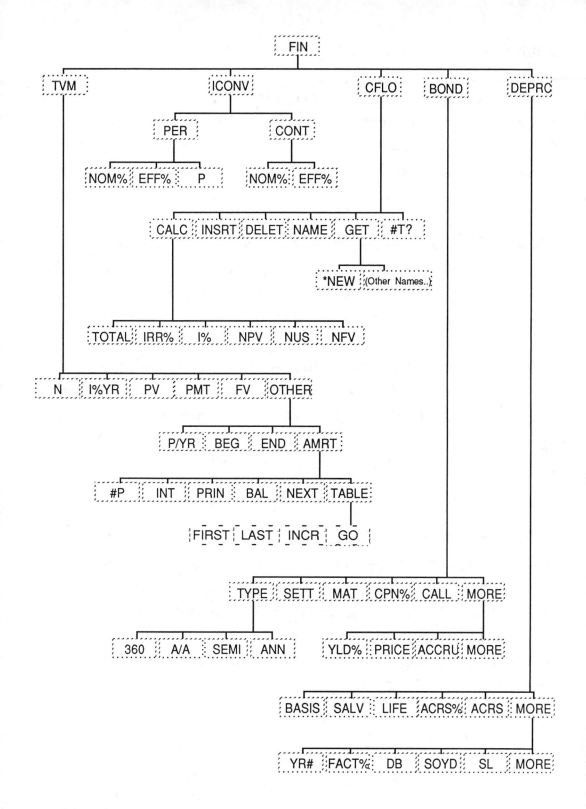

MAIN Routes vs. Side Trips

One more thing to notice about navigating through menus: Sometimes you can be working at one menu and need to take a short trip to do a "side calculation" at another menu—to get a number or adjust some mode, etc. But then you want to go back to the first menu and continue.

Like This: Suppose you're working in the TVM menu (so you've pressed ■ MAIN FIN TVM . But, once there, you realize that you want to do an exponential interest calculation like the kind you did on page 48.

Easy: Just go right to the MATH Menu: Press ■ MATH . And once you're done with that menu, just press (EXIT) and voilá!—you're back at the TVM Menu directly—*not* at the MAIN Menu. The machine remembers where you were before your EXP calculation.

Moral of the Story: Except for ■ MAIN and (EXIT), any operation that's available to you *on the keyboard* (i.e. *not* via menu keys) is regarded as a temporary "side trip." So while you do arithmetic, use the Stack, change the DiSPlay setting, use the PRINTER or MATH Menus, etc., your HP 17BII doesn't forget "where you were" in the menu system—and it returns you there when you finish with the keyboard.

Playing "What-If?" with Menu Keys

So now you know the basics of moving around in the menus.

But of course, menu keys are not just "traveling keys." They're also keys that can give you answers—hard numbers. For example, you've already used the  key to give you the date and day of the week.

But the real beauty of menu calculations is how they let you play with complicated formulas—which often have several different variables in them. And since each variable has its own key on the menu, you can vary them—one at a time—to see the effect on your answer.

This means that you can play the "What-If?" game that's so useful in making good decisions. You can ask questions like *what if* the rent goes up by $100?" "*What if* that interest rate were 2 points higher?"

And your calculator will show you the answers.

Watch This: From the MAIN Menu, press **BUS** and then **%CHG**:

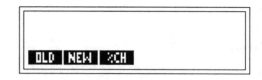

And here's the problem you want to solve:

The retail trade per square foot in one shop was $75 this year. Last year it was $64. By what percentage did this trade increase in a year?

Related question: *What if* you were looking for a 20% increase? What level of trade would that have required this year?

Solution: ⑥④ **OLD** ⑦⑤ **NEW** **%CH**

<u>Answer:</u> %CHANGE=17.19
That was the actual percentage increase in the per-square-foot retail trade.

Now specify the 20% target increase: ②⓪ **%CH**
And find what the NEW trade (i.e. this year's) would have had to be in order to meet that target: **NEW**

Answer: NEW=76.80

The General Idea

See the basic pattern?

With the first calculation, you specified known values for two variables, OLD and NEW, and calculated the unknown variable, %CH. Then, for the second part, you specified your desired %CH and OLD values and calculated NEW instead.

> You can calculate any one of the three values
> —if you know the other two.

And Notice: You can *review* the current values in each of the variables—anytime you want.

Here's How: Press (RCL) **OLD** and see: $OLD=64.00$
Press (RCL) **NEW** and see: $NEW=76.80$
Press (RCL) **%CH** and see: $\%CHANGE=20.00$

You use the (RCL) key to *ReCaLl* values from variables. There are actually three storage *registers* built into the machine, registers named OLD, NEW, and %CH. This is where the calculator stores the values you give it when you're playing "What-If?"

That's the heart of it, then: You store values in all menu variables except one, then calculate that one. And you can play this "What-If?" with *any* of the menu variables.

Now press EXIT to back up one level to the BUSiness Menu... and try some more examples....

If: A broker buys a property for $12/ft² and then sells it for $15/ft². What's the markup as a percentage of cost?

What is the markup as a percentage of price?

Solution: From the BUSiness Menu, press MU%C. This is the "MarkUp as a % of Cost" Menu.

So use it: Press 1 2 COST and 1 5 PRICE.
Then calculate: M%C

Answer: MARKUP%C=25.00

To find the markup as a percentage of price, go back to the BUSiness Menu (EXIT) and press MU%P.

Then press M%P.

Answer: MARKUP%P=20.00

Hmmm...

Question: Why didn't you need to key in the COST and PRICE in the MU%P Menu, as you did in the MU%C Menu?

Answer: Simple: The COST and PRICE variable registers in the MU%P Menu are *the same* as in the MU%C Menu. They are *shared variables*—shared between more than one menu. Since you had already stored the 12 and the 15 in the COST and PRICE registers, those values were still there, ready to calculate either M%C or M%P!

And they're still there now—which you can prove by recalling them:

Press (RCL) COST and see COST=12.00
Press (RCL) PRICE and see PRICE=15.00

One More: If the appraised value of a property decreased by 36% this year and 25% last year, what was its total percentage decrease in value over these two years?

Solution: From the BUS Menu, choose the **%CHG** option. Then, since you don't have the actual values to work with, just start with a convenient number—say, 100—to represent the property's value two years ago: Press ①⓪⓪ **OLD**

One year later, the value was 36% less than that. That is, the %CH was -36. So press ③⑥⊕/⊖ **%CH**.

Now solve for the NEW level: **NEW**.... NEW=64.00
So if the value was 100 two years ago, then it was just 64 one year later.

Now do the second year. The NEW value from the first year is the OLD value for the second year, so you would press ⑥④ **OLD**. Next, you key in the value decrease in the second year: ②⑤⊕/⊖ **%CH**, and solve for the NEW (and that's the current) value: **NEW**....NEW=48.00

So, what was the percent change for the two years? Your NEW level is now correct, but your OLD level needs to be 100 for the entire two-year period, right?

Press ①⓪⓪ **OLD** **%CH**
<u>Answer:</u> %CHANGE=-52.00

The property's value dropped 52% over two years.

Review

That's what you need to know about menus and "moving around" in your HP 17B_{II}. Just keep in mind these few important things:

- When in doubt, look at your display. It will orient you, showing you your current menu choices, error messages, instructions, etc.

- You can always get "Home" to the MAIN Menu quickly, via ■ (MAIN).

- You can always "retrace your steps" (toward Home) with (EXIT).

- When there are more than six menu items, you'll find a second "page" for that menu, by choosing **MORE**.

- You can play "What-If?" with the formulas you find in the menu system. Each variable is matched with a *register*, where you store the value you want to use in the formula.

- Even short quizzes can be helpful....

Menu Quiz

Take a "solo drive" with some percentage problems and with some "What-Iffing." Try these (the answers are on the next page, as usual):

1. There's a calculation key called PRICE in the BOND Menu. Your mission: Starting from the MAIN Menu, find it (don't bother to calculate with it), then report back to the MAIN Menu ASAP.

2. Using what you know about menus, see if you can figure out how to set the correct time and date in your calculator.

3. If you're in the middle of an arithmetic problem and you suddenly decide to change menus ("move") for some reason, what happens to your calculation?

4. A holder of a note wished to sell it and offered a 10% discount off of the face value. The buyer then turned around and re-sold the note by adding 10% to the price he had just paid for it. Did he sell it for face value?

5. The most severe drop in the history of the U.S. stock market occurred in the period between September 3, 1929 and July 8, 1932. During that time, an industrial stocks average fell from 452 to 58. If the same percentage drop happened with a beginning average level of, say, 2735, where would the bottom level be?

6. A football field is 100 yards long. If it's 45 yards wide and you increase both its width and its length by 9%, by what percentage would this increase its area?

Menu Quiz Answers

1. From the MAIN Menu, press **FIN** **BOND** **MORE**, and there on the second page of the BOND Menu, you'll see the choice called **PRICE**. Notice that, as usual, if you press **MORE** at this point, you'll flip-flop between the pages of the BOND Menu (see page 58 if you don't remember this). Then press ■**MAIN** to "fly home" again.

2. From the Main Menu, press **TIME** (obviously), and then **SET** (because you want to *set* the time and date). That brings you to another menu. Now, just pressing **DATE** or **TIME** on that menu won't set the correct time or date in the display. What do you do?

    Ask for **HELP**! ...See? It shows you how to key in the number to represent the correct time and date. For example, if today is February 28, 1990, and it's 2:25 p.m., press ②·②⑧①⑨⑨⓪ **DATE**, then ②·②⑤ (then **A/PM** if necessary) and **TIME** to get 2:25 in the afternoon. Now set your *correct* date and time, and watch the information in the display change.

3. Absolutely nothing happens to your calculation-in-progress. Try it: Press ②⊕③ (or ②ENTER③, for RPN), change menus (e.g. EXIT), then ⊟ (or ⊕, for RPN), to finish your addition.

4. Use the MU%P Menu and, say, a $100 note: Press ⌈1⌉⌈0⌉⌈0⌉ **PRICE** ⌈1⌉⌈0⌉ **MZP** **COST**....   Result: COST=90.00

That's what the buyer paid for the note. Then he resold it simply by adding 10% to this figure. That is, he used the MU%C Menu and, since the 90.00 was already stored in the COST register, he did this: ⌈1⌉⌈0⌉ **MZC** **PRICE**....   Result: PRICE=99.00
That's *not* the face value.

5. This is a %CHG problem. From the BUS Menu, press **ZCHG**, then ⌈4⌉⌈5⌉⌈2⌉ **OLD** ⌈5⌉⌈8⌉ **NEW** **ZCH**. Result: %CHANGE=-87.17

That's the *percent* change of the 1929-1932 crash (negative because the change was downward). Now key in the hypothetical high level, ⌈2⌉⌈7⌉⌈3⌉⌈5⌉ **OLD**, and calculate what the corresponding low level would be: **NEW**....   Result: NEW=350.95

6. You need a %CHANGE calculation, so go to the %CHG Menu. Then start by computing the area before the enlargement:
⌈4⌉⌈5⌉⌈×⌉⌈1⌉⌈0⌉⌈0⌉⌈=⌉   (or ⌈4⌉⌈5⌉⌈INPUT⌉⌈1⌉⌈0⌉⌈0⌉⌈×⌉ for RPN)
Answer: 4,500.00   Press **OLD**—this is the OLD area.

Next, you need to find the dimensions of the enlarged field:
⌈(⌉⌈1⌉⌈0⌉⌈0⌉⌈+⌉⌈9⌉⌈%⌉⌈)⌉⌈×⌉⌈(⌉⌈4⌉⌈5⌉⌈+⌉⌈9⌉⌈%⌉⌈=⌉   (for ALG), or
⌈1⌉⌈0⌉⌈0⌉⌈ENTER⌉⌈9⌉⌈%⌉⌈+⌉⌈4⌉⌈5⌉⌈ENTER⌉⌈9⌉⌈%⌉⌈+⌉⌈×⌉   (for RPN)
Answer: 5,346.45   This is the NEW area; press **NEW**.

Finally, **ZCH** gives you the increase in area: %CHANGE=18.81
(If you had decreased it, the %CH would have been negative).

Where Do You Want To Go Next?

You've come to a fork in the road.

Since you now know the basics of arithmetic and menus on your HP 17Bɪɪ, it's really up to you now to decide where to read next.

Of course, the recommended choice is to keep going, straight through the book. Each topic takes only a short amount of time to cover, but it teaches you a lot about the calculator and how versatile and powerful it really is.

But granted, you may not be interested in all the topics, so here's where you can read the road signs and make your own choice.

(You'll find similar "forks in the road" at the ends of later chapters, too, so you'll have this kind of choice through the rest of the Course....)

Where Do You Want To Go Next?

5. THE TIME VALUE OF MONEY: TVM

Problem Understanding = Problem Solving

Now that you know the basics of math and arithmetic, it's time to start on financial problem solving. But first, consider this:

"You never really understand something
until you can explain it to someone else."

This is certainly true for solving problems on your HP 17Bɪɪ. To get it to solve your problems, you must explain the problem to it—in the "picture language" it understands. And of course, that means you need to figure out that picture for yourself first. To repeat:

You must understand and define a problem
for yourself before you can possibly "explain"
it to your calculator.

This Course trains you to do exactly that—understand and define problems. That makes the actual button-pushing very easy—almost an afterthought. So don't be too impatient to start hitting keys here. Just park your calculator for a moment, sit back, and consider carefully the details that surround even simple finance calculations.

And don't skip over this part! Even if you've seen some of this before, it will pay you to review it now....

What Is TVM?

TVM, of course, stands for the Time Value of Money.

TVM assumes that money earns *interest* simply through the passage of time. When you're not using it yourself, you're renting it out (loaning it) for someone else to use. Therefore, when you ask "How much money do I have?" you must also ask "What time is it?" Under TVM's assumption, the first question is meaningless without the second one.

So for the purposes of calculations, the old cliché is very useful:

Time is money.

Thus, even when *amounts* of money differ, they may still be equivalent because of the *time* difference between them. For example, if $1.00 today earns 10% annual interest, it will be worth $1.10 this time next year. And you can say this with an "equals" in it:

"$1.00 now *equals* $1.10 next year."

Time adds the extra Value to the Money. So (assuming that 10% annual interest rate), you could correctly view the face value of a dollar-bill as being any one of these equivalent amounts of money:

$$\$1.00_{\text{now}} \ = \ \$1.10_{\text{next year}} \ = \ \$2.59_{\text{ten years from now}}$$

How Does Interest Behave?

OK, so borrowed money earns interest over time. Everybody knows that. But how, exactly? If you were to watch the pennies of interest accrue in your bank account, what would the pattern look like?

It all depends on what kind of interest you're earning.

Basically, there are two forms of interest: **Simple** and **Compound**. Here's how they differ:

Simple Interest is the less common method: The amount of money earned periodically as interest is defined as a set percentage of the amount *originally loaned*.

Example: Suppose you earn **Simple Interest** at 1% per month in your bank account (not bad). And suppose you deposit $100.00 there for 12 months. How much interest will you earn over the entire 12 months?

Solution: There will be exactly $12.00 in interest, because you earn 1% of the *original* $100.00 every month. That's $1 per month for 12 months. Simple to calculate—just like the name—**Simple Interest.**

Compound Interest, on the other hand, is much more widely used: The amount of interest earned per period is defined as a set percentage of the amount owed *as of the beginning of that period*, including any past interest that has been earned but not yet paid.

Example: Take that same $100.00 for 12 months, earning 1% per month, but this time it's **Compound Interest**. How much is earned over 12 months?

Solution: The first month is easy: 1% of $100.00 = $1.00
So after one month, the total amount owed is $101.00.

Now comes the second month: 1% of $101.00 = $1.01
So after 2 months, the total owed is $102.01. Etc.:

After	Amount Owed
Month 3	$ 103.03
Month 4	$ 104.06
Month 5	$ 105.10
Month 6	$ 106.15
Month 7	$ 107.21
Month 8	$ 108.29
Month 9	$ 109.37
Month 10	$ 110.46
Month 11	$ 111.57
Month 12	$ 112.68

So if it's not paid immediately, Compound Interest earns *more* than Simple Interest.

Again, here's the difference between the two types of interest:

With **Simple Interest**, no matter what month you're talking about, the interest earned in that month is always based upon the *original amount*—the amount owed *at the beginning of the loan.*

With **Compound Interest**, the interest earned in any given month is based upon the amount owed at the beginning of *that month.* Therefore, interest is earned not only on the original amount but also on all other interest already earned (but not yet paid). Hence the name, *Compound* **Interest**.

(Don't worry—you're going to put these ideas into practice in just a few more pages. Just grin and bear it for now; it's very important to cover these things first.)

Here's a pictorial summary of the behaviors of each of these types of interest:

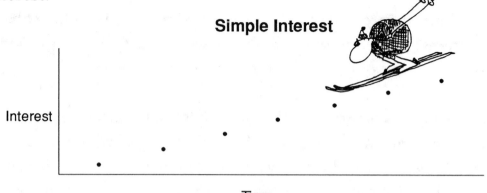

Simple Interest

Interest

Time

Compound Interest

Interest

Time

As you know (and is illustrated here), Compound Interest grows faster than Simple Interest. That's why Compound Interest is used much more widely—and on your HP 17Bɪɪ.

So you won't hear much more about Simple Interest here; anytime you see just the word "interest," it will mean Compound Interest.

Again, all this may seem obvious. But don't overlook these subtleties:

Subtlety #1: In either form of interest, there is only one time period which is the Defined Interest Period (D.I.P.), and only one Defined Interest Rate (D.I.R.) corresponding to that period. No other numbers can be used to calculate compounding interest. Don't be mislead by quoted annualized values! They may be *nominal*—not *effective*—rates.

The examples with the $100.00 for 12 months stated specifically that interest accrues at 1% per month. Therefore the D.I.P. is 1 month, and the corresponding D.I.R. is 1%. But it's conventional to quote interest rates on an annual basis, using a simplified, "thumbnail" approximation, called a *nominal* rate. For example, a bank would quote the above rate as "12% A.P.R. (Annual Percentage Rate)."

That's the nominal rate. But now ask the bank for your *effective* (i.e. your actual) interest earned on $100.00 over 12 months. They do not simply multiply your starting $100.00 by 12% A.P.R. (that would be simple interest). Instead, they divide the quoted A.P.R. by the number of D. I. P.'s per year (12), to get the D.I.R.* Then they go through exactly the same compounding calculation as you did on page 78—one period at a time.

To put it succinctly: A *nominal* rate is a *simple-interest* annualized approximation often used to *quote* interest rates. The *effective* rate it stands for is then calculated—by *compounding* the D.I.R. for a year's worth of D.I.P.'s.

*Canadian lenders do it slightly differently. The Appendix shows you how to convert between the Canadian method and the U.S. method—which is used by the HP 17BII.

Subtlety #2:   In your 12-month account problem, you never stopped to ponder how much interest you had earned after, say, 2.5 months, or 5.79 months, or 9.61 months.

And why not?

Because you weren't given any rules.

The D.I.R. and D.I.P. define only what the loan balance will be at *one point* in each period (the end). There must be other definitions to determine how that balance goes *between* points.

That's why the points on the graph on page 80 aren't connected with lines. Knowing only the D.I.R. and the D.I.P., nobody can tell you how those lines should be drawn. For all you know, those lines might be drawn like this:

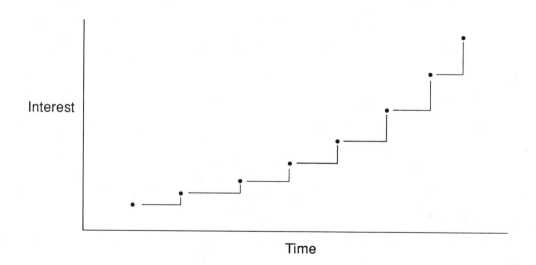

Or maybe interest might accrue like this....

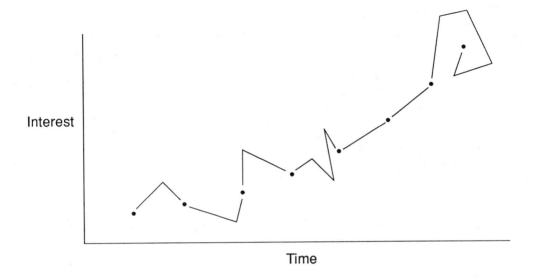

Interest

Time

...Or who-knows-what-else. All you know is the balance at one point in each Defined Interest Period.

"Then how <u>do</u> I picture my $100.00 compound-interest bank account—if I can't draw a nice smooth curve of some kind?

"And what if I deposit into—or withdraw from—my account during those 12 months? How do I include that information in the picture?

"And how does this apply for other kinds of investments?"

Funny you should ask.... ☞

Getting the Picture Right

Whether it's a note, mortgage, lease or another financial scenario, the underlying TVM principles are the same. But each financial industry may use its own set of terms, so it's best to omit the words altogether—*draw a picture*—to analyze the scenario. The picture must show:

- The numerical *value* of the transaction;
- The *direction* of the transaction (*paying* or *receiving* the money), usually shown with (), or ±, or a debit/credit designation.
- The *time* of the transaction. Time adds value to money!

There are many ways to "draw the picture." Here are two of them:

Using a T-Bar

Suppose you invest $100 now, then $10 more at the end of every month for 6 months. In return you receive $40 at the end of month 2, and then your original $100, plus $30 more, at the end of month 6. Here's how a *T-bar*—a chronological table of cash-flows—would represent this:

Month (m)	$Cash-flow
0	(100.00)
1	(10.00)
2	(10.00) + 40.00
3	(10.00)
4	(10.00)
5	(10.00)
6	(10.00) + 100.00 + 30.00

To be sure you build a correct T-bar, follow these rules:

1. "Either a borrower or a lender be!" When buying money market shares or putting money into a savings account, you're a *lender*. If you're taking out a mortgage to buy or build a piece of property, then clearly you're a *borrower*. The same scenario will look different, depending upon which view you take. So pick one perspective and *stick with it*.

2. The signs (negative vs. positive) of the cash-flows denote the directions of the transactions. A *positive* amount means that you *receive* money; a *negative* amount means you *pay* money.

3. The cash-flows proceed forward in time from top to bottom in the chart—and the *same period of time* separates each cash-flow. This period must be the D.I.P. (Defined Interest Period) to match the assumptions of your HP 17Bɪɪ.

4. When multiple transactions occur simultaneously, *you combine them* into one net transaction. For example, these two scenarios are entirely equivalent:

m	$		*m*	$
0	(100.00)		0	(100.00)
1	(10.00)		1	(10.00)
2	(10.00) + 40.00		2	30.00
3	(10.00)		3	(10.00)
4	(10.00)		4	(10.00)
5	(10.00)		5	(10.00)
6	(10.00) + 100.00 + 30.00		6	120.00

Using a Cash-Flow Diagram

A **cash-flow diagram** is a good way to represent and understand an investment scenario *visually*. For example, observe how a cash-flow diagram would represent this same T-bar scenario:

Month (m)	$Cash-flow
0	(100.00)
1	(10.00)
2	(10.00) + 40.00
3	(10.00)
4	(10.00)
5	(10.00)
6	(10.00) + 100.00 + 30.00

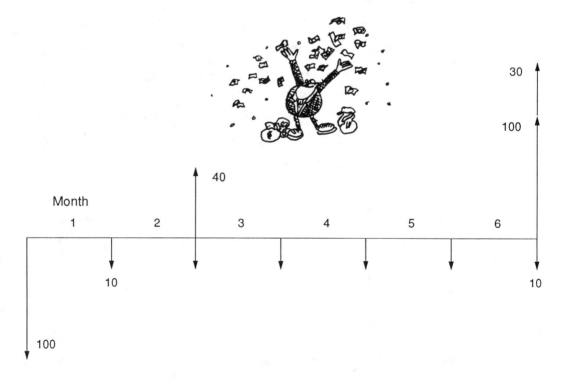

Of course, just as with T-bars, there are certain rules for drawing cash-flow diagrams—and you'll notice a lot of similarities:

1.   "Either a borrower or a lender be!" In drawing the diagram, *pick one perspective and stick with it.*

2.   The cash-flows proceed forward in time from left to right on the diagram—and the *same period of time* separates each cash-flow. This period must be the D.I.P. (Defined Interest Period) to match the assumptions of your HP 17Bɪɪ.

3.   The *directions* of the vertical arrows denote the directions of the transactions. An *upward* arrow means that you *receive* money; a *downward* arrow means that you *pay* money:

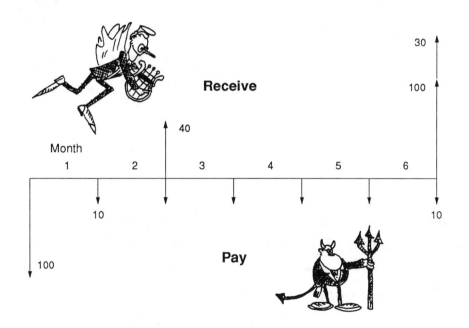

4. Whenever multiple transactions occur simultaneously, *you can net them together.* This:

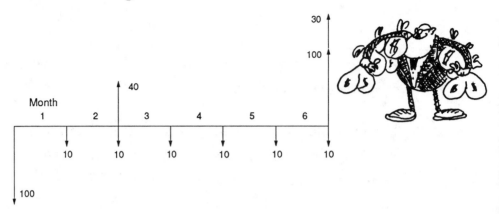

is the same as this:

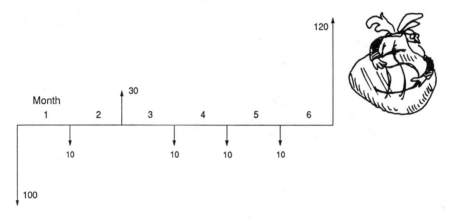

Whichever method you choose—T-bar or diagram—use it! You can't solve a problem if you can't describe it correctly first.

> *The first thing to do in any financial calculation is to*
> **Get the Picture Right.**
> *Either create a T-bar or draw a cash-flow diagram.*

Discounting Cash-Flows

One of the real values of TVM is that you can use it to make the scenario simpler—actually *adjust* cash-flow amounts to get a clearer picture of the situation. Think back to your $100.00 sitting in the bank account for 12 months (page 78). Of course, you can withdraw your money from the account at any time, but suppose you want to see your options for withdrawing at the end of each of the first six months. Here's how those six options look on T-bars:

m	$	*m*	$	*m*	$
0	(100.00)	0	(100.00)	0	(100.00)
1	101.00	1	0.00	1	0.00
2	0.00	2	102.01	2	0.00
3	0.00	3	0.00	3	103.03
4	0.00	4	0.00	4	0.00
5	0.00	5	0.00	5	0.00
6	0.00	6	0.00	6	0.00

m	$	*m*	$	*m*	$
0	(100.00)	0	(100.00)	0	(100.00)
1	0.00	1	0.00	1	0.00
2	0.00	2	0.00	2	0.00
3	0.00	3	0.00	3	0.00
4	104.06	4	0.00	4	0.00
5	0.00	5	105.10	5	0.00
6	0.00	6	0.00	6	106.15

Each of these withdrawal amounts is equivalent to any other, *considering the time involved*. This is indeed the *Time* Value of Money.

And here's how these same six variations look on cash-flow diagrams—
it's like playing "What-If?" with your withdrawal:

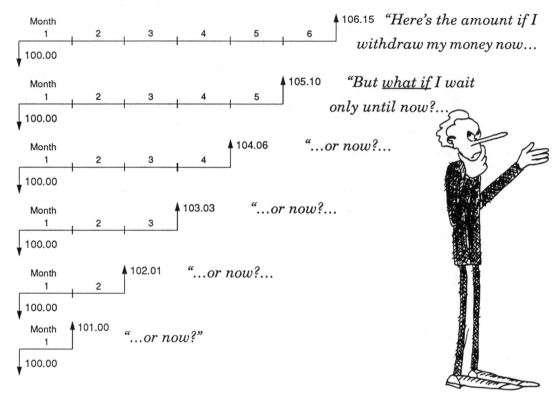

The point is, each of these scenarios is entirely equivalent. You are
really just "sliding" one cash-flow (your proposed withdrawal) *across
time*. The earlier in time the cash-flow's position becomes, the smaller
its amount becomes. This process is called **discounting**, and it's one
of the fundamental tools offered by TVM analysis.

To repeat: You can slide any cash-flow across a cash-flow diagram (or
up/down the list of a T-bar) and retain complete accuracy as long as you
adjust it according to the prevailing interest rate. If the cash-flow is
sent forward in time, it increases in amount; if it goes back in time, it
decreases (and is said to be *discounted*).

So here's what you know about the Time Value of Money so far:

- You know the difference between the two types of interest. Rates are often *quoted* with *nominal* (simple-interest) annual values but *calculated* via *effective* (compound-interest) periodic values;

- You know that the HP 17Bɪɪ's TVM uses Compound Interest;

- You know how to draw T-bars and/or cash-flow diagrams;

- You know that you can slide cash-flows along the timeline and keep the picture entirely accurate, as long as you adjust those cash-flows according to the prevailing interest rate.

What you *don't* know (yet) is how to draw a diagram for your HP 17Bɪɪ. After all, it's supposed to do the calculating. How can the machine possibly "see" or "understand" a picture that you've drawn on paper?

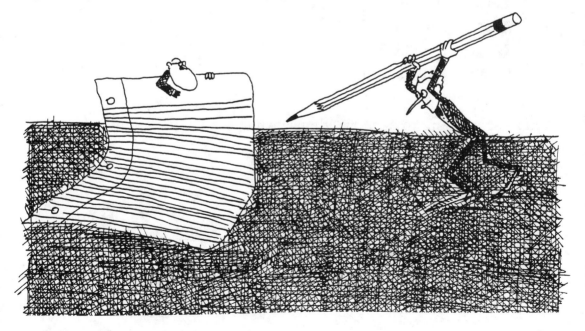

Drawing the Picture for Your Calculator

Time to rev up your machine. From the MAIN Menu, choose these menu selections: **FIN** **TVM**.

You'll see something like this:

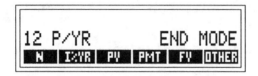

```
12 P/YR           END MODE
 N  I%YR  PV  PMT  FV OTHER
```

(Change the display setting back to FIX 2, also)

This is the TVM Menu. The first five selections here are the keys you use to draw a cash-flow diagram for your calculator:

N	Number of Defined Interest Periods (D.I.P.'s)
I%YR	Interest % rate per YeaR
PV	Present Value
PMT	PayMenT
FV	Future Value

You're soon going to be very adept with these keys.

The keys form a picture frame over a cash-flow scenario:

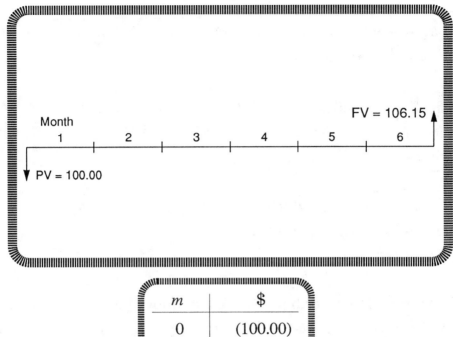

or:

m	$
0	(100.00)
1	0.00
2	0.00
3	0.00
4	0.00
5	0.00
6	106.15

The first thing to look for in this picture is a pattern of steady, regular cash-flows—one per D.I.P.—throughout the timeline. If you have *un-even* or *irregular* cash-flows along the timeline (except for the ends), you can't use TVM (as shown above, the cash-flows may be $0.00, but they must be level and regular throughout).

The reason for this restriction is TVM's **PMT** (PayMenT) key. When de-scribing a cash-flow scenario to your calculator, you must put this steady, level cash-flow amount into the PMT register on the TVM Menu.

And here's what the other four TVM keys mean to your picture frame:

N represents the Number of periods (D.I.P.'s) from one side of the picture frame to the other.

PV is the Present Value, which is the net cash-flow (if any) that occurs at the *left* side of the picture frame *besides* any PMT cash-flow that may also occur there.

FV is the Future Value, which is the net cash-flow (if any) that occurs at the *right* side of the picture frame *besides* any PMT cash-flow that may also occur there.

So, for example, to describe the diagram under your picture frame on the previous page (your $100 bank account, assuming you wait until after month 6 to withdraw), here's what you would tell your HP 17BII:

$$
\begin{aligned}
N &= 6 \\
PMT &= 0.00 \\
PV &= -100.00 \\
FV &= 106.15
\end{aligned}
$$

Notice again that anytime you have a cash-flow paid *out*, you show it on your diagram with a *downward* arrow, and you tell it to your calculator with a minus sign (remember the +/− key?). By opening your bank account, you *loan* the bank $100.00, so this is an *out*flow of cash (downward) on your diagram—a *negative* 100.00 in your calculator.

But what about I%YR—the fifth key on your TVM Menu? The interest is the "glue" that holds the picture frame together.

All you really know is that the D.I.R. is 1% per month, right? But notice that **OTHER** item on your menu. Press it. Here's what you'll see:

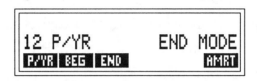

This is the second page of the TVM Menu. Here you can vary certain parameters that affect the outcome of TVM calculations.

For example, notice the message: 12 P/YR Your HP 17BII is telling you its current assumption about the picture you're "drawing" for it: 12 payments per year.

Is this correct for your bank account problem? You don't really make any PMT's (withdrawals or deposits), do you? No, but there *are* 12 PMT's per year, nevertheless—*because the number of payments per year is always the number of periods (D.I.P.'s) per year.* There's *always* one PMT per period—even if it's zero; that's what you mean by a PMT—that steady, level, once-per-period cash-flow.

Since the D.I.P. is one month, there are indeed 12 payments per year—no need to change that message (which you could do by using the **P/YR** key).

Now [EXIT] to return to the TVM Menu.

OK, so there are 12 PMT's per year. How does this help you determine the interest rate in your "picture frame?"

It helps a lot: It means that you can *key in the I%YR as an A.P.R.* (recall the discussion on page 81). That is, I%YR is the annualized approximation you use to *conveniently specify* the interest rate. And, just like the bank with its quoted, *nominal* A.P.R., the calculator knows that it's supposed to divide the I%YR by the number of PMT's per year to get the actual D.I.R. to do its compounding:*

Therefore, saying that   A.P.R. ÷ D.I.P.'s/Year = D.I.R.

...is really saying that   I%YR ÷ PMTS/YR = D.I.R.

And in this problem, that's   12% ÷ 12 = 1%

Seem complicated? The point is, *all you need to key in* is the 12%—the I%YR. Then, as long as the machine knows the right number of PMTS/YR, it knows how to convert the annualized I%YR to the actual D.I.R.

*Just like a *U.S.* bank, that is. For a Canadian mortgage, you need to perform a quick conversion to arrive at the correct A.P.R. to match the HP 17BII's U.S. assumptions. See the Appendix.

So now you know all five TVM variables in the picture of your bank account—the scenario where you withdraw after the sixth month:

N	I%YR	PV	PMT	FV
6	12.00	0.00	-100.00	106.15

And here's the completed picture frame around the scenario:

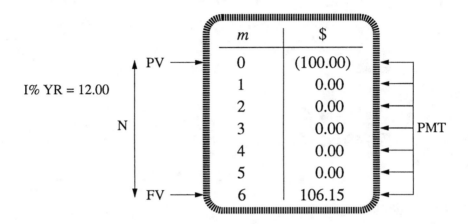

or:

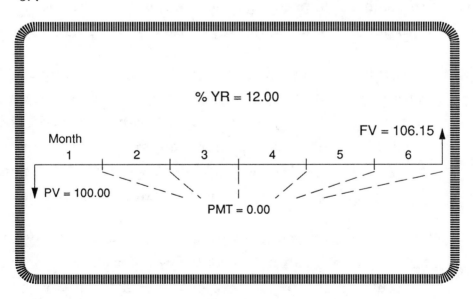

Of course, normally, you need the calculator to *compute* one of these five variables for you—after you tell it the values for the other four. But you can always test your calculator to see if it agrees with these values. Do that now: Give it any four of the five values and see if it comes up with the missing value—the missing piece of the "picture...."

Verify: Try solving for Future Value. That means you need to key in the other four TVM values. From the TVM Menu, press

⑥ **N**

① ② **I%YR**

① ⓪ ⓪ +/− **PV**

⓪ **PMT** **FV** ....   Result: **FV=106.15**   Right on.

Things to notice and remember:

1. Remember that pressing a menu key can mean either to store or to calculate—depending upon what you did just previously.

2. You could have keyed in the N, the I%YR, the PV, and the PMT *in any order*—just so you have them all in there when you ask for the FV. You may solve for any of the five variables, but always specify the other four; never ignore a variable or assume it's zero. The machine will use whatever value it happens to find in that variable's register; that value had better be right.

3. The machine obeyed its own sign convention: Since your PV was negative (meaning cash out of your pocket), it figured that FV must be the payoff—when the cash comes back—and

therefore, positive. In fact, the machine *insists* that PV and FV be of opposite sign—to keep this idea of investment and return. If you give it a PV and FV of the same sign (when solving for PMT, for example), it beeps with a `NO SOLUTION` message, because you *must* have at least one investment and one return in any meaningful TVM problem.

4. **Most importantly**, now that you have all the parameters in the TVM registers, you can play "What-If" simply by changing the number of months you leave your money in there. For example, by pressing 1 N FV , you change the analysis to the case where you withdraw your money after 1 month. By pressing 2 N FV , you do the 2-month scenario, etc. You use the TVM keys to "slide" a cash-flow (your withdrawal) up and down the timeline—just as you did on paper (page 90).

So, what if you let your account grow for a full 12 months? How about 50 years (600 months)? The answers to each of these are merely variations on the same procedure. You're varying one parameter (N, the number of periods), preserving three others, and checking to see how this affects the fifth parameter (Future Value). And remember: as with all menus, you never need to re-key in any number once it's stored in a TVM Menu register. It's there to be used—or varied—over and over again.

Drawing the Picture for Your Calculator

A Typical Mortgage Problem

Now it's time to put TVM into practice with something more exciting than a bank account. After all, what's life without a good mortgage?

Like This One: You're buying a $110,000 property by paying down $10,000 and financing the rest on a 30-year mortgage with monthly payments. The quoted A.P.R. is 12.00%. What is the monthly payment?*

Solution: You can't solve this problem until you fill in some details that aren't specifically spelled out:

- Is the monthly payment at the beginning or at the end of the month?

- What is the D.I.P.?

- What is the D.I.R.?

- Why do you care about these things?

---

*If you already know how to solve this, go to page 108. Note: Laws for quoting mortgage rates in Canada differ slightly from the U.S. To use the HP 17Bıı under Canadian rules, see the Appendix.

BEGIN or END?

Does it make any difference whether the payment is at the beginning or at the end of a month? After all, isn't the beginning of one month the same as the end of the previous one? Compare the two scenarios:

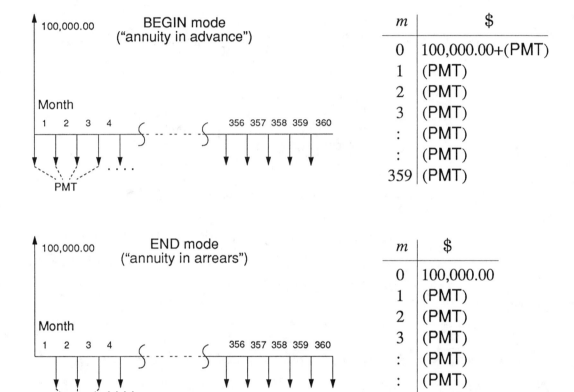

m	$
0	100,000.00+(PMT)
1	(PMT)
2	(PMT)
3	(PMT)
:	(PMT)
:	(PMT)
359	(PMT)

m	$
0	100,000.00
1	(PMT)
2	(PMT)
3	(PMT)
:	(PMT)
:	(PMT)
360	(PMT)

As you can see, in the first case, a payment is due at the beginning of the loan—right when you sign the papers. This reduces the balance sooner, so there is *less interest* to be paid on the borrowed money. With less interest to be paid, the PMT amount (which covers both principal and interest) will be less; indeed it does matter whether the payment is at the beginning or at the end of the month.

So what about your mortgage? Which is it—BEGIN or END?

In a real contract, it would have to be stated, of course, but for this problem, just assume the more common case—the END of the month. So, how do you tell your HP 17Bᴵᴵ to assume this too?

Like This: From the TVM Menu, press OTHER and see this again:

Notice the two keys, there, BEG and END.

Press them alternately and notice the change in the message in your display (but be sure to leave it in END MODE for this problem).

Don't forget to set this mode to match the specifications of the loan you're computing. And remember to check this for each new TVM problem. Except when you first arrive at the TVM Menu, you can't usually tell which of these two modes your calculator is using.

Next detail to clear up:

What's the D.I.P.?

The problem says 12% A.P.R.—and it's compound interest, of course—but it doesn't say how *often* this interest compounds. Is it yearly? After all, A.P.R. does stand for <u>Annual</u> Percentage Rate.*

Well, yes and no: Yes—that's what A.P.R. means, but no—the compounding isn't yearly. It's monthly.

How do you know? Because the payments are specified as monthly, and unless told otherwise, you can assume that the payment period is the same as the compounding period (and vice versa).

Thus, the Defined Interest Period (D.I.P.)—the period over which interest *actually* compounds—is a month. And now you need to tell your HP 17Bɪɪ this detail also....

Clue It In: From the second "page" of the TVM Menu (use `OTHER` to get there), press `1` `2` `P/YR`. (Your display probably already shows 12 P/YR, but do this anyway, just for practice.)

Now `EXIT` back to the TVM Menu.

---

*Remember that Canadian quoted rates must be converted to an equivalent U.S. A.P.R., which will be different than this 12%. For details, see the Appendix.

And so what's the D.I.R.? What's the monthly rate of interest that corresponds to an A.P.R. of 12.00%?

It's "12% divided by 12 months/year," or 1%/month (recall the discussions on pages 81 and 96). You may sleep better tonight knowing this, but you don't need to tell your calculator—it will *assume* it.*

*The nominal A.P.R. used to compute a loan payment
is exactly what I%YR means to the HP 17B$_{II}$.*

That is, to arrive at the actual interest rate to use in its calculations, a bank would take this *nominal* A.P.R. and divide it by the number of compounding periods in a year.

So whenever you see a nominal A.P.R. specified for the purposes of computing a payment or a balance, just make sure that your P/YR is set properly and then use that A.P.R. as your I%YR.*

---

*It's this assumption that forces Canadian lenders and borrowers to do a little interest conversion before supplying the HP 17B$_{II}$ with an "A.P.R." Again, see the Appendix for details.

The Typical Solution

Finally, you're ready to solve this mortgage problem. Here's the scenario in diagrams again. Notice how it takes your perspective—the borrower. The loan amount is shown as positive (you *receive* it), and each PMT amount is negative (you *pay* it).

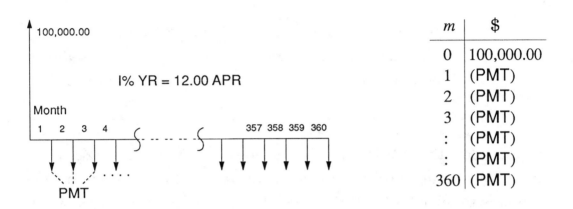

Simply by looking at the picture, you can read off the values you need for the TVM registers:

Read 'em Off: At the TVM Menu: ③⓪✕①②═ (ALG) *or*
                                      ③⓪INPUT①②✕ (RPN) **N**
                     ①② **I%YR** ①⓪⓪⓪⓪⓪ **PV** ⓪ **FV** .
                     Then press **PMT** to calculate the payment.
                     <u>Answer</u>: PMT=-1,028.61

Note how the HP 17BII knows that this PMT must be negative (a cash *outflow*). It obeys the sign convention.

Question: How did you know that FV (Future Value) was zero?

Answer: The problem didn't specifically say there's anything left to pay at the end of the 30 years, so you can safely assume there isn't. That is, the payments completely *amortize* (literally: "kill") the loan in 360 months.

If it were otherwise, the problem would have specified an amount then due in a lump-sum payment—called a *balloon* payment—at the end of the 360-month term.

So you know that FV is zero. But even so, *don't ignore it.* Zero is a number just like any other, and your calculator always uses four TVM numbers to solve for the fifth. If you had forgotten to specify your FV for this problem, your machine would not have assumed zero. It would have used the number it found in the FV register—no matter what that value was or when it was put in there.

Remember! A number in the continuous memory of the HP 17BII is like a budget deficit: It won't melt back to zero just because you ignore it.

The Typical Mortgage Checklist

Review in your mind the checklist of all the little invisible steps you took to actually calculate the payment on that $100,000 mortgage.

1.   You got a verbal description of the loan.

2.   You decided on the *annuity* mode. In other words, do the payments come at the END of the month (also called "annuity in arrears") or at the BEGINning of the month (also called "annuity in advance")?

3.   You interpreted the terms of the loan in order to arrive at the proper D.I.P. and thus the D.I.R. You set the P/YR accordingly so that the A.P.R. given in the problem could be used directly as your I%YR.

4.   You drew the correct picture of the problem from your perspective as a borrower, thus establishing the directions of the cash-flows (up or down on the diagram, + or - in your calculator).

5.   You observed that since no mention was made of any balloon payment, the mortgage must be completely amortized after the 360th payment. So the Future Value (FV) was zero.

6.   You plugged in all known values: N = 360 months, I%YR = 12.00, PV = 100,000, FV = 0. Then you solved for PMT.

7.   You realized that most of the real problem is in defining it; the keystrokes are easy.

Variations on a Theme

So there you have it: a $1028.61 monthly mortgage payment, assuming that your payment comes due at the END of the month.

Question: *What if* it were at the BEGINning of the month? What would your payment amount be? From the comparison diagrams on page 101, can you tell whether it's more or less than the END mode payment?

Solution: Don't touch any of the values you now have in the five TVM registers. Just go to the OTHER Menu and change the annuity mode from END to BEGIN.

Now (EXIT) back to the TVM Menu, and solve for PMT. <u>Answer</u>: PMT=-1,018.43

About ten bucks a month *less*—not a whole lot, you might think. But over 360 months, that works out to be over $3,600 in interest saved.

And keep in mind how you're saving this interest—it's not from a lower rate: With BEGIN mode, you're still paying the same interest *rate*, but you save money, because you are borrowing for a slightly shorter *time*.

From the diagram on page 101, you can see that you're actually making each payment one month earlier than in the END mode scenario.

Well, in either BEGIN or END mode, that payment's a little steep for your budget. But you do want the house, so now you're going to use the "What-If?" abilities of your HP 17BII to shop for better loan terms....

O Joy: Up jumps a lender who offers you all the same terms—360 months, payment at the end of each month, etc.—*and* it's only a 10.5% A.P.R.(!) What will your payment be?

Easy: Again, leave all your TVM parameters alone, except for the ones you're now going to vary:

Press **OTHER END**, to set the annuity mode. Then (EXIT). Now, the only thing you need to change is the I%YR, right?

Prove this by *recalling* each of the five TVM registers (menu variables are just registers you (STO) into and (RCL) from):

(RCL) **N**	N=360.00	Don't change this.
(RCL) **I%YR**	I%YR=12.00	Change this.
(RCL) **PV**	PV=100,000.00	Don't change this.
(RCL) **PMT**	PMT=-1,018.43	Recalculate this after changing I%YR.
(RCL) **FV**	FV=0.00	Don't change this.

OK, so change the interest rate: (1)(0)(·)(5) **I%YR**.... And recalculate **PMT**: PMT=-914.74

Well... that's better—about $100 lower on the payment. But what if it's still too high? Suppose your absolute limit for a principal-and-interest payment is $900.00. That's fine—but it will mean that at the end of the 360th month, you'll have a lump-sum balloon payment to make, to pay off the remaining balance. After all, you *know* there'll be a remaining balance—the machine just told you that it will take $914.74/month to *completely* amortize this loan in 360 months. If you pay even slightly less per month than that, there'll be some leftover to pay at the end.

So here's how the scenario looks:

m	$
0	100,000.00
1	(900.00)
2	(900.00)
3	(900.00)
:	(900.00)
:	(900.00)
360	(900.00)+(FV)

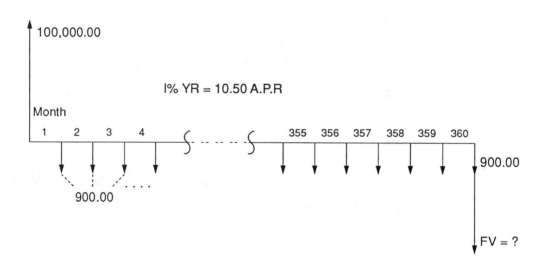

What you want to know is: How much is that final balloon payment?

Find Out: Again, three of the five TVM parameters are already correct (the term, N; the interest rate, I%YR; and the Present Value, PV). What you will do now is *specify* the payment (rather than calculate it), and then find the Future Value that would result.

Press ⑨⓪⓪⊕ **PMT** (remember why it should be negative?), and solve for the remaining balance: **FV**

Answer: FV=-37,089.98

Remember the definition of Future Value! This represents the amount you would have to pay *over and above* your final (360th) payment—and it's negative, as it should be, to indicate who's paying it (yep—it's you). Since this is an END mode problem, your last PMT occurs at the same time as this balloon payment.

As you can see, then, you could lump those last two cash-flows together and write just one check if you wanted. Just be sure that you don't forget what each part means. Sometimes the terms of a contract won't itemize this final combined payment, and if you try to confirm such terms by using that *combined* total as your Future Value ... well, that's not what your HP 17BII means by Future Value. You need to subtract out the amount of the final PMT.

Looking at the T-bar and cash-flow diagram on the previous page here, you can see how clearly and succinctly it shows all this information. ***You'll never get confused if you get the picture right.***

So, here's what you've decided: You want to borrow $100,000.00 at 10.5% A.P.R., repaying it in 360 end-of-month installments of $900.00, plus a final balloon payment of $37,089.98 ...OK?...

No? *Now* what's wrong?

Oh—the balloon's a bit much, eh? It's amazing what "a little less" each month adds up to over thirty years, isn't it? All right, but you realize, of course, that a lower balloon will demand a slightly higher monthly payment; you'll be breaking your $900.00 monthly payment ceiling—by few more bucks a month now—to save thousands over thirty years.

How big a balloon payment could you stand—say, $20,000? Fine. Now check to see what PMT this will demand.

Not Much More: As usual, change only the values you need to (this is routine by now, no?): Press ②⓪⓪⓪⓪ (+/−) **FV** to specify the balloon amount. Then press **PMT** to find the corresponding payment.

<u>Answer</u>: PMT=-906.79

See how powerful this "What-If?" ability is? And you can review your variables at any time with the (RCL) key ((RCL) **N**, (RCL) **I%YR**, etc.):

360	10.50	100,000.00	−906.79	−20,000.00
N	I% YR	PV	PMT	FV

So you can live with those terms. The only problem is, your lender with the 10.5% A.P.R. won't agree to anything less than full amortization—no balloons. In fact, he's encouraging you to consider even *higher* payments, to shorten the term of the loan down to 25, 20, even 15 years.

Of course, you already know you can't afford this much every month, but now that you've got a machine like the HP 17BII, it doesn't hurt to play some more "What-If?" So, *what if* you had the same financing rate and amount, but only, say, a 20-year term? Your scenario would be:

m	$
0	100,000.00
1	(PMT)
2	(PMT)
3	(PMT)
:	(PMT)
:	(PMT)
240	(PMT)

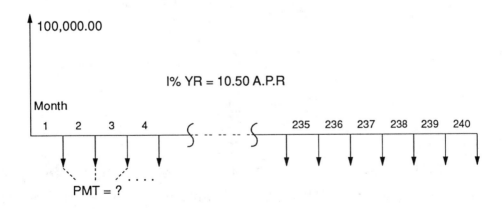

Play With the Term: Find the payment amount necessary to fully amortize this loan in 25, 20, and 15 years.

Solution: Change only what you need to, and leave the rest of the five parameters alone:
②⑤Ⓧ①②(ALG) or ②⑤(INPUT)①②Ⓧ(RPN) ▮N▮ (a shorter term). Then ⓪ ▮FV▮ (no balloon), and solve for ▮PMT▮....
<u>Answer</u>: PMT=-944.18

Not much more than the $914.74—for 5 years' fewer payments! What about 20 years?
②⓪Ⓧ①②(ALG) or ②⓪(INPUT)①②Ⓧ(RPN) ▮N▮, then ▮PMT▮....
<u>Answer</u>: PMT=-998.38

Try 15 years:
①⑤Ⓧ①②(ALG) or ①⑤(INPUT)①②Ⓧ(RPN) ▮N▮, then ▮PMT▮....
<u>Answer</u>: PMT=-1,105.40

Did you realize that for less than $200 more per month, you could cut your mortgage term in *half*? Not bad—if you could scrape together that extra $200/month. But you can't, so you shake the fellow's hand, thank him for his eye-opening offer, and head on down the road....

Feeling slightly discouraged at this point, you start to wonder if you can really afford this house after all....

Sigh: You had set your upper monthly payment limit at $900.00, but even that was pushing it. What you *really* wanted to get away with was about $800.00 or less—and no balloon.

Check: How much house could you finance at 10.5% A.P.R., with 30 years of $800 end-of-month payments?

Here's how the TVM registers should look right now (and you can verify these with the (RCL) key, remember?):

180	10.50	100,000.00	−1,105.40	0.00
N	I% YR	PV	PMT	FV

This time, you're varying the PMT and calculating the Present Value—the amount you can finance over 30 years:

(3)(0)(×)(1)(2) (ALG) *or* (3)(0)(INPUT)(1)(2)(×) (RPN) ▮N▮
(8)(0)(0)(+/−) ▮PMT▮   (the payment you'd like to make)
▮PV▮   (find how much you could finance)
Answer: PV=87,456.61

So if you could come up with about $22,500 for a down-payment on that $110,000 house, you'd have an $800.00 monthly payment. But you've only got $10,000 for a down-payment, and you *do* want the house, so stick to your $900 limit (with a $20,000 balloon) and keep looking....

The next bank down the road seems to have a better deal for you. Here's a lender who will loan you $100,000 in exchange for $906.79 end-of-month payments for 360 months. Period.

Same payments—but no $20,000 balloon—what a deal!

"Uh... what's the catch?"

This: There's a *loan fee* (also known as "points") due and payable at the moment you sign the papers. This fee is 2% of the amount financed, but it's not an early installment on the loan; you still have to pay 360 full payments of $906.79 each.

Is this really a better deal than the $20,000 balloon? Better find out. Start with the T-bar and diagram:

m	$
0	100,000.00+(2,000.00)
1	(906.79)
2	(906.79)
:	(906.79)
360	(906.79)

100,000.00

Month
1 2 3 4 .... 356 357 358 359 360

2,000   906.79 ...   ... 906.79

Still, it's hard to tell which is the better deal for you. How can you use your TVM calculations to help?

Think about it: On page 112, you *know* you're paying 10.5% A.P.R.— that's what you specified to calculate your PMT. But this lender here just pulled a payment amount out of the air. What's the interest rate he was using to do this?

Hmm... Let your HP 17Bɪɪ tell you. Here are the current contents of the TVM registers:

360	10.50	87,456.61	−800.00	0.00
N	I% YR	PV	PMT	FV

You need to change only PV and PMT. First, press ⑨⑧⓪⓪⓪ **PV** . Since you net together all simultaneous cash-flows, what with the $2000 fee (2% of $100,000), you're *not* getting a $100,000 loan. It's a $98,000 loan—but you're still paying $906.79 a month for 30 years.

So press ⑨⓪⑥·⑦⑨⁺⁄⁻ **PMT** then **I%YR**, to find the *real* A.P.R.....   <u>Answer:</u> I%YR=10.64

Aha! That loan fee effectively raised the rate *above* 10.5% A.P.R. you're looking for—not so good!

By using just fundamental TVM skills and your HP 17Bɪɪ's "What-If?" ability, you saved yourself from an expensive mistake (and the calculator probably paid for itself several times over)!

Interest CoNVersions

More confident now, you continue your search for the elusive Perfect Mortgage.... Finally, you find a bank that agrees to your payments, balloon, and a 10.35% rate(!)—but this is a rate that compounds *daily*.

That calls for a little thought.... An *effective* yield is higher than a *nominal* (quoted) rate, since interest compounds. For example, your $100 bank account yields you $112.68 after one year—because the 12% quoted A.P.R. is actually compounded at 1% per month for 12 months.

But when competing for borrowers, a lender wants to put his rates in the best possible light. So, if he's allowed to quote a 10.35% nominal rate alongside its higher effective yield, he'll probably want to emphasize the nominal rate—the lower number is simply more attractive to the loan shopper.

The point is, the more often you compound, the bigger this difference becomes—between the nominal rate and the effective yield. And you can prove this.

Prove It: Use the HP 17Bɪɪ to find the *effective* yield on a nominal annual rate of 10.35%, compounded:

(i) annually; (ii) semi-annually; (iii) quarterly;
(iv) monthly; (v) semi-monthly; (vi) weekly; (vii) daily

Like So: (EXIT) from the TVM Menu and notice the **ICNV** selection. This is a side-calculations menu for converting between interest rates. So press **ICNV**.... Then, since you want *periodic* interest conversions (converting from one period to another), press **PER**. Here's what you'll see:

```
┌─────────────────────────────────────┐
│ COMPOUNDING P TIMES/YR               │
│ [NOM%][EFF%]  P                      │
└─────────────────────────────────────┘
```

Just like any other "What-If?" menu, you key in any two variables and solve for the third. Here you know the NOMinal rate (10.35%) and you have some values to try for P (the number of Periods to be compounded) to see what EFFective yields they produce:

(1)(0)(·)(3)(5) **NOM%** (1) **P** **EFF%** ....EFF%=10.35
10.35% compounded once a year is just 10.35%.
But now try (2) **P** **EFF%** ....   EFF%=10.62
That's the effective yield for *semi-annual* compounding.
And (4) **P** **EFF%** ....EFF%=10.76 (quarterly)
Well, you get the idea. Try the rest of the compounding periods (P = 12, 24, 52, and 365) on your own.

As you'll see, the effective rate for 10.35% compounded daily is 10.90.

"This lender is charging me 10.90% ??? That's way too high!"

Not so fast. That's the *effective* rate. You're trying to compare that to a 10.5% *nominal* rate—like comparing apples and oranges. Besides, a nominal rate is what the HP 17BII needs for its I%YR, since it then converts this to a D.I.R. according to its assumptions.

So, what nominal rate—compounded monthly—*is* equivalent to 10.35% compounded daily? Use the ICNV Menu to find out....

Do It: At the (periodic) interest conversion Menu: 1 0 · 3 5 NOM%
3 6 5 ■ P ■ EFF%.... EFF%=10.90
You've already done this much.

Now just 1 2 ■ P ■ NOM%.... NOM%=10.39

See? You can use this menu to work in either direction—from nominal to effective or vice versa.

That's the A.P.R. this bank is really quoting you. It's higher than it looked—but it's still less than the A.P.R. you were hoping for! And that means you'll actually have a slightly *smaller* payment or balloon than you were willing to accept.

Go for the smaller payment....

Choose: Leaving the interest conversion (`10.39`) right where it is, go back into the TVM Menu (`EXIT` `EXIT` `TVM`). Then, once you're there, the first thing you do is press `STO` `I%YR` (don't just press `I%YR`, because that would be asking the calculator to *calculate* I%YR, which is not what you want).

Now you're ready to figure your payment:

`N=360.00`	(don't touch it)
`I%YR=10.39`	(you just stored this—don't touch it)
`PV=100,000.00`	(you'll probably need to key this in)
`FV=-20,000.00`	(key this in, too)

Solve for `PMT`: `PMT=-898.64`

That's less than your $906.79 for the monthly compounding case, which makes sense: The equivalent A.P.R. here is 10.39, rather than 10.5.

At last—a mortgage with a $20,000.00 balloon <u>and</u> payments of less than $900! All your shopping around and "What-Iffing" with your HP 17Bɪɪ has finally paid off. Congratulations (take a bow).

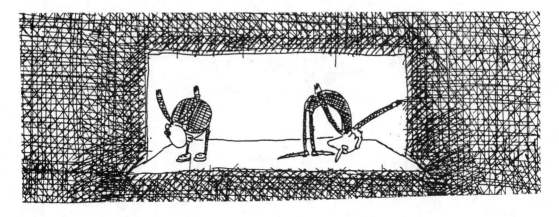

Interest CoNVersion Review

Here's a summary of how to convert an interest rate with differing compound and payment periods, using the ICNV Menu. Remember that the idea is to find the rate to use in TVM (with TVM's assumptions) that produces the same *effective* result as the quoted rate:

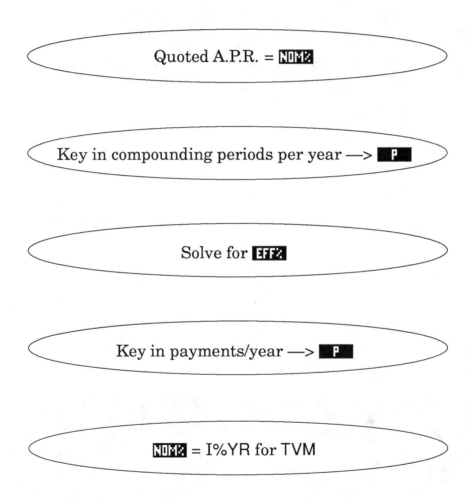

And keep in mind that this conversion can go in either direction.

One more conversion example—just to be sure you've got it....

Example: You're making monthly payments on a $88,500 loan for 25 years. The rate is 12.75%, compounded *daily*. What's the equivalent I%YR you would use in TVM?

Solution: At the ICNV Menu, convert the daily-compounding rate to an equivalent monthly-compounding rate:

　　　　1 2 · 7 5 NOM%
　　　　3 6 5 ▮ P ▮
　　　　EFF% .... (EFF%=13.60)
　　　　1 2 ▮ P ▮
　　　　NOM% .... Answer: NOM%=12.82

Notice that each step here matches the step on the opposite page—no magic, no mystery.

By now, you should know how to handle these types of problems:

- A simple, fully-amortized loan with annuity either in arrears (END) or in advance (BEGIN);

- A loan with a balloon payment;

- A loan with prepaid fees (also called "prepaid finance charges" or "points up front");

- Conversion of an interest rate that compounds over a different period of time than the payment period;

If those are the typical kinds of problems you face each day, then you might wish to skip now to the quiz (on page 140).

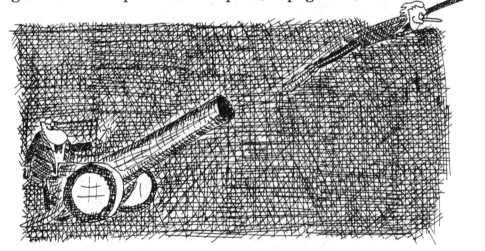

Or, if you want to explore some other kinds of TVM before you try the quiz, then just continue on right here....

5. *The Time Value of Money: TVM*

AMoRTization Schedules

The most common questions you'll want to answer after you know the terms of a mortgage are:

"How much interest and principal am I paying every year? And what's my remaining balance?"

Well, the HP 17BII has an additional feature on the TVM Menu to help you answer these very questions.

Try This: From the TVM Menu, select **OTHER**. Notice the item here that you haven't used yet: Press **AMRT**, and see this:

An AMoRTization schedule is an itemized computation of the amounts of principal and interest ("P and I") paid over any given number of periods within the term of a mortgage. You'll want to know at least the amount of interest you've paid each year, because it's usually tax-deductible.

The AMRT Menu is a set of side calculations—much like the ICONV Menu—but AMRT has an added advantage: *It uses the values directly from your TVM registers;* that's why it's located on the TVM Menu.

To get a feel for AMRT, look at your original house loan again: It was a 30-year, fully-amortized mortgage for $100,000 at 10.5% A.P.R., with monthly payments in arrears, and a balloon of $20,000 at the end (this was before you found that attractive 10.35% loan).

Try This: Use the AMRT Menu to find the principal and interest you would pay in each of the first three years—and the remaining balance still due after the third year.

Solution: First, fill in the usual TVM parameters:

[EXIT][EXIT] to return to the TVM Menu, then
[3][6][0] N
[1][0][·][5] I%YR
[1][0][0][0][0][0] PV
[2][0][0][0][0][+/−] FV
OTHER [1][2] P/YR END [EXIT]
PMT .... Result: PMT=-906.79

This payment ought to look familiar. It was what you had settled on as "acceptable," with a $20,000 balloon.

Now go to the AMRT Menu, by pressing OTHER AMRT. Then just follow the displayed directions:

```
KEY #PMTS; PRESS {#P}
 #P | INT |PRIN| BAL |NEXT|TABLE
```

Since you want to look at 12 payments (one year) at a time, just press ①② **#P**....

```
#P=12 PMTS: 1-12
#P | INT |PRIN | BAL |NEXT |TABLE
```

The display tells you that the numbers you'll get when you calculate INTerest, PRINcipal or BALance now will be for payments 1-12. So, do it:

INT .... INTEREST=-10,481.09
PRIN .... PRINCIPAL=-400.39
BAL .... BALANCE=99,599.61

Notice that your payments show as negative numbers here—because AMRT follows the same sign conventions as the rest of the TVM Menu. That makes sense, right?

But here's the best part: To amortize the NEXT set of 12 payments, just press **NEXT** and you're ready. Not bad, eh?

You can go all the way through the life of the loan this way. To start over from the beginning of the loan, just (EXIT) from the AMRT Menu, then re-enter it again with the **AMRT** key.

Play around with the AMRT Menu items on your own a little bit. Notice especially the selection called **TABLE**. It lets you *print* any portion of the amortization schedule, if you have a printer.

One other note about AMRT: As you know, your HP 17BII uses 12 digits in its arithmetic, including the TVM calculations. *But AMRT is a rare exception to this rule.*

Look: Recall the current value in the PMT register (from TVM, press [RCL] **PMT**). You'll see this: PMT=-906.79

But now SHOW all of its digits (press ■ SHOW).... That's what the payment *really* works out to be (to nine decimal places, at least): PMT=-906.791435594

But nobody writes a check for that much, right? So even though this is the amount you would need to pay every month to *exactly* amortize that 30-year mortgage, you won't be paying that. To be accurate, you need to use the true amount to the nearest penny (here it would be rounded down: 906.790000000).

So key it in: [9][0][6][·][7][9][+/-] **PMT**. And now *recalculate* the **FV**....

You get FV=-20,003.61   What does this mean?

This: Since you had to round your payment down slightly (by a fraction of a penny), you've technically (mathematically) *underpaid* your loan by $3.61. Therefore, your $20,000 balloon payment at the end of the loan is *increased* slightly.

AMRT uses the TVM values, too, but it doesn't use unrealistic "penny fragments" that those TVM registers may hold. Except for the I%YR variable (which is always used to 12 digits), the AMRT Menu uses TVM values only up to the *displayed* number of digits.

In other words, if you have your display set to FIX 2 digits (for dollars and cents), the AMRT calculations will automatically round its own copies of PV and PMT in the same way—so that you always end up with a realistic and verifiable amortization schedule.

Prove It: Go back and run the AMRT example on pages 126-127 again—but with a DSP ALL setting.... Then try it with a FIX 4 setting.... See how the results differ slightly?

So although you'll normally keep a FIX 2 setting, it's instructive to see and understand this difference—to avoid any unnecessary misunderstandings with the bank.

Other Side Calculations

The TVM Menu is designed to handle one basic kind of interest-bearing situation—an amortized installment loan (such as a mortgage). The TVM Menu can handle *only* regular installments over regular periods, with interest compounding each period. So while it's very useful for analyzing investments with cash-flow diagrams, sometimes you need to do other, preliminary calculations simply to construct those diagrams. That's where the "side calculations" menus come in handy.

You've already seen how to use one of these side calculations menus—the ICNV Menu—when you need to determine a proper I%YR to use in the TVM Menu. But there are a couple other such side calculations menus that you ought to look at now....

Do This: Go to the MAIN Menu (press ■MAIN). Press **FIN**....
There, alongside the TVM selection you've come to know and love, you'll see several other choices:

You've already seen the ICNV Menu. And CFLO is another major cash-flow diagram analysis tool (like TVM)—the subject of the next chapter. But the two other choices are indeed side calculations menus: **BOND** and **DEPRC**.

Bonds

A bond is just another kind of loan, but it has different conventions than those of the TVM Menu. A bond is simply a piece of paper that acknowledges an interest-bearing debt from the *issuer* of the bond (the borrower) to the *holder* (the lender). The issuer usually makes *interest-only* payments once or twice a year. The bond specifies the amount of this interest (the *coupon rate*), when it is paid (the *coupon dates*), and when the principal amount is to be repaid (the *maturity date*):

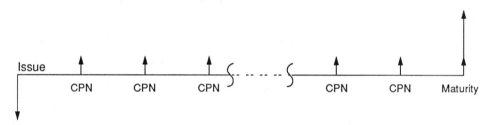

Furthermore, bonds are generally designed to be *negotiable*. That is, they may be freely traded at any time* and for any price.* Thereafter the issuer must pay the interest (and the principal, at maturity) to the *new* holder. This makes for some complications when calculating your yield or the price you should pay, because the dates upon which you buy or sell a bond may not coincide with its coupon dates or maturity date:

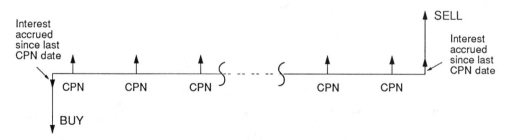

This is why you can't put a bond scenario on a TVM-compatible cash-flow diagram—because the time periods may be *irregular*.

*within all applicable laws and the terms of the bond's original issuance, of course.

Try One: On July 3, 1990, you buy a municipal bond that matures on August 30, 1994 for $100. The bond's coupon rate is 6.75%, with semi-annual payments, calculated on a 30/360-day basis (30 days/month and 360 days/year). What is your yield to maturity if you paid a price of $96.50?

Solution: Press the **BOND** selection and see this menu:

| TYPE | SETT | MAT | CPN% | CALL | MORE |

First, specify the TYPE of bond you have: Press **TYPE**, then **SEMI** and **360** to select the coupon payment frequency and the calendar basis, respectively.

Now [EXIT] and key in the SETTlement date (the date when you buy the bond): [7][.][0][3][1][9][9][0] **SETT** ...
...and the MATurity date: [8][.][3][0][1][9][9][4] **MAT** ...
...and the CouPoN percentage rate: [6][.][7][5] **CPN%** ...
...and the CALL (maturity) value: [1][0][0] **CALL** ....

Now **MORE**, [9][6][.][5] **PRICE** **YLD%** ....
Answer: YLD%=7.75

Easy, no? There's not a lot more to say about calculating with bonds on the HP 17BII. Just key in all the particulars and grind out the answers. You'll get some more hands-on practice in the upcoming quiz, but here are some reminders and things to consider about the BOND Menu:

- No matter whether the coupon is paid annually or semi-annually, the rate you key in is the *annualized* coupon rate.

- Key in dates according to the current date format. This example assumed that your HP 17BII was in MM.DDYYYY date mode.*

- Sometimes a bond may have one or more optional "pay-off" dates—earlier than the maturity date. This is a *call date,* and the HP 17BII allows for it (just key it in as the MATurity date) *as long as it coincides with a coupon date* (a date when interest is paid).

- A call value may be different from $100, but the maturity value must be $100, the conventional basis for face value. Thus, all calculated values represent *percentages of the face value* of your bond. The "pay-off" value—whether it's the face value or some other call value—must always go into the CALL register. However, for convenience, the calculator automatically puts 100.00 into the CALL register whenever you press ▉CLEAR DATA).

- Unlike some of the other "What-If?" menus you've seen, most of the values on the BOND Menu are for input only; you can't solve for them. Only PRICE or YLD% may be your unknown—and you must key in one to get the other.

- When you buy a bond on any date other than a coupon date, in addition to the price, the seller is also due the unpaid interest accrued since the last coupon date. So after calculating either the price or yield (whichever is your unknown), just press ▉ACCRU.
  <u>Result</u> (for this example): ACCRU=2.31

*You can change this format: Press ▉MAIN TIME SET M/D, then ▉MAIN FIN BOND to return to the BOND Menu. Date formats are covered in Chapter 8.

Depreciation

The final topic of this chapter is another "side-calculation" menu you may need when constructing a TVM diagram.

Usually, when you think of the Time Value of Money, it's an investment or account that gains value over time. But depreciation occurs when an asset *loses* value over time. It starts at its cost or other BASIS value, then, over its useful LIFE, depreciates to its SALVage value. The total value lost over the LIFEtime is called the *total depreciable value*.

Example: You're buying a piece of equipment for $40,000. You estimate it to have a useful life of 5 years and a salvage value of $10,000. What amounts should you recognize as depreciation in each of those five years?

Answer: First of all, identify the BASIS value. Usually, this is the cost: $40,000. You know the SALVage value is $10,000, and so the total depreciable value—the difference—is $30,000. This is the total capital value you expect the asset to *lose* over its 5-year LIFE.

Now, that doesn't answer the main question: What fraction (percentage) of the depreciable value should you depreciate each year—for tax and accounting purposes—for this asset? There are several standard methods to compute this—different methods for different assets. The HP 17BⅡ gives you four such methods. Consider each, as it would treat your $40,000 asset:

SL: **Straight Line.** This is the easiest method to compute (and to understand). It simply *prorates* the total depreciable value, reducing it evenly over the LIFE of the asset. That is, the same percentage of the original value is taken each year. Your asset has a total depreciable value is $30,000, so you simply depreciate $6,000/year for each of the 5 years of its useful life.

Do It: From the MAIN Menu, press **FIN** **DEPRC**.... This is the "side-calculations" DEPReCiation Menu.

First, key in the values you know: ④⓪⓪⓪⓪**BASIS**①⓪⓪⓪⓪ **SALV** ⑤ **LIFE**. Then press **MORE** to see the menu's next page.

Now just key in each year you're interested in and ask for the SL amount of depreciation for that year:

① **YR#** **SL**	Result: SL=6,000.00
② **YR#** **SL**	Result: SL=6,000.00
③ **YR#** **SL**	Result: SL=6,000.00
④ **YR#** **SL**	Result: SL=6,000.00
⑤ **YR#** **SL**	Result: SL=6,000.00
⑥ **YR#** **SL**	Result: SL=0.00

As you can see, Straight-Line depreciation is just that—steady and uniform. And notice that it's smart enough to catch your "Year 6" error. The HP 17Bɪɪ won't let you take depreciation beyond the asset's SALVage value (provided that you haven't changed depreciation methods in midstream).

DB: **Declining Balance.** This method reduces the *total remaining* value of the asset by the same *fraction* each year. That fraction is expressed as a percentage of the fraction necessary for a *Straight-Line* depreciation to *zero* (no salvage value).

For example, with your five-year asset, a straight-line depreciation to zero Salvage Value would require that you depreciate 20% (of the original value) per year. A Declining Balance factor of, say, "150%" would therefore depreciate 30% (that's 1.5 times—or 150%—as fast as the SL 20%) per year.

But *unlike SL,* DB is depreciating this 30% off of the *Remaining* Depreciable Value. As that value declines, so does the amount of depreciation in each successive year. Here are the two methods, side by side:

	Straight Line (20% of *total BASIS value* per year)		Declining Balance (30% of *total remaining value* per year)	
Year	$ deprec.	Remaining Value	$ deprec.	Remaining Value
0	--	$40,000	--	$40,000
1	$8,000	32,000	$12,000	28,000
2	8,000	24,000	8,400	19,600
3	8,000	16,000	5,880	13,720
.				
.				
.				

And so on.

Do It: From the previous example, you're already within the DEPRC Menu, with your known values already in the BASIS, SALV and LIFE registers.

So press **MORE**, if necessary, and key in the Declining Balance FACTor, as a percentage: ①⑤⓪ **FACT%**. This is how fast the declining balance rate begins its depreciations, compared to a Straight-Line/no-salvage pace. Then, as usual, key in each year and ask for the amount of depreciation for that year:

① **YR#** **DB**	<u>Result</u>: DB=12,000.00
② **YR#** **DB**	<u>Result</u>: DB=8,400.00
③ **YR#** **DB**	<u>Result</u>: DB=5,880.00
④ **YR#** **DB**	<u>Result</u>: DB=3,720.00
⑤ **YR#** **DB**	<u>Result</u>: DB=0.00

Notice that if the depreciation rate is too fast, there may be one or more years at the end in which the depreciation is *zero*—as in year 5 here. Or, if the rate is too slow, then there may be a big chunk of depreciable value left for the final year—and it will *all* be taken that year.

SOYD: Sum Of the Years' Digits. This method—like the DB method—weights the depreciation toward the beginning. But it does so by depreciating a decreasing percentage of the total depreciable value (whereas DB takes a *constant* percentage of the total *remaining* value). The pattern of SOYD's percentage decreases is determined by the Sum Of the Years' Digits. For example, your $40,000 asset has a total depreciable value of $30,000 and a 5-year LIFE. And the sum of those five years' *digits* is 1+2+3+4+5 = 15. *So:*

Year	fraction depreciated	$ amount of deprec.
1	5/15	$10,000
2	4/15	8,000
3	3/15	6,000
4	2/15	4,000
5	1/15	2,000
Total	15/15	$30,000

Go: Using the existing asset data (BASIS, LIFE and SALVage), key in each year and ask for the depreciation for that year:

     ① ▮YR#▮ ▮SOYD▮   Result: SOYD=10,000.00

     ② ▮YR#▮ ▮SOYD▮   Result: SOYD=8,000.00

     ③ ▮YR#▮ ▮SOYD▮   Result: SOYD=6,000.00

     ④ ▮YR#▮ ▮SOYD▮   Result: SOYD=4,000.00

     ⑤ ▮YR#▮ ▮SOYD▮   Result: SOYD=2,000.00

ACRS: Accelerated Cost Recovery System. This method isn't really much of a calculation. ACRS simply *assigns* percentages of the total depreciable value to be taken in each year in the asset's LIFE. These percentages don't necessarily follow a mathematical formula, but they must add up to 100% of the *BASIS* value over the asset's LIFE (*ACRS ignores the SALVage value*). Here's an example of how ACRS depreciation percentages and amounts might look for your 5-year asset:

Year	percentage depreciated	$ amount of deprec.
1	25	$10,000
2	15	6,000
3	20	8,000
4	20	8,000
5	20	8,000
Total	100	$40,000

So: Using the existing asset data (the BASIS value) do this:

②⑤ ACRS% ACRS	Result: ACRS=10,000.00
①⑤ ACRS% ACRS	Result: ACRS=6,000.00
②⓪ ACRS% ACRS	Result: ACRS=8,000.00
②⓪ ACRS% ACRS	Result: ACRS=8,000.00
②⓪ ACRS% ACRS	Result: ACRS=8,000.00

As you can see, these ACRS calculations are little more than simple percentage calculations—where *you* key in the percentages. So beware: The HP 17BII doesn't check these percentages to see if they add up to 100—nor does it check to see if the BASIS or LIFE has been exceeded.

TVM Quiz

It's time to put it all together. On the following pages are quiz problems that combine and reinforce the various TVM concepts and tools you've studied in this chapter.

Don't blur over these problems! This is where you'll do most of your real learning. You don't know how much you really understand until you do some problems where the answers aren't given right away.* Most problems will require you to build a cash-flow diagram or T-bar—and you may need to do "side-calculations" to get those values.

The problems are grouped according to subject matter, so that you can concentrate on one area, if that's your main concern. However, you will learn far more if you try them all, rather than concentrating on your immediate interest, because all the problems give you practice with menus, problem-solving, and (in most cases) the TVM Menu and cash-flow diagrams. Whatever else you do, be sure to use a diagram or a T-bar for any situation where you need any help in visualizing the nature and timing of the cash-flows!

Enjoy these—and take all the time you need to understand them *well*. There's nobody looking over your shoulder here.

---

* The answers *are* given here—they're just collected all together, following the problems.

TVM Review

1. If Benjamin Franklin saved (and thus earned) a single penny, investing it on January 1, 1750, in a tax-free account earning 5% per year (compounded annually), what would that account balance be on January 1, 2000? When would it reach $1,000? What if the interest compounds *daily*?

2. How much will you need to invest every month for 5 years, in a fund that typically earns 12% (compounded monthly), to accumulate a 15% down payment on a $130,000 home? What if home prices are rising at 6% per year in the meantime?

3. If your money can earn 8% interest (compounded daily) in a liquid account, and you win a $1 million lottery jackpot, would you rather receive it tax-free but paid out at $50,000/year over 20 years, or in a taxable lump-sum now? Your tax bracket is 33%.

4. A fast-food hamburger that went for $0.89 twenty years ago now costs $2.59. Using this as a cost-of-living index, what has been the average annual inflation rate over those twenty years?

5. How long does it take to pay down a 30-year, $100,000 mortgage at 10%, (monthly payments in arrears) to 75% of the original balance? How about 50% of the balance? 25%?

6. What is the balance after 48 end-of-month payments of $188 on a loan of $7,500 at 12.5%, compounded monthly? What if the first payment is due three months from the date of the loan?

7. If you can earn 6.5% in an account (compounded daily), and you are selling a truck for $15,000, would you accept $500 down and a note for $15,000 more—due in 1 year?

8. How long would it take to double your money in each of these accounts?

    a. 7.5%, compounded monthly;

    b. 7.5% compounded daily;

    c. 5% compounded annually;

    d. 10% compounded annually;

    e. 15% compounded annually;

What yearly-compounded rate doubles your money in 10 years?

9. If, on your 25th birthday (happy birthday), you begin to pay $2000 per year for 7 years into a (tax-deferred) IRA yielding a 10% A.P.R., and then you *stop* paying into that account for 28 subsequent years, how does the resulting year-end balance compare with a similar account that you open on your 32nd birthday, into which you pay $2000 for *every year* up through your 60th year?

10. As a lessor, what should you pay for a 5-year office lease with monthly rent (due in advance) of $900? Your discount rate is 8%. Then, for a 12% yield, what should you sell the lease for in 3 years?

11. A mortgage was written at 9.5% A.P.R. It amortizes totally in 30 years of monthly payments (in arrears). If the payment amount is $924.94, what was the loan amount?

12. If the loan from the previous problem instead had $850 payments—and annuity in advance—what would the remaining balance be after the 360th month? After the 120th month?

13. Compare these interest rates: A $20,000 car lease with monthly payments of $440 (in advance) and a buyout of $5000 in five years; or a credit card charging 16.5% A.P.R., compounded daily.

14. A finance company charges 2 points for a $100,000 loan at 12% A.P.R., compounded daily (on a 360-day year), with quarterly payments (in arrears) that will amortize the loan in 15 years.

   a. What is the payment amount?

   b. What is the remaining balance after 10 years?

   c. If the balance is actually paid in a balloon payment at that 10-year point, what is the A.P.R. earned by the finance company? Would that A.P.R. be different if the loan is carried to term (15 years)? Why?

Residential Real Estate

15. You're buying a $103,000 home, putting 10% down and financing the balance at 11% A.P.R., with monthly payments in arrears. Your maximum payment (principal and interest) is $900.

   a. Can you totally amortize this loan in 20 years?

   b. If you were to make the payment necessary to amortize the loan in 20 years, how much interest would you save, compared to a 30-year amortization?

16. How long will it take to pay off a 30-year, $100,000 mortgage at 10%, if you make 26 payments/year, each *half* the normal monthly payment? What is this payment amount? Calculate the amortization schedule for each of the first two years.

17. A prospective home-buyer wants to accelerate the pay-down of her mortgage by adding an extra $20 of payment toward principal in each monthly installment. The $85,000, 9.5% mortgage would normally amortize in 30 years of monthly payments (in arrears), how much sooner will the borrower pay this off? Calculate the amortization schedule for each of the first two years.

18. What is the amount of the first payment on a 30-year, $72,000 loan at 12% (monthly payments, in arrears), with constant payments to principal? How much is the last payment?

19. The rates for a 30-year, $90,000 Adjustable Rate Mortgage (ARM) are: Year 1: 9.0%   Year 2: 9.5%   Year 3: 10.0%

Year 4: 10.5%   Year 5: 11.0%

Find the payments and year-end balances for the first five years.

20. A couple is buying a $90,000 home. Their gross monthly income is $3500. They pay $200 per month toward other long-term debt. Insurance on the home will be about $30/month; taxes are $2,250 annually. With a 30-year mortgage at a fixed rate of 10%, for what amount of financing could they qualify under each of the following four sets of qualifying rules?* Calculate the corresponding principal-and-interest payments, also.

(*Note:* Applicable qualifying rules may now be different):

Conventional: *Maximum* PITI (Principal, Interest, Taxes and Insurance, plus any mortgage insurance/association dues) is the *lesser* of
- 28% of Gross Income ($GI)   *or*
- 36% of $GI, less long-term debt pmt. ($LTD).

Use 25% of $GI and 33% of $GI, respectively, if the down-payment is less than 10%.

FNMA: Maximum PITI is 28% of $GI.

GNMA: Maximum PITI is 36% of $GI, less $LTD.

FHA: Maximum PITI is the *lesser* of
- 29% of Gross Income ($GI)   *or*
- 41% of $GI, less long-term debt pmt. ($LTD).

*Assume no mortgage insurance or other association dues in this example.

Commercial Investment

21. For a 10% yield-to-maturity, what price (and accrued interest) can you pay on 7/28/90 for a 7% bond (semiannual coupons, actual calendar basis) maturing on 9/9/99? Then what's your yield-to-call if the bond is callable at 88.125 on 3/9/95?

22. At the beginning of a tax year, you buy a small office building with improvements valued at $75,000, a $10,000 computer, and then landscape the property with $5000 in shrubs. Estimated salvage values for these new assets: $15,000, $500 and $0, respectively. What depreciation can you take for each in tax years 3 and 4?:

Property examples	Class	Allowed Depr. Method
vehicles, office/lab equip.	5 years	200% DB or SL
roads, shrubbery,	15 years	150% DB or SL
nonresidential real prop.	31.5 years	SL

23. Use the Band of Investment method (weighting current market expectations for mortgage and equity funds by the Loan-to-Value ratio on a property) to compute the NOI, cap rate and value of this property:

	Office	Warehouse
Rent ($/ft²/year)	7.80	4.07
Floor area (ft²)	2,277	2,005
Vacancy rate (%)	0.5	1.0

Taxes: $3,647   Mngmt: $3,060   Maint.: $2,318

Insurance: $773   Loan-to-Value: 70%

Mortgage rate: 12.75%   Equity return rate: 14%

24. An investor is considering the purchase of a small office building appraised at $750,000, of which 70% is improved.

The proposal:

$250,000 cash down
First mortgage: $350,000 at 10.5% for 20 years (1.5 points)
Second mortgage: $150,000 at 12% for 10 years (2 points)
Costs of closing and acquisition: $2,000

Maximum gross rent potential: $125,000/yr
Projected vacancy/loss rate: 6%
Insurance: $3,000/yr
Maintenance and management: $12,000/yr

Property tax rate: 2.5%
Rent, expenses and prop. values to follow inflation: 5%/yr.

In five years, the investor expects to sell the property (through a broker, for a 6% commission), at a cap rate of 11.5% on the Net Operating Income projected for Year 6. The investor's income tax bracket is 33%; capital gains are 100% taxable.

Find the net (after-tax) cash-flow for the initial investment and for each of the five years of operation. For Year 1, find the Gross Rent Multiplier, cap rate, equity return rate, and the after-tax cash return rate.

25. If inflation is 5% per year, and your tax bracket is 27%, what will be the real value (i.e. the buying power in terms of today's dollars) of a $1000 investment (today) into a taxable account earning 10% per year—for 25 years? 40 years?

26. Assuming a 5% annual inflation rate and an income tax rate of 28%, if you invest $2,000 of *buying power* at the end of each year into a growth-oriented mutual fund that earns 15% per year, what buying power will accumulate in this account over 30 years? What is the equivalent annual growth rate of this buying power? What if the account were tax-deferred—like an IRA?

27. Your monthly salary is $3333.20 per month, with annual cost-of-living raises (5% a year). If, for 35 years, you invest 5% of each monthly paycheck into a growth-oriented mutual fund IRA (tax-deferred until withdrawal) averaging 15% growth per year, what gross income (today's dollars) could then you draw for 30 years of retirement if you roll the account into a more secure bond fund at 10%? What is the rollover amount? What if, in addition to that 5%, you were also allowed to invest the 7.65% that now goes for Social Security and Medicare? Repeat the problem for a taxable account (28% income tax bracket).

TVM Quiz Solutions

1. From the investor's perspective:

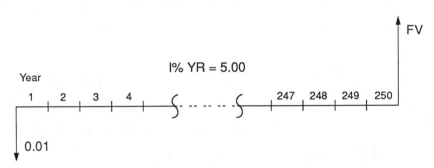

From the TVM Menu, press **OTHER** and set your annuity mode (to END MODE) and P/YR (to 1). Then (EXIT) to TVM, and:
(2)(5)(0) **N** (5) **I%YR** (.)(0)(1)(+/−) **PV** (0) **PMT**
FV .... Answer: FV=1,983.01 (in the year 2000)

Then (1)(0)(0)(0) **FV** **N** .... Result: N=235.97
(+)(1)(7)(5)(0)(=) (ALG) *or* (1)(7)(5)(0)(+) (RPN) Result: 1985.97
So the account balance reaches $1000 toward the end of 1985.

For daily compounding, you just change the number of payments per year: Press **OTHER** and set P/YR to 365 (don't worry about leap years). Then (EXIT) to TVM, and:
(2)(5)(0)(×)(3)(6)(5) (ALG) *or* (2)(5)(0)(INPUT)(3)(6)(5)(×) (RPN) **N**
FV .... Answer: FV=2,681.08 (in the year 2000)

Then (1)(0)(0)(0) **FV** **N** .... Result: N=84,050.11
(÷)(3)(6)(5)(+)(1)(7)(5)(0)(=) (ALG) *or* (3)(6)(5)(÷)(1)(7)(5)(0)(+) (RPN)
Result: 1980.27 The balance reaches $1000 in early 1980.

2. From your perspective:

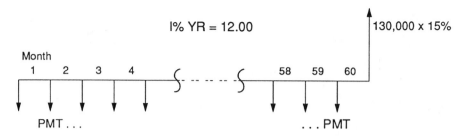

From the TVM Menu, press **OTHER** and set your annuity mode (to
BEG MODE) and **P/YR** (to **12**). Then EXIT to TVM, and:
⑤✕①② (ALGebraic) *or* ⑤ INPUT ①②✕ (RPN) **N**
①② **I%YR** ⓪ **PV**
①③⓪⓪⓪⓪✕①⑤% (ALGebraic) *or*
①③⓪⓪⓪⓪ INPUT ①⑤% (RPN) **FV**
Then solve: **PMT** ....   Answer: PMT=-236.40

But if the prices of houses are increasing at 6% per year, then you
must first compute what a 15% down payment will be in 5 years:

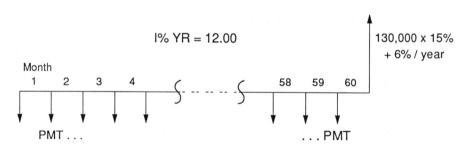

From the TVM Menu, press **OTHER** and set **P/YR** to **1**. Then EXIT
and: ⑤ **N** ⑥ **I%YR** RCL **FV** +/− **PV** ⓪ **PMT**
FV ....   Answer: FV= 26,095.40
Now re-calculate your monthly investment: **OTHER** ①② **P/YR**
EXIT ⑤✕①② (ALGebraic) *or* ⑤ INPUT ①②✕ (RPN) **N**
①② **I%YR** ⓪ **PV**
Then solve: **PMT** ....   Answer: PMT=-316.36

3. The question is: "Which is greater—a lump sum of $1 million, less 33%, or the Present Value of this scenario, discounted at 8%?"

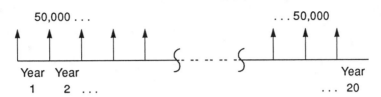

I% YR = 8.00 (daily)

The lump-sum: $\boxed{1}\boxed{0}\boxed{0}\boxed{0}\boxed{0}\boxed{0}\boxed{0}\boxed{-}\boxed{3}\boxed{3}\boxed{\%}\boxed{=}$ (ALGebraic) *or*
$\boxed{1}\boxed{0}\boxed{0}\boxed{0}\boxed{0}\boxed{0}\boxed{0}\boxed{INPUT}\boxed{3}\boxed{3}\boxed{\%}\boxed{-}$ (RPN)   Result: **670,000.00**
To analyze the above scenario, first you must find the equivalent *yearly* discount rate: $\boxed{EXIT}$ from TVM and press **ICNV** **PER** $\boxed{8}$ **NOM%**
$\boxed{3}\boxed{6}\boxed{5}$ **P** **EFF%**....   Result: **EFF%=8.33**
Then $\boxed{EXIT}\boxed{EXIT}$ **TVM**, $\boxed{STO}$ **I%YR**. Then press **OTHER** and set your annuity mode (to **BEG MODE**) and **P/YR** (to 1).
Then $\boxed{EXIT}$ and: $\boxed{2}\boxed{0}$ **N** $\boxed{5}\boxed{0}\boxed{0}\boxed{0}\boxed{0}$ **PMT** $\boxed{0}$ **FV**
PV....   Answer: **PV=-519,064.88**
So those 20 later payments are equivalent to $519,064.88 now. Looks like the lump-sum is the better deal.

4. A simple rate calculation problem—but the TVM sign conventions still need to treat it as an investment/return scenario:

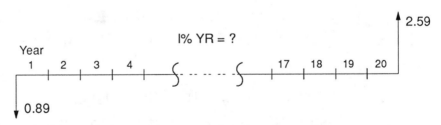

From the TVM Menu, press **OTHER** and set **P/YR** to 1. Then $\boxed{EXIT}$
$\boxed{2}\boxed{0}$ **N** $\boxed{.}\boxed{8}\boxed{9}\boxed{+/-}$ **PV** $\boxed{0}$ **PMT** $\boxed{2}\boxed{.}\boxed{5}\boxed{9}$ **FV**
Then solve: **I%YR**....   Answer: **I%YR=5.49**

5. The basic picture:

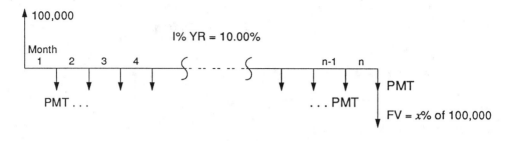

First, find the payment amount: At the TVM Menu, press **OTHER** and set END MODE and 12 P/YR. Then (EXIT) and:

(3)(0)(×)(1)(2) (ALGebraic) *or* (3)(0)(INPUT)(1)(2)(×) (RPN) **N**
(1)(0) **I%YR** (1)(0)(0)(0)(0)(0) **PV** (0) **FV**
PMT .... Result: PMT=-877.57

Now find the number of payments (months) to reach those specified balances (Future Values):

(RCL) **PV** (+/−)
(×)(7)(5)(%)(=) (ALGebraic) *or* (7)(5)(%) (RPN) **FV**
N ....Result: N=209.92   (about 17.5 years)

(RCL) **PV** (+/−)
(×)(5)(0)(%)(=) (ALGebraic) *or* (5)(0)(%) (RPN) **FV**
N .... Result: N=282.40   (about 23.5 years)

(RCL) **PV** (+/−)
(×)(2)(5)(%)(=) (ALGebraic) *or* (2)(5)(%) (RPN) **FV**
N .... Result: N=327.34   (a little more than 27 years)

Note: If you do a lot of this sort of calculation, you may want to use a Solver formula—see the note on page 311 in Chapter 9.

6. The conventional loan, from the borrower's perspective:

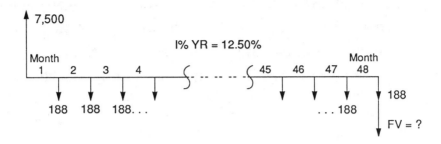

From the TVM Menu, press <kbd>OTHER</kbd>, set END MODE and 12 P/YR.
Then <kbd>EXIT</kbd> and:
<kbd>4</kbd><kbd>×</kbd><kbd>1</kbd><kbd>2</kbd> (ALGebraic) *or* <kbd>4</kbd><kbd>INPUT</kbd><kbd>1</kbd><kbd>2</kbd><kbd>×</kbd> (RPN) <kbd>N</kbd>
<kbd>1</kbd><kbd>2</kbd><kbd>.</kbd><kbd>5</kbd> <kbd>I%YR</kbd> <kbd>7</kbd><kbd>5</kbd><kbd>0</kbd><kbd>0</kbd> <kbd>PV</kbd> <kbd>1</kbd><kbd>8</kbd><kbd>8</kbd><kbd>+/−</kbd> <kbd>PMT</kbd>
Then solve: <kbd>FV</kbd>....   <u>Answer</u>: FV=-702.21

The same loan, but with 90 days before the first payment is due:

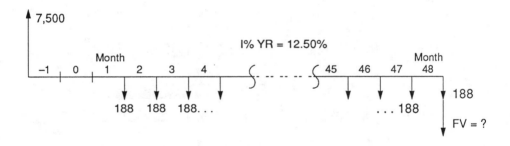

First you calculate how much $7500 becomes with 2 months of
accrued interest: <kbd>2</kbd> <kbd>N</kbd> <kbd>0</kbd> <kbd>PMT</kbd>
<kbd>FV</kbd>....   <u>Result</u>: FV=-7,657.06

Now use this result as the "amount loaned" (after a sign change)
for a repeat of the above conventional loan calculation:
<kbd>+/−</kbd> <kbd>PV</kbd> <kbd>4</kbd><kbd>8</kbd> <kbd>N</kbd> <kbd>1</kbd><kbd>8</kbd><kbd>8</kbd><kbd>+/−</kbd> <kbd>PMT</kbd>
<kbd>FV</kbd>....   <u>Answer</u>: FV=-960.49

7. You're looking for $15,000 now, and the buyer is offering $500 now. So, is the *present* value of receiving $15,000 *a year from now* equal to the difference ($14,500)? Or, to put it differently, what rate of interest are you earning if you *assume* this equivalency? Is it better or worse than 6.5% compounded daily? Here's the picture:

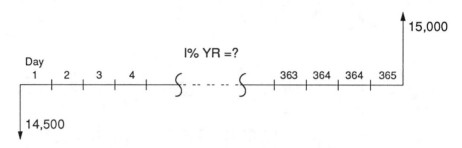

From the TVM Menu, press **OTHER** and set P/YR to 365. (EXIT) to TVM, and:

(3)(6)(5) **N** (1)(4)(5)(0)(0)(+/−) **PV** (0) **PMT** (1)(5)(0)(0)(0) **FV**
I%YR.... Answer: I%YR=3.39   Better insist on cash now.

8. Just double a dollar: (1)(+/−) **PV** (0) **PMT** (2) **FV**

    a. Set 12 P/YR and (EXIT)(7)(·)(5) **I%YR** **N** ....
    Result: N=111.25 (111.25 *months*—about 9.27 years)

    b. Set 365 P/YR and (EXIT) **N** ....
    Result: N=3,373.66 (3,373.66 *days*—about 9.24 years)

    c. Set 1 P/YR and (EXIT)(5) **I%YR** **N** ....
    Result: N=14.21

    d. (1)(0) **I%YR** **N** ....   Result: N=7.27

    e. (1)(5) **I%YR** **N** ....   Result: N=4.96

In 10 years exactly : (1)(0) **N** **I%YR**   Result: I%YR=7.18

9. You're comparing the Future Values of these two scenarios:

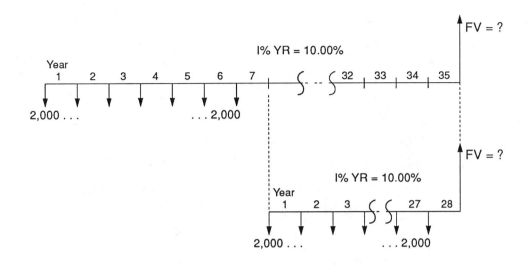

From TVM, press `OTHER` `1` `P/YR` `BEG` `EXIT`.

To begin in the first scenario, find the account balance after 7 years of saving: `7` `N` `10` `I/YR` `0` `PV` `2000` `+/−` `PMT` `FV` .... Result: FV=20,871.78

Now let that amount accrue for another 28 years, with no further payments into the account. This FV becomes the PV now (i.e. you are moving the entire TVM "picture frame" forward in time):
`+/−` `PV` `0` `PMT` `28` `N` `FV`
Answer: FV=300,991.75

The second scenario: `0` `PV` `2000` `+/−` `PMT` `FV`
Answer: FV=295,261.86

Just 7 early years of saving are better than 28 later years.
That's the Time Value of Money.

10. The first problem, from your (the new lessor's) perspective:

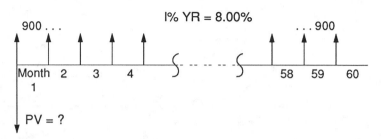

From the TVM Menu, press **OTHER** and set your annuity mode (to BEG MODE) and P/YR (to 12). Then (EXIT) to TVM, and:

⑤⊗①② (ALGebraic) *or* ⑤(INPUT)①②⊗ (RPN) **N**

⑧ **I%YR** ⑨⓪⓪ **PMT** ⓪ **FV**

Solve: **PV** ....   Answer: PV=-44,682.50

To find its price for sale in 3 years to yield you 12%:

③⊗①② (ALGebraic) *or* ③(INPUT)①②⊗ (RPN) **N**

①② **I%YR** **FV** ....   Answer: FV=24,773.44

11. From the lender's perspective:

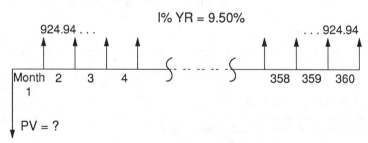

From the TVM Menu, press **OTHER** and check your annuity mode (should be END MODE) and P/YR (should be 12). Then (EXIT) to TVM, and:

③⓪⊗①② (ALGebraic) *or* ③⓪(INPUT)①②⊗ (RPN) **N**

⑨•⑤ **I%YR** ⑨②④•⑨④ **PMT** ⓪ **FV**

Then solve: **PV** ....   Answer: PV=-110,000.04

12. A variation on the previous problem:

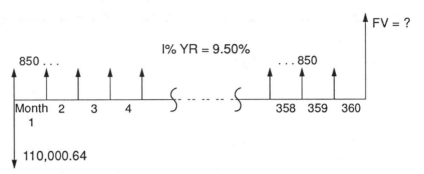

Change only what you have to from the previous problem: At the TVM Menu, press `OTHER` `BEG` (EXIT). Then ⑧⑤⓪ `PMT` `FV` to find the balloon payment after 30 years: FV=138,675.02

Yikes! What's *that*? How can a $110,000 mortgage produce this howling monster $138,000 balloon?

It can—if the monthly mortgage payment is not enough to cover all of the monthly interest. And $850 a month just doesn't do it. Instead of covering all interest plus paying a little principal (like a normal mortgage payment), $850 pays only *part* of the interest and never touches the principal. That astronomical balloon is the result of the unpaid interest compounding for 30 years.*

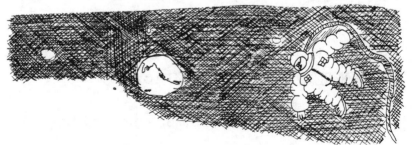

Indeed, look how far this *negative amortization* gets in just 10 years: ①②⓪ `N` `FV` .... FV=112,807.98

*When asked to name the most awesome force in the universe, Albert Einstein is said to have once replied, "compound interest."

13. This is just a comparison of two interest rates, but you'll need to do some calculating before you can compare them directly.

Here's the car loan diagram:

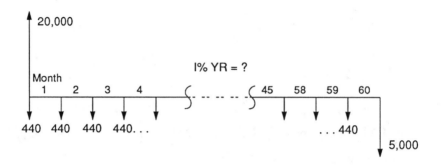

At the TVM Menu (set 12 P/YR and BEGIN MODE):
⑥⓪ **N** ②⓪⓪⓪⓪ **PV** ④④⓪(+/-) **PMT**
⑤⓪⓪⓪(+/-) **FV**
I%YR   <u>Answer</u>: I%YR=17.22

As for the credit card rate, you don't even need a TVM calculation —just a quick trip to the ICNV Menu:
From the TVM Menu, press (EXIT)**ICNV** **PER**, then ③⑥⑤ **P**
①⑥·⑤**NOM%**, and solve:
EFF% ....   <u>Result</u>: EFF%=17.93
Now find the corresponding nominal rate in a 12-period year:
①②**P** **NOM%**....<u>Result</u>: NOM%=16.61

That's better than the 17.22% of your car loan.

14. Here's the situation:

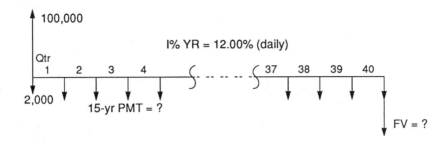

Your first problem is to match the interest rate (daily) to the payment schedule (quarterly). That's an Interest CoNVersion side calculation: From the TVM Menu, press (EXIT) ICNV PER

Then (1)(2) NOM% (3)(6)(0) P EFF%   EFF%=12.75
And (4) P NOM%   NOM%=12.18
Now (EXIT)(EXIT) TVM and (STO) I%YR.

a. The payment amount: Press OTHER END and (4) P/YR, then (EXIT) to TVM and (6)(0) N (1)(0)(0)(0)(0)(0) PV (0) FV PMT ....   Answer: PMT=-3,648.16

b. The remaining balance after 10 years (40 payments): (4)(0) N FV ....   Answer: FV=-54,050.52

c. The finance company really loaned $98,000: (9)(8)(0)(0)(0) PV I%YR .... Answer: I%YR=12.59

d. Same calculation, but take the loan to term: (6)(0) N (0) FV I%YR .... Answer: I%YR=12.56

The term of the loan *does* affect the A.P.R. The finance charge is the same in either case, but its impact on the yield percentage is "distributed" over more time in the latter case. (Analogy: The same $3 tip adds 15% to a $20 dinner tab but only 10% to a $30 tab.)

15. Here's the scenario:

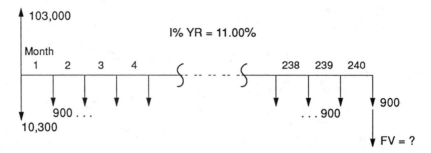

If FV comes up negative, it represents a balloon you'll have to pay at the end of the term. If FV is positive, this means that you have actually *overpaid* the loan (thus it shows a positive balance). Set 12 P∕YR and END mode. Then, at the TVM Menu: ②⓪✕①②
(ALG) *or* ②⓪ INPUT ①②✕ (RPN) N ①① I%YR
①⓪③⓪⓪⓪ and ➖①⓪% (ALG) *or* INPUT ①⓪%➖ (RPN) PV
⑨⓪⓪+/− PMT FV .... Answer: FV=-49,201.69

This is a balloon that you'd need to *pay* (it's negative), so $900 is *not* enough to amortize the mortgage in 20 years. And how much interest would a true 20-year amortization save? Compare these:

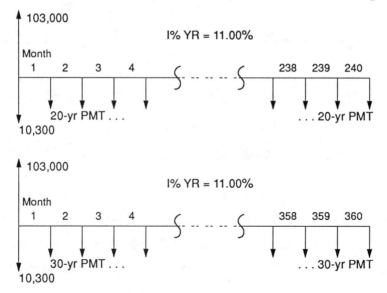

Each amortizing PMT pays all interest accrued on the loan balance in that period, *plus* it pays a little on the principal. The next month, there's a little less interest to pay and so a little more room to pay on principal, etc. Look at this diagram:

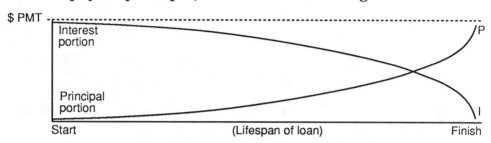

Since in both cases, the loan is totally amortized, the principal paid is the same—the amount financed: $92,700. So the difference in interest paid is simply the difference in totals paid:

Press ⓪ ▮Fⱽ▮ to specify total amortization of the 20-year case, then ▮PMT▮.... Result: PMT=-956.84

Then ⊗ RCL ▮N▮ ⊜(ALGebraic) *or* RCL ▮N▮ ⊗ (RPN) and STO ①
to store this (to read more about storage registers, see Ch. 7).

The 30-year case: ③⓪⊗①②(ALG) *or* ③⓪INPUT①②⊗ (RPN)
▮N▮ ▮PMT▮   (Result: PMT=-882.80)
And ⊗ RCL ▮N▮ ⊜(ALGebraic) *or* RCL ▮N▮ ⊗ (RPN), then
⊖RCL①⊜(ALGebraic) *or* RCL①⊖ (RPN)
Answer: -88,168.09

That's the *face value* of the difference in interest paid. But you can't equate amounts of money unless they are transacted at the same time—not true here. You can't say simply that "the 20-year case saves $88,168.09 in interest." After all, an extra $882.80/month for ten years can earn a lot of interest—far more than its face value. You can earn the added value of *time*.

16.

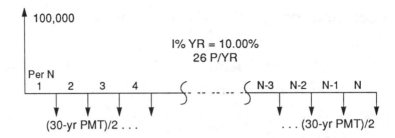

Find the normal monthly payment: At the TVM Menu, press OTHER, then set END MODE and 12 P/YR. (EXIT) and:

3 0 X 1 2 (ALGebraic) *or* 3 0 INPUT 1 2 X (RPN) N

1 0 I%YR 1 0 0 0 0 0 PV 0 FV

PMT .... Result: PMT=-877.57

Now divide this in half to get the bi-weekly payment amount:

÷ 2 = (ALGebraic) *or* 2 ÷ (RPN)   <u>Answer</u>: -438.79

Press PMT, then OTHER to set 26 P/YR.

Now (EXIT) and solve for N ....   Result: N=544.93

That's about 545 *bi-weekly* periods. Divide this by 26, to find that it will take just under 21 years to amortize the loan with 26 "half-monthly-payments" per year.

The amortization schedule: Press OTHER AMRT

2 6 #P	#P=26 PMTS: 1-26
INT	INTEREST=-9,930.16
PRIN	PRINCIPAL=-1,478.38
BAL	BALANCE=98,521.62
NEXT	#P=26 PMTS: 27-52
INT	INTEREST=-9,774.98
PRIN	PRINCIPAL=-1,633.56
BAL	BALANCE=96,888.06

<u>Note</u>: If you do a lot of this sort of calculation, you may want to use a Solver formula—see the note on page 311 in Chapter 9.

17.

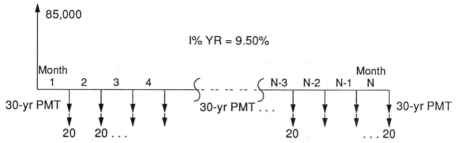

First, find the normal monthly payment amount: At the TVM Menu, press **OTHER**, then set END MODE and 12 P/YR. Then (EXIT) and:

(3)(0)(×)(1)(2) (ALGebraic) *or* (3)(0)(INPUT)(1)(2)(×) (RPN) **N**
(9)(•)(5) **I%YR** (8)(5)(0)(0)(0) **PV** (0) **FV**
PMT ....   Result: PMT=-714.73

Now include the extra $20: (−)(2)(0)(=)(ALGebraic)*or*(2)(0)(−)(RPN)
Result: -734.73   Now use this as the PMT (press **PMT**),
and solve for **N** ....   Result: N=313.92

That's about 314 *months*. Divide this by 12, to find that it will take a little over 26 years to amortize the loan with this additional $20 monthly payment toward principal.

The amortization schedule: Press **OTHER** **AMRT**

(1)(2) **#P**	#P=12 PMTS: 1-12
INT	INTEREST=-8,041.85
PRIN	PRINCIPAL=-774.91
BAL	BALANCE=84,225.09
NEXT	#P=12 PMTS: 13-24
INT	INTEREST=-7,964.92
PRIN	PRINCIPAL=-851.84
BAL	BALANCE=83,373.25

Note: If you do a lot of this sort of calculation, you may want to use a Solver formula—see the note on page 311 in Chapter 9.

18. In a conventional mortgage, each monthly payment covers all of that month's interest, plus a little bit of principal. The total payment amount stays constant, but the portions paid to interest and principal shrink and grow, respectively, throughout the term of the loan (recall page 161). But if you specify that the portion paid to principal must remain constant, then the total payment will not—it will shrink as the interest portion shrinks.

To find the steady amount of each monthly payment that goes to principal, divide the starting principal by the number of months:
⑦②⓪⓪⓪÷③⑥⓪ (ALG) *or* ⑦②⓪⓪⓪INPUT③⑥⓪÷ (RPN)
<u>Result</u>: **200.00**   Knowing that, you know this:

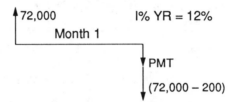

At the TVM Menu, press **OTHER**, set **END MODE** and **12 P/YR**. Then
(EXIT) and: ① **N** ①② **I%YR** ⑦②⓪⓪⓪ **PV**
and ⊟②⓪⓪⩵+/- (ALG) *or* ②⓪⓪⊟+/- (RPN) **FV**
PMT .... <u>Result</u>: **PMT=-920.00**   The first payment.

For the last payment, you know that this is the situation:

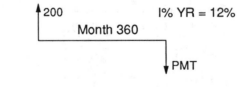

②⓪⓪ **PV** ⓪ **FV** **PMT** .... <u>Result</u>: **PMT=-202.00**

<u>Note</u>: If you do a lot of this sort of calculation, you may want to use a Solver formula—see the note on page 311 in Chapter 9.

19. Each time the rate changes in an ARM, you recompute the payment, using the new rate and the remaining term of the loan to amortize the remaining balance. At the TVM Menu, set END MODE and 12 P/YR. Then (EXIT) and:

Year 1: ③⓪☒①② (ALGebraic) *or* ③⓪(INPUT)①②☒ (RPN) **N**
⑨ **I%YR** ⑨⓪⓪⓪⓪ **PV** ⓪ **FV** **PMT**....
      Result: PMT=-724.16   Monthly payment.
①② **N** **FV** ....FV=-89,385.12   Year-end balance.

Year 2: (+/-) **PV** ⑨•⑤ **I%YR** ⓪ **FV**
②⑨☒①② (ALGebraic) *or* ②⑨(INPUT)①②☒ (RPN) **N** **PMT**....
      Result: PMT=-756.26   Monthly payment.
①② **N** **FV** ....FV=-88,775.47   Year-end balance.

Year 3: (+/-) **PV** ①⓪ **I%YR** ⓪ **FV**
②⑧☒①② (ALGebraic) *or* ②⑧(INPUT)①②☒ (RPN) **N** **PMT**....
      Result: PMT=-788.29   Monthly payment.
①② **N** **FV** ....FV=-88,166.10   Year-end balance.

Year 4: (+/-) **PV** ①⓪•⑤ **I%YR** ⓪ **FV**
②⑦☒①② (ALGebraic) *or* ②⑦(INPUT)①②☒ (RPN) **N** **PMT**....
      Result: PMT=-820.21   Monthly payment.
①② **N** **FV** ....FV=-87,551.99   Year-end balance.

Year 5: (+/-) **PV** ①① **I%YR** ⓪ **FV**
②⑥☒①② (ALGebraic) *or* ②⑥(INPUT)①②☒ (RPN) **N** **PMT**....
      Result: PMT=-851.99   Monthly payment.
①② **N** **FV** ....FV=-86,927.97   Year-end balance.

Note: If you do a lot of ARM calculations, you may want to use a Solver formula—see the note on page 311 in Chapter 9.

20. For conventional, FNMA and GNMA loans, suppose the comparison is between 28% of $GI and 36% of $GI less $LTD, unless the amount of financing is 90% or more of the home value:

⟦3⟧⟦5⟧⟦0⟧⟦0⟧⟦×⟧⟦2⟧⟦8⟧⟦%⟧⟦=⟧ (ALGebraic) *or* ⟦3⟧⟦5⟧⟦0⟧⟦0⟧⟦INPUT⟧⟦2⟧⟦8⟧⟦%⟧ (RPN)
Result: 980.00

and ⟦3⟧⟦5⟧⟦0⟧⟦0⟧⟦×⟧⟦3⟧⟦6⟧⟦%⟧⟦−⟧⟦2⟧⟦0⟧⟦0⟧⟦=⟧ (ALGebraic) *or*
⟦3⟧⟦5⟧⟦0⟧⟦0⟧⟦INPUT⟧⟦3⟧⟦6⟧⟦%⟧⟦2⟧⟦0⟧⟦0⟧⟦−⟧ (RPN)
Result: 1,060.00

For FHA loans, compare 29% of $GI and 41% of $GI less $LTD:

⟦3⟧⟦5⟧⟦0⟧⟦0⟧⟦×⟧⟦2⟧⟦9⟧⟦%⟧⟦=⟧ (ALGebraic) *or* ⟦3⟧⟦5⟧⟦0⟧⟦0⟧⟦INPUT⟧⟦2⟧⟦9⟧⟦%⟧ (RPN)
Result: 1,015.00

and ⟦3⟧⟦5⟧⟦0⟧⟦0⟧⟦×⟧⟦4⟧⟦1⟧⟦%⟧⟦−⟧⟦2⟧⟦0⟧⟦0⟧⟦=⟧ (ALGebraic) *or*
⟦3⟧⟦5⟧⟦0⟧⟦0⟧⟦INPUT⟧⟦4⟧⟦1⟧⟦%⟧⟦2⟧⟦0⟧⟦0⟧⟦−⟧ (RPN)
Result: 1,235.00

Conventional: Maximum PITI is $980—unless the financing is 90% or more. Now find the maximum mortgage payment by subtracting the monthly insurance and taxes:

⟦9⟧⟦8⟧⟦0⟧⟦−⟧⟦3⟧⟦0⟧⟦−⟧⟦(⟧⟦2⟧⟦2⟧⟦5⟧⟦0⟧⟦÷⟧⟦1⟧⟦2⟧⟦=⟧ (ALGebraic) *or*
⟦9⟧⟦8⟧⟦0⟧⟦INPUT⟧⟦3⟧⟦0⟧⟦−⟧⟦2⟧⟦2⟧⟦5⟧⟦0⟧⟦INPUT⟧⟦1⟧⟦2⟧⟦÷⟧⟦−⟧ (RPN)
Result: 762.50

At the TVM Menu, press ⟦+/−⟧ **PMT** . Then press **OTHER**, set END MODE and 12 P⁄YR. Then ⟦EXIT⟧ and:

⟦3⟧⟦0⟧⟦×⟧⟦1⟧⟦2⟧ (ALGebraic) *or* ⟦3⟧⟦0⟧⟦INPUT⟧⟦1⟧⟦2⟧⟦×⟧ (RPN) **N**
⟦1⟧⟦0⟧ **I⁄YR** ⟦0⟧ **FV** **PV** ....
Result: PV=86,887.50

But this is over 90% of the value of the $90,000 home ($81,000), so test whether the 25%/33% limits can improve upon this 90% limit:

⟦3⟧⟦5⟧⟦0⟧⟦0⟧⟦×⟧⟦2⟧⟦5⟧⟦%⟧⟦=⟧ (ALGebraic) *or* ⟦3⟧⟦5⟧⟦0⟧⟦0⟧⟦INPUT⟧⟦2⟧⟦5⟧⟦%⟧ (RPN)

Result: 875.00

and ③⑤⓪⓪×③③%－②⓪⓪＝ (ALGebraic) or

③⑤⓪⓪ INPUT ③③% ②⓪⓪ － (RPN)

Result: 955.00

So maximum PITI is $875:

⑧⑦⑤－③⓪－（②②⑤⓪÷①②＝ (ALGebraic) or

⑧⑦⑤ INPUT ③⓪ － ②②⑤⓪ INPUT ①②÷－ (RPN)

Result: 657.50   At the TVM Menu, press +/− **PMT**.

Then **PV** ....   Result: PV=74,922.66

So the maximum conventional financing is 90%, or $81,000.

FNMA: Maximum PITI is $980, so the maximum financing is $86.887.50, as you just calculated for the conventional case.

GNMA: Maximum PITI is $1,060:

①⓪⑥⓪－③⓪－（②②⑤⓪÷①②＝ (ALGebraic) or

①⓪⑥⓪ INPUT ③⓪ － ②②⑤⓪ INPUT ①②÷－ (RPN)

Result: 842.50   At the TVM Menu, press +/− **PMT**.

Then **PV** ....   Result: PV=96,003.57

FHA: Maximum PITI is $1,015:

①⓪①⑤－③⓪－（②②⑤⓪÷①②＝ (ALGebraic) or

①⓪①⑤ INPUT ③⓪ － ②②⑤⓪ INPUT ①②÷－ (RPN)

Result: 797.50   At the TVM Menu, press +/− **PMT**.

Then **PV** ....   Result: PV=90,875.78

Note: If you do a lot of home loan qualifying calculations, you may want a Solver formula—see the note on p. 311 in Chapter 9.

21. Just a quick review problem with bonds: From the Main Menu, press `FIN` `BOND` `TYPE` `A/A` `SEMI` `EXIT`.

Then `7` `·` `2` `8` `1` `9` `9` `0` `SETT` `9` `·` `0` `9` `1` `9` `9` `9` `MAT` `7` `CPN%`
`MORE` `1` `0` `YLD%`   `PRICE`.... PRICE=82.31   For a 10% YTM.
                        `ACCRU`.... ACCRU=2.68
`MORE` `3` `·` `0` `9` `1` `9` `9` `5` `MAT` `8` `8` `·` `1` `2` `5` `CALL`
`MORE` `YLD%` ....   YLD%=9.75   The yield-to-call.

Note: If you often need bond calculations that also account for taxes and commissions, see the note on page 311 in Ch. 9.

22. Take the greater of the two allowed depreciations whenever you have a choice. From the Main Menu, press `FIN` `DEPRC`.

The building: `7` `5` `0` `0` `0` `BASIS` `1` `5` `0` `0` `0` `SALV`
`3` `1` `·` `5` `×` `1` `2` (ALG) *or* `3` `1` `·` `5` `INPUT` `1` `2` `×` (RPN) `LIFE`
The HP 17BII won't accept non-integer input, but SL depreciation is uniform; just multiply the *monthly* depreciation by 12:
Pick any period: `MORE` `1` `YR#` `SL` .... SL=158.73
`×` `1` `2` `=` (ALG) *or* `1` `2` `×` 1,904.76

The computer: `MORE` `1` `0` `0` `0` `0` `BASIS` `5` `0` `0` `SALV` `5` `LIFE`
`MORE` `2` `0` `0` `FACT%`
`3` `YR#` `DB` ....DB=1,140.00 `SL` ....SL=1,900.00
`4` `YR#` `DB` ....DB=864.00 `SL` ....SL=1,900.00*

The shrubs: `MORE` `5` `0` `0` `0` `BASIS` `0` `SALV` `1` `5` `LIFE`
`MORE` `1` `5` `0` `FACT%`
`3` `YR#` `DB` ....DB=405.00 `SL` ....SL=333.33
`4` `YR#` `DB` ....DB=364.50 `SL` ....SL=333.33

*Caution! The RDV of the computer is only $1200 in Year 4 if you've been using 200% DB in the previous years. If you do a lot of MACRS calculations, see the note on page 311 in Chapter 9.

23. The gross rents, less vacancies:

$\boxed{7}\boxed{\cdot}\boxed{8}\boxed{\times}\boxed{2}\boxed{2}\boxed{7}\boxed{7}\boxed{-}\boxed{\cdot}\boxed{5}\boxed{\%}$

$\boxed{+}\boxed{(}\boxed{(}\boxed{4}\boxed{\cdot}\boxed{0}\boxed{7}\boxed{\times}\boxed{2}\boxed{0}\boxed{0}\boxed{5}\boxed{-}\boxed{1}\boxed{\%}\boxed{=}$ (ALG) *or*

$\boxed{7}\boxed{\cdot}\boxed{8}\boxed{\text{INPUT}}\boxed{2}\boxed{2}\boxed{7}\boxed{7}\boxed{\times}\boxed{\cdot}\boxed{5}\boxed{\%}\boxed{-}$

$\boxed{4}\boxed{\cdot}\boxed{0}\boxed{7}\boxed{\text{INPUT}}\boxed{2}\boxed{0}\boxed{0}\boxed{5}\boxed{\times}\boxed{1}\boxed{\%}\boxed{-}\boxed{+}$ (RPN)

(Result: 25,750.54)

Less operating expenses:

$\boxed{-}\boxed{3}\boxed{6}\boxed{4}\boxed{7}\boxed{-}\boxed{3}\boxed{0}\boxed{6}\boxed{0}\boxed{-}\boxed{2}\boxed{3}\boxed{1}\boxed{8}\boxed{-}\boxed{7}\boxed{7}\boxed{3}\boxed{=}$ (ALG) *or*

$\boxed{3}\boxed{6}\boxed{4}\boxed{7}\boxed{-}\boxed{3}\boxed{0}\boxed{6}\boxed{0}\boxed{-}\boxed{2}\boxed{3}\boxed{1}\boxed{8}\boxed{-}\boxed{7}\boxed{7}\boxed{3}\boxed{-}$ (RPN)

Result: 15,952.54   The NOI—leave it in the History Stack.

Now find the cap rate by weighting each portion of the investment by its expected return rate (this is the Band of Investment method for determining a cap rate):

$\boxed{\cdot}\boxed{1}\boxed{2}\boxed{7}\boxed{5}\boxed{\times}\boxed{7}\boxed{0}\boxed{\%}\boxed{+}\boxed{(}\boxed{(}\boxed{\cdot}\boxed{1}\boxed{4}\boxed{\times}\boxed{3}\boxed{0}\boxed{\%}\boxed{=}$ (ALG) *or*

$\boxed{\cdot}\boxed{1}\boxed{2}\boxed{7}\boxed{5}\boxed{\text{INPUT}}\boxed{\cdot}\boxed{7}\boxed{\times}\boxed{\cdot}\boxed{1}\boxed{4}\boxed{\text{INPUT}}\boxed{\cdot}\boxed{3}\boxed{\times}\boxed{+}$ (RPN)

Result: 0.13   The cap rate, as a decimal.

Then divide the NOI by the cap rate:

$\boxed{\div}\boxed{\blacksquare}\boxed{\text{LAST}}\boxed{=}\boxed{\blacksquare}\boxed{1/x}$ (ALG) *or*

$\boxed{\div}$ (RPN)

Result: 121,543.19   The property value.

Note: If you do a lot of this sort of calculation, you may want to use a Solver formula—see the note on page 311 in Chapter 9.

24. At TVM , press **OTHER**. Set END MODE and 12 P/YR.
[EXIT] and amortize the first mortgage:

[2][0][X][1][2] (ALG) *or* [2][0][INPUT][1][2][X] (RPN) **N**
[1][0][•][5] **I%YR** [3][5][0][0][0][0] **PV** [0] **FV**
Then solve: **PMT** ....   Answer: PMT=-3,494.33

The amortization schedule: Press **OTHER AMRT**, then:

[1][2] **#P**	#P=12 PMTS: 1-12	(Year 1)
INT	INTEREST=-36,493.20	
PRIN	PRINCIPAL=-5,438.76	
BAL	BALANCE=344,561.24	
NEXT	#P=12 PMTS: 13-24	(Year 2)
INT	INTEREST=-35,893.83	
BAL	BALANCE=338,523.11	
NEXT	#P=12 PMTS: 25-36	(Year 3)
INT	INTEREST=-35,228.41	
BAL	BALANCE=331,819.56	
NEXT	#P=12 PMTS: 37-48	(Year 4)
INT	INTEREST=-34,489.63	
BAL	BALANCE=324,377.23	
NEXT	#P=12 PMTS: 49-60	(Year 5)
INT	INTEREST=-33,669.48	
BAL	BALANCE=316,114.75	

Now [EXIT][EXIT] and do the second mortgage:

[1][0][X][1][2] (ALGebraic) *or* [1][0][INPUT][1][2][X] (RPN) **N**
[1][2] **I%YR** [1][5][0][0][0][0] **PV** [0] **FV**
Then solve: **PMT** ....   Answer: PMT=-2,152.06

The amortization schedule: Press `OTHER` `AMRT`, then:

`1``2` `#P`	#P=12 PMTS: 1-12	(Year 1)
`INT`	INTEREST=-17,554.96	
`PRIN`	PRINCIPAL=-8,269.76	
`BAL`	BALANCE=141,730.24	
`NEXT`	#P=12 PMTS: 13-24	(Year 2)
`INT`	INTEREST=-16,506.14	
`BAL`	BALANCE=132,411.66	
`NEXT`	#P=12 PMTS: 25-36	(Year 3)
`INT`	INTEREST=-15,324.34	
`BAL`	BALANCE=121,911.28	
`NEXT`	#P=12 PMTS: 37-48	(Year 4)
`INT`	INTEREST=-13,992.60	
`BAL`	BALANCE=110,079.16	
`NEXT`	#P=12 PMTS: 49-60	(Year 5)
`INT`	INTEREST=-12,492.02	
`BAL`	BALANCE=96,746.46	

Annual debt service:

`3``4``9``4``.``3``3``+``2``1``5``2``.``0``6``×``1``2``=` (ALG) *or*

`3``4``9``4``.``3``3``INPUT``2``1``5``2``.``0``6``+``1``2``×` (RPN)

Result: 67,756.68   The mortgage payments.

Annual depreciation:

`7``5``0``0``0``0``×``7``0``%``÷``3``1``.``5``=` (ALG) *or*

`7``5``0``0``0``0``INPUT``7``0``%``3``1``.``5``÷` (RPN)

Result: 16,666.67   The 31.5-year SL cost recovery.

Annual deduction for points:

[3][5][0][0][0][0][×][1][·][5][%][+][(][(][1][5][0][0][0][0][×][2][%][)][)][÷][5][=] (ALG)

or [3][5][0][0][0][0][INPUT][·][0][1][5][×][1][5][0][0][0][0][INPUT]

[·][0][2][×][+][5][÷] (RPN)

Result: **1,650.00**   The annual points deduction.

Initial Cash-Flow ("Year 0"): Down-payment, points and COA:

[2][5][0][0][0][0][+][(][(][3][5][0][0][0][0][×][1][·][5][%][)]

[+][(][(][1][5][0][0][0][0][×][2][%][)][)][+][2][0][0][0][=][+/−] (ALG) or

[2][5][0][0][0][0][INPUT][3][5][0][0][0][0][INPUT][·][0][1][5][×][+]

[1][5][0][0][0][0][INPUT][·][0][2][×][+][2][0][0][0][+][+/−] (RPN)

Result: **−260,250.00**   The initial cash-flow.

Year 1: Each yearly cash-flow is the NOI (rents less operating expenses), less income taxes, plus tax relief for depreciation and interest and prorated points (and, for Year 1, costs of acquisition), less debt service:

[1][2][5][0][0][0][−][6][%]	(rent)
[−][3][0][0][0]	(− insurance)
[−][1][2][0][0][0]	(− mnt./mgmt.)
[−][(][(][7][5][0][0][0][0][×][2][·][5][%][)][)]	(− prop. taxes)
[=]	(= NOI: **83,750.00**)
[−][3][3][%]	(−income taxes)
[+][(][(][1][6][6][6][6][·][6][7]	(+ tax relief...
[+][3][6][4][9][3][·][2][+][1][7][5][5][4][·][9][6]	...
[+][2][0][0][0][+][1][6][5][0][×][3][3][%][)][)]	...)
[−][6][7][7][5][6][·][6][8]	(− debt serv.)
[=](ALG)	

or (RPN): $\boxed{1}\boxed{2}\boxed{5}\boxed{0}\boxed{0}\boxed{0}\boxed{\text{INPUT}}\boxed{6}\boxed{\%}\boxed{-}$ (rent)

     $\boxed{3}\boxed{0}\boxed{0}\boxed{0}\boxed{-}$ (− insurance)

     $\boxed{1}\boxed{2}\boxed{0}\boxed{0}\boxed{0}\boxed{-}$ (− mnt./mgmt.)

     $\boxed{7}\boxed{5}\boxed{0}\boxed{0}\boxed{0}\boxed{0}\boxed{\text{INPUT}}\boxed{\cdot}\boxed{0}\boxed{2}\boxed{5}\boxed{\times}\boxed{-}$ (− prop. taxes)

                                            (= NOI: 83,750.00)

     $\boxed{3}\boxed{3}\boxed{\%}\boxed{-}$ (−income taxes)

     $\boxed{1}\boxed{6}\boxed{6}\boxed{6}\boxed{6}\boxed{\cdot}\boxed{6}\boxed{7}\boxed{\text{INPUT}}$ (+ tax relief...

         $\boxed{3}\boxed{6}\boxed{4}\boxed{9}\boxed{3}\boxed{\cdot}\boxed{2}\boxed{+}\boxed{1}\boxed{7}\boxed{5}\boxed{5}\boxed{4}\boxed{\cdot}\boxed{9}\boxed{6}\boxed{+}$ ...

         $\boxed{2}\boxed{0}\boxed{0}\boxed{0}\boxed{+}\boxed{1}\boxed{6}\boxed{5}\boxed{0}\boxed{+}\boxed{\cdot}\boxed{3}\boxed{3}\boxed{\times}\boxed{+}$ ...)

     $\boxed{6}\boxed{7}\boxed{7}\boxed{5}\boxed{6}\boxed{\cdot}\boxed{6}\boxed{8}\boxed{-}$ (− debt serv.)

<u>Result</u>: 12,896.21   The Year 1 cash-flow.

<u>Year 2</u>: Each year, the NOI increases by the inflation rate:

$\boxed{8}\boxed{3}\boxed{7}\boxed{5}\boxed{0}\boxed{+}\boxed{5}\boxed{\%}$ (NOI + inflation adj.)

     $\boxed{-}\boxed{3}\boxed{3}\boxed{\%}$ (−income taxes)

     $\boxed{+}\boxed{(}\boxed{(}\boxed{1}\boxed{6}\boxed{6}\boxed{6}\boxed{6}\boxed{\cdot}\boxed{6}\boxed{7}\boxed{+}\boxed{3}\boxed{5}\boxed{8}\boxed{9}\boxed{3}\boxed{\cdot}\boxed{8}\boxed{3}$ (+ tax relief...

         $\boxed{+}\boxed{1}\boxed{6}\boxed{5}\boxed{0}\boxed{6}\boxed{\cdot}\boxed{1}\boxed{4}\boxed{+}\boxed{1}\boxed{6}\boxed{5}\boxed{0}\boxed{\times}\boxed{3}\boxed{3}\boxed{\%}\boxed{)}\boxed{)}$ ...)

     $\boxed{-}\boxed{6}\boxed{7}\boxed{7}\boxed{5}\boxed{6}\boxed{\cdot}\boxed{6}\boxed{8}$ (− debt serv.)

$\boxed{=}$ (ALG) *or* (RPN):

$\boxed{8}\boxed{3}\boxed{7}\boxed{5}\boxed{0}\boxed{\text{INPUT}}\boxed{5}\boxed{\%}\boxed{+}$ (NOI + inflation adj.)

     $\boxed{3}\boxed{3}\boxed{\%}\boxed{-}$ (−income taxes)

     $\boxed{1}\boxed{6}\boxed{6}\boxed{6}\boxed{6}\boxed{\cdot}\boxed{6}\boxed{7}\boxed{\text{INPUT}}\boxed{3}\boxed{5}\boxed{8}\boxed{9}\boxed{3}\boxed{\cdot}\boxed{8}\boxed{3}\boxed{+}$ (+ tax relief...

         $\boxed{1}\boxed{6}\boxed{5}\boxed{0}\boxed{6}\boxed{\cdot}\boxed{1}\boxed{4}\boxed{+}\boxed{1}\boxed{6}\boxed{5}\boxed{0}\boxed{+}\boxed{\cdot}\boxed{3}\boxed{3}\boxed{\times}\boxed{+}$ ...)

     $\boxed{6}\boxed{7}\boxed{7}\boxed{5}\boxed{6}\boxed{\cdot}\boxed{6}\boxed{8}\boxed{-}$ (− debt serv.)

<u>Result</u>: 14,497.94   The Year 2 cash-flow.

Year 3: Each year, the NOI increases by the inflation rate:

8 3 7 5 0 + 5 % + 5 %   (NOI + inflation adj.)
  − 3 3 %   (−income taxes)
  + ((1 6 6 6 6 · 6 7 + 3 5 2 2 8 · 4 1   (+ tax relief...
      + 1 5 3 2 4 · 3 4 + 1 6 5 0 × 3 3 %)) ...)
  − 6 7 7 5 6 · 6 8   (− debt serv.)
= (ALG) or (RPN):

8 3 7 5 0 INPUT 5 % + 5 % +   (NOI + inflation adj.)
  3 3 % −   (−income taxes)
  1 6 6 6 6 · 6 7 INPUT 3 5 2 2 8 · 4 1 +   (+ tax relief...
      1 5 3 2 4 · 3 4 + 1 6 5 0 + · 3 3 × + ...)
  6 7 7 5 6 · 6 8 −   (− debt serv.)

Result: 16,834.26   The Year 3 cash-flow.

Year 4: Each year, the NOI increases by the inflation rate:

8 3 7 5 0 + 5 % + 5 % + 5 %   (NOI + inflation adj.)
  − 3 3 %   (−income taxes)
  + ((1 6 6 6 6 · 6 7 + 3 4 4 8 9 · 6 3   (+ tax relief...
      + 1 3 9 9 2 · 6 + 1 6 5 0 × 3 3 %))   ...)
  − 6 7 7 5 6 · 6 8   (− debt serv.)
= (ALG) or (RPN):

8 3 7 5 0 INPUT 5 % + 5 % + 5 % +   (NOI + inflation adj.)
  3 3 % −   (−income taxes)
  1 6 6 6 6 · 6 7 INPUT 3 4 4 8 9 · 6 3 +   (+ tax relief...
      1 3 9 9 2 · 6 + 1 6 5 0 + · 3 3 × +   ...)
  6 7 7 5 6 · 6 8 −   (− debt serv.)

Result: 19,244.19   The Year 4 cash-flow.

Year 5: When the property sells (at a price based upon a cap rate and projected Year 6 NOI), the lenders are repaid from the net sale proceeds, and capital gains are realized on the difference between the net proceeds and the unrecovered cost:

8 3 7 5 0 + 5 % + 5 % + 5 % + 5 % + 5 %   (Year 6 NOI)

÷ . 1 1 5 - 6 % =   (net sale proceeds: 873,697.97)

- 3 1 6 1 1 4 . 7 5 - 9 6 7 4 6 . 4 6   (-mortgage balances)

- ((8 7 3 6 9 7 . 9 7 -   (- tax on capital gains...

(7 5 0 0 0 0 - ((5 × 1 6 6 6 6 . 6 7))) × 3 3 %))...)

+ ((8 3 7 5 0 + 5 % + 5 % + 5 % + 5 %   (+ Year 5 NOI)

- 3 3 %   (-income taxes)

+ ((1 6 6 6 6 . 6 7 + 3 3 6 6 9 . 4 8   (+ tax relief...

+ 1 2 4 9 2 . 0 2 + 1 6 5 0 × 3 3 %)) ...)

- 6 7 7 5 6 . 6 8))   (- debt serv.)

= (ALGebraic)

or (RPN):

8 3 7 5 0 INPUT 5 % + 5 % + 5 % + 5 % + 5 % +   (Year 6 NOI)

. 1 1 5 ÷ 6 % -   (net sale proceeds: 873,697.97)

3 1 6 1 1 4 . 7 5 - 9 6 7 4 6 . 4 6 -   (-mortgage balances)

8 7 3 6 9 7 . 9 7 INPUT   (- tax on capital gains...

5 INPUT 1 6 6 6 6 . 6 7 × +/- 7 5 0 0 0 0 + - . 3 3 × -...)

8 3 7 5 0 INPUT 5 % + 5 % + 5 % + 5 % +   (NOI + infl. adj.)

3 3 % -   (-income taxes)

1 6 6 6 6 . 6 7 INPUT 3 3 6 6 9 . 4 8 +   (+ tax relief...

1 2 4 9 2 . 0 2 + 1 6 5 0 + . 3 3 × + ...)

6 7 7 5 6 . 6 8 -   (- debt serv.)

+

Result: 414,242.63   The Year 5 cash-flow.

The GRM (Gross Rent Multiplier) is Price÷Rents$_{max}$:

$\boxed{7}\boxed{5}\boxed{0}\boxed{0}\boxed{0}\boxed{0}\boxed{\div}\boxed{1}\boxed{2}\boxed{5}\boxed{0}\boxed{0}\boxed{0}\boxed{=}$ (ALG) *or*

$\boxed{7}\boxed{5}\boxed{0}\boxed{0}\boxed{0}\boxed{0}\boxed{\text{INPUT}}\boxed{1}\boxed{2}\boxed{5}\boxed{0}\boxed{0}\boxed{0}\boxed{\div}$ (RPN)

Result: **6.00**   The GRM.

The cap rate is NOI$_1$÷Price:

$\boxed{8}\boxed{3}\boxed{7}\boxed{5}\boxed{0}\boxed{\div}\boxed{7}\boxed{5}\boxed{0}\boxed{0}\boxed{0}\boxed{0}\boxed{\times}\boxed{1}\boxed{0}\boxed{0}\boxed{=}$ (ALG) *or*

$\boxed{8}\boxed{3}\boxed{7}\boxed{5}\boxed{0}\boxed{\text{INPUT}}\boxed{7}\boxed{5}\boxed{0}\boxed{0}\boxed{0}\boxed{0}\boxed{\div}\boxed{1}\boxed{0}\boxed{0}\boxed{\times}$ (RPN)

Result: **11.17**   The cap rate, as a percentage.

The equity return rate is the ratio of the net cash-flow, mortgage principal payments and appreciation, to the down-payment:

$\boxed{1}\boxed{2}\boxed{8}\boxed{8}\boxed{5}\boxed{\cdot}\boxed{4}\boxed{1}\boxed{+}\boxed{5}\boxed{4}\boxed{3}\boxed{8}\boxed{\cdot}\boxed{7}\boxed{6}\boxed{+}\boxed{8}\boxed{2}\boxed{6}\boxed{9}\boxed{\cdot}\boxed{7}\boxed{6}\boxed{+}$

$\boxed{(}\boxed{(}\boxed{7}\boxed{5}\boxed{0}\boxed{0}\boxed{0}\boxed{0}\boxed{\times}\boxed{5}\boxed{\%}\boxed{)}\boxed{\div}\boxed{2}\boxed{5}\boxed{0}\boxed{0}\boxed{0}\boxed{\times}\boxed{1}\boxed{0}\boxed{0}\boxed{=}$ (ALG) *or*

$\boxed{1}\boxed{2}\boxed{8}\boxed{8}\boxed{5}\boxed{\cdot}\boxed{4}\boxed{1}\boxed{\text{INPUT}}\boxed{5}\boxed{4}\boxed{3}\boxed{8}\boxed{\cdot}\boxed{7}\boxed{6}\boxed{+}\boxed{8}\boxed{2}\boxed{6}\boxed{9}\boxed{\cdot}\boxed{7}\boxed{6}\boxed{+}$

$\boxed{7}\boxed{5}\boxed{0}\boxed{0}\boxed{0}\boxed{0}\boxed{\text{INPUT}}\boxed{\cdot}\boxed{0}\boxed{5}\boxed{\times}\boxed{+}\boxed{2}\boxed{5}\boxed{0}\boxed{0}\boxed{0}\boxed{\div}\boxed{1}\boxed{0}\boxed{0}\boxed{\times}$ (RPN)

Result: **25.64**   The equity return rate, as a percentage.

The after-tax cash return rate is the Year 1 cash-flow divided by the initial cash-flow:

$\boxed{1}\boxed{2}\boxed{8}\boxed{8}\boxed{5}\boxed{\cdot}\boxed{4}\boxed{1}\boxed{\div}\boxed{2}\boxed{6}\boxed{0}\boxed{2}\boxed{5}\boxed{0}\boxed{\times}\boxed{1}\boxed{0}\boxed{0}\boxed{=}$ (ALG) *or*

$\boxed{1}\boxed{2}\boxed{8}\boxed{8}\boxed{5}\boxed{\cdot}\boxed{4}\boxed{1}\boxed{\text{INPUT}}\boxed{2}\boxed{6}\boxed{0}\boxed{2}\boxed{5}\boxed{0}\boxed{\div}\boxed{1}\boxed{0}\boxed{0}\boxed{\times}$ (RPN)

Result: **4.95**   The after-tax cash return rate, as a percentage.

Note: If you do a lot of these lengthy income property analyses, you may want to use a Solver formula—see the note on page 311 in Chapter 9.

25. Suppose that $1.00 today will buy a loaf of bread. Then, with 5% inflation, that loaf will cost $1.05 this time next year. So, how many loaves can you buy then if your dollar has increased—by earning interest—to $1.10? It's 1.10÷1.05. Do that arithmetic:

①▪①÷①▪⓪⑤＝ (ALG) *or* ①▪① INPUT ①▪⓪⑤÷ (RPN)

The same value that bought 1 loaf this year will buy 1.0476 loaves next year. So your real buying power has grown by 4.76%.

But that doesn't take taxes into account. If interest is taxable at 27%, then 27% of the $0.10 interest earned by your dollar goes you-know-where. So:

▪①－②⑦%＋①÷①▪⓪⑤－①×①⓪⓪＝ (ALG) *or*

▪① INPUT ②⑦%－①＋①▪⓪⑤÷①－①⓪⓪× (RPN)

This is the *after-tax* growth rate of your real buying power—as a percentage: **2.19**. This is what you should use as your interest rate in the TVM Menu to grow your $1000 investment:

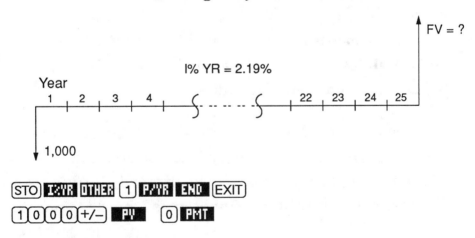

STO I%YR OTHER ① P/YR END EXIT
①⓪⓪⓪+/− PV ⓪ PMT

②⑤ N FV ....   Answer: FV=1,718.94
And ④⓪ N FV ....   Answer: FV=2,379.12

Note: If you do a lot of tax and inflation calculations, you may want a Solver formula—see the note on page 311 in Chapter 9.

26. Find the growth rate of the buying power in the taxable account:

⎡•⎤⎡1⎤⎡5⎤⎡−⎤⎡2⎤⎡8⎤⎡%⎤⎡+⎤⎡1⎤⎡÷⎤⎡1⎤⎡•⎤⎡0⎤⎡5⎤⎡−⎤⎡1⎤⎡×⎤⎡1⎤⎡0⎤⎡0⎤⎡=⎤ (ALG) *or*

⎡•⎤⎡1⎤⎡5⎤⎡INPUT⎤⎡2⎤⎡8⎤⎡%⎤⎡−⎤⎡1⎤⎡+⎤⎡1⎤⎡•⎤⎡0⎤⎡5⎤⎡÷⎤⎡1⎤⎡−⎤⎡1⎤⎡0⎤⎡0⎤⎡×⎤ (RPN)

Answer: 5.52

Now use this as your interest rate in the TVM Menu:

⎡STO⎤ **I%YR** **OTHER** ⎡1⎤ **P/YR** **END** ⎡EXIT⎤

⎡2⎤⎡0⎤⎡0⎤⎡0⎤⎡+/−⎤ **PMT** ⎡0⎤ **PV**

⎡3⎤⎡0⎤ **N** **FV** ....   Answer: FV=145,472.28

This is the *buying power* (in terms of today's dollars) in your taxable account after 30 years. The actual *face-value* amount of dollars will be higher, but those dollars won't buy as much then.

Repeat this calculation for the IRA—a tax-deferred account (no tax on interest while it's growing):

⎡1⎤⎡•⎤⎡1⎤⎡5⎤⎡÷⎤⎡1⎤⎡•⎤⎡0⎤⎡5⎤⎡−⎤⎡1⎤⎡×⎤⎡1⎤⎡0⎤⎡0⎤⎡=⎤ (ALG) *or*

⎡1⎤⎡•⎤⎡1⎤⎡5⎤⎡INPUT⎤⎡1⎤⎡•⎤⎡0⎤⎡5⎤⎡÷⎤⎡1⎤⎡−⎤⎡1⎤⎡0⎤⎡0⎤⎡×⎤ (RPN)

Answer: 9.52

Now use this as your interest rate in the TVM Menu:

⎡STO⎤ **I%YR** **FV** ....   Answer: FV=300,718.13

What a difference an IRA makes!

But keep in mind that the level $2,000 PMT amount you're using here is also in terms of buying power ("today's dollars"). To hold that buying power *investment* amount steady, its *face value* must increase every year by 5%. Inflation is a hard taskmaster.

27. Since you're saving a level *percentage* of your inflation-adjusted income, you're investing a level amount of buying power (today's dollars) each month. So you can just use today's income numbers—if you adjust the growth rate of the account to reflect the true growth rate of its buying power instead of its face value:*

[.][1][5][÷][1][2][+][1][÷][(][(][.][0][5][÷][1][2][+][1][)][)]
[−][1][×][1][2][0][0][=] (ALG) *or*

[.][1][5][INPUT][1][2][÷][1][+][.][0][5][INPUT][1][2][÷][1][+][÷]
[1][−][1][2][0][0][×] (RPN)

(Result: 9.96)   Use this as the interest rate in TVM:

[STO] **I%YR** **OTHER** [1][2] **P/YR** **END** [EXIT]

[3][3][3][3][.][2][×][5][%][=] (ALG) *or* [3][3][3][3][.][2][INPUT][5][%] (RPN)

[+/−] **PMT** [0] **PV**

[3][5][×][1][2] (ALGebraic) *or* [3][5][INPUT][1][2][×] (RPN) **N**

FV ....Answer: FV=626,011.09   The rollover amount.

Use this as a Present Value to amortize over 30 years of retirement in an account paying 10%: [+/−] **PV** [0] **FV**

[3][0][×][1][2] (ALGebraic) *or* [3][0][INPUT][1][2][×] (RPN) **N**

[.][1][÷][1][2][+][1][÷][(][(][.][0][5][÷][1][2][+][1][)][)]
[−][1][×][1][2][0][0][=] (ALG) *or*

[.][1][INPUT][1][2][÷][1][+][.][0][5][INPUT][1][2][÷][1][+][÷]
[1][−][1][2][0][0][×] (RPN)

(Result: 4.98) **I%YR** **PMT** ....Answer: PMT=3,352.63

Your monthly retirement income—in today's dollars.

---

*For simplicity here, you may assume that all rates are *nominal* rates that compound monthly (otherwise—if they were *effective* annual rates—you'd need to use the ICNV Menu to find the corresponding nominal rates to use in the TVM Menu).

Repeat for the taxable scenario:*

⟨·⟩⟨1⟩⟨5⟩⟨−⟩⟨2⟩⟨8⟩⟨%⟩⟨÷⟩⟨1⟩⟨2⟩⟨+⟩⟨1⟩⟨÷⟩⟨(⟩⟨(⟩⟨·⟩⟨0⟩⟨5⟩⟨÷⟩⟨1⟩⟨2⟩⟨+⟩⟨1⟩⟨)⟩

⟨−⟩⟨1⟩⟨×⟩⟨1⟩⟨2⟩⟨0⟩⟨0⟩⟨=⟩ (ALG) *or*

⟨·⟩⟨1⟩⟨5⟩⟨INPUT⟩⟨2⟩⟨8⟩⟨%⟩⟨−⟩⟨1⟩⟨2⟩⟨÷⟩⟨1⟩⟨+⟩⟨·⟩⟨0⟩⟨5⟩⟨INPUT⟩⟨1⟩⟨2⟩⟨÷⟩⟨1⟩⟨+⟩⟨÷⟩

⟨1⟩⟨−⟩⟨1⟩⟨2⟩⟨0⟩⟨0⟩⟨×⟩ (RPN)

(Result: 5.78) **I%YR**

⟨3⟩⟨3⟩⟨3⟩⟨3⟩⟨·⟩⟨2⟩⟨×⟩⟨5⟩⟨%⟩⟨=⟩ (ALG) *or* ⟨3⟩⟨3⟩⟨3⟩⟨3⟩⟨·⟩⟨2⟩⟨INPUT⟩⟨5⟩⟨%⟩ (RPN)

⟨+/−⟩ **PMT** ⟨0⟩ **PV**

⟨3⟩⟨5⟩⟨×⟩⟨1⟩⟨2⟩ (ALGebraic) *or* ⟨3⟩⟨5⟩⟨INPUT⟩⟨1⟩⟨2⟩⟨×⟩ (RPN) **N**

FV ....Answer: FV=225,536.96 The rollover amount.

Then: ⟨+/−⟩ **PV** ⟨0⟩ **FV**

⟨3⟩⟨0⟩⟨×⟩⟨1⟩⟨2⟩ (ALGebraic) *or* ⟨3⟩⟨0⟩⟨INPUT⟩⟨1⟩⟨2⟩⟨×⟩ (RPN) **N**

⟨·⟩⟨1⟩⟨−⟩⟨2⟩⟨8⟩⟨%⟩⟨÷⟩⟨1⟩⟨2⟩⟨+⟩⟨1⟩⟨÷⟩⟨(⟩⟨(⟩⟨·⟩⟨0⟩⟨5⟩⟨÷⟩⟨1⟩⟨2⟩⟨+⟩⟨1⟩⟨)⟩

⟨−⟩⟨1⟩⟨×⟩⟨1⟩⟨2⟩⟨0⟩⟨0⟩⟨=⟩ (ALG) *or*

⟨·⟩⟨1⟩⟨INPUT⟩⟨2⟩⟨8⟩⟨%⟩⟨−⟩⟨1⟩⟨2⟩⟨÷⟩⟨1⟩⟨+⟩⟨·⟩⟨0⟩⟨5⟩⟨INPUT⟩⟨1⟩⟨2⟩⟨÷⟩⟨1⟩⟨+⟩⟨÷⟩

⟨1⟩⟨−⟩⟨1⟩⟨2⟩⟨0⟩⟨0⟩⟨×⟩ (RPN)

(Result: 2.19) **I%YR** **PMT** ....Answer: PMT=855.32

And what if you could also invest the 7.65% of your income that now goes toward Social Security and Medicare (a total of 12.65% of your income)? Your answers would be *proportionately* higher. So just multiply each answer above by (12.65÷5):

	IRA (tax-deferred) acct.	Taxable acct.
Rollover:	1,583,808.06	570,608.52
Ret. income:	8,482.15	2,163.96

Note: If you do a lot of retirement calculations, you may want to use a Solver formula—see the note on page 311 in Chapter 9.

*Again, for simplicity here, you may assume that you pay monthly taxes on your interest—not generally true, but note that this leads to a slightly more conservative (lower) growth rate, which, if you're going to go wrong with assumptions in retirement planning, is the side on which to err.

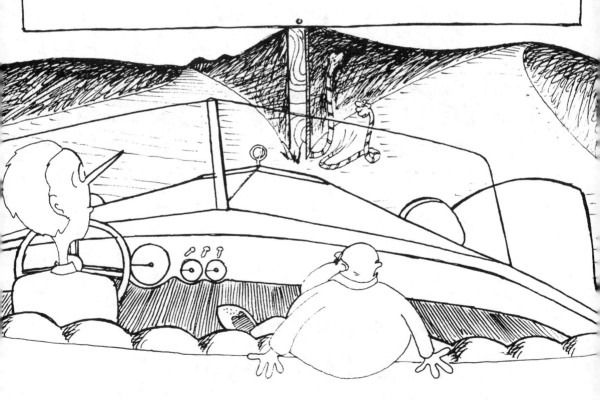

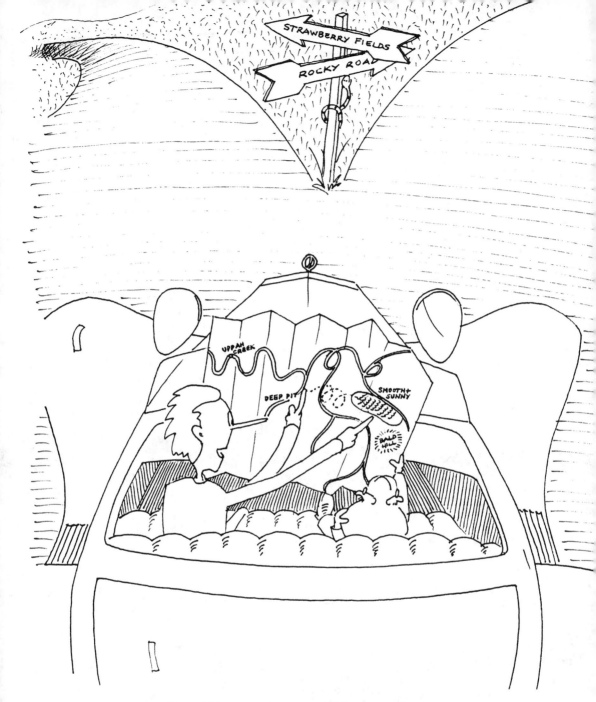

6. ROUGHER ROADS:
THE CFLO MENU

Problems with Uneven Payments

So far, all the various finance problems you've been solving have had one thing in common: that smooth, level PMT cash-flow happening once every period. But the real world isn't always so neat and tidy. Often, you'll run into situations where the periodic cash-flow amounts vary, sometimes quite often, like this:

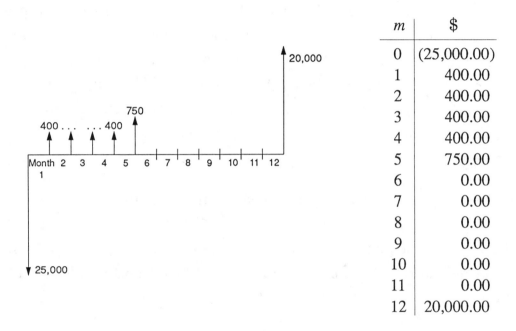

m	$
0	(25,000.00)
1	400.00
2	400.00
3	400.00
4	400.00
5	750.00
6	0.00
7	0.00
8	0.00
9	0.00
10	0.00
11	0.00
12	20,000.00

The HP 17BII can handle the above situation: the amounts are uneven, but at least there's still a cash-flow for every period (zero is a cash-flow). But if cash-flows occur at irregular time intervals, the machine cannot analyze that. It can analyze scenarios only where at least the cash-flow *occurrences* are regular—once per period.

The above picture does indeed fall within those limitations, but how do you analyze it? Certainly not with the TVM keys—there's no level PMT. You must use the CFLO Menu instead....

Go Find It: From the MAIN Menu, press **FIN**, but instead of **TVM**, hit **CFLO**. You'll see something like this:

```
FLOW(0)=?
CALC INSR DELET NAME GET #T?
```

This is a CFLO list, a list specially designed for representing cash-flow diagrams. Any value you key in (and then press INPUT) will go into the list. For example, if you were to key in a value now, it would be put into the list as Cash-Flow 0, since that's what the machine is prompting you for now.

So, how do you translate your cash-flow diagram into numbers to key into a CFLO list? You've already seen how the variables in the TVM Menu "draw the picture" for your calculator. But now you're working under a different set of circumstances, because there's no level PMT value.

Instead, to draw a picture of an *uneven* cash-flow situation, you use the concept of cash-flow *groups*.

Cash-Flow Groups

Here's that uneven cash-flow scenario again:

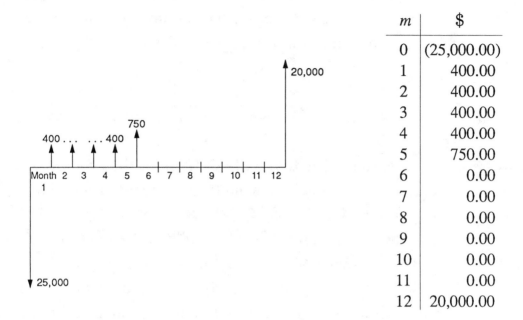

m	$
0	(25,000.00)
1	400.00
2	400.00
3	400.00
4	400.00
5	750.00
6	0.00
7	0.00
8	0.00
9	0.00
10	0.00
11	0.00
12	20,000.00

Notice that you could describe it quite succinctly like this:

"The initial cash-flow is –25,000.00.

"The amount of the first cash-flow group is 400.00. The number of times this occurs in a row is 4.

"The amount of the next cash-flow group is 750.00. The number of times it occurs in a row is 1.

"The amount of the next cash-flow group is 0.00. The number of times it occurs in a row is 6.

"The amount of the next cash-flow group is 20,000.00. The number of time it occurs in a row is 1."

That's the whole idea right there. Notice, however, that you treat the very first cash-flow, FLOW(0), separately. It usually represents the investment (a negative) cash-flow in the scenario. But other than that, you just read off the groups from your T-bar (top to bottom) or diagram (left to right), note how many times each cash-flow amount occurs in a row, and key this information into your CFLO list.

Do It: Key in the cash-flow scenario from the previous page.

Like So: First, of course, go to the CFLO Menu so that your display looks like that shown on page 184. Now, watch your display as you press ■ CLEAR DATA ▉YES▉. Next, press ▉#T?▉ until the display briefly shows #TIMES PROMPTING: ON (if this feature were turned off, the machine would assume only one cash-flow in each group—handy when that's the situation, but in this case, you do need to key in groups of different sizes—you need the prompting). Now, watch your display:

2 5 0 0 0 +/- INPUT
4 0 0 INPUT
4 INPUT
7 5 0 INPUT
1 INPUT
0 INPUT   (you must key all flows—even if they're zero)
6 INPUT
2 0 0 0 0 INPUT
1 INPUT

See how this works? You just read off each group.

Keep in mind that FLOW(0) always occurs just "1 time in a row." It's the first cash-flow group *after* that which is called FLOW(1).

Also, notice that every time you key in a cash-flow amount, the machine starts out by assuming that this flow occurs only once. That is, it puts a 1 in there for the #TIMES= , so that if this is the case, you don't need to key in 1; you just press (INPUT)—very handy.

Change Values: Go to the top of the list and step down through it to check it. Then change the cash-flow *amounts* (not the number of times each occurs) as follows:

FLOW(0):   -22,000.00
FLOW(1):   250.00
FLOW(2):   400.00

FLOW(4):   25,000.00

Solution: Press ■▲ (to jump to the top), then ▼▼▼▼▼▼ ▼▼, and check the display against your diagram. Then ■▲ once again, and change the numbers:

2 2 0 0 0 +/- INPUT
2 5 0 INPUT
▼ 4 0 0 INPUT
▼▼▼ 2 5 0 0 0 INPUT

(You can change the numbers in any order, but it just means more moving around with ▼ and ▲.)

With the changed numbers, your situation now looks like this:

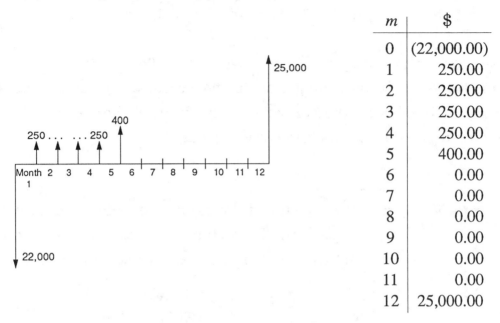

m	$
0	(22,000.00)
1	250.00
2	250.00
3	250.00
4	250.00
5	400.00
6	0.00
7	0.00
8	0.00
9	0.00
10	0.00
11	0.00
12	25,000.00

Now, before you do any calculations, you should NAME your list so that the machine will save it: (EXIT) NAME, then type FRED (INPUT).* Then CALC.

Look: You'll see this menu:

This is the CALCulations Menu, where you "crunch" your answers after drawing the correct picture. Notice the message, telling you that you must key in an interest rate, I%, before you can calculate NPV, NUS, and NFV. Why? What are those calculations anyway?

---

*You type alphabetical characters via menu selections, where each character is a two-step process. For example, to type FRED, you would press FGHI F RSTUV R ABCDE E ABCDE D .

What Is NPV?

Suppose this cash-flow scenario ("FRED") is a real-life situation—an investment opportunity you're being offered to help your friend, Fred, to get a business started over the course of the next year.

The budding entrepreneur figures that he needs $22,000 up front. He offers to demonstrate his good faith and ability to manage cash by paying a little something back over the first five months ($250 for four months and then one month of $400). Then, if you'll give him until the end of the year with no further payments, he'll pay you off with an even $25,000 at that time.

The pitch: Over the year-long scenario, he claims that you'll be earning an A.P.R. of about 19.175%.

Would you do it? How can you verify his claim?

Go back to the basics: The Time Value of Money is the interest value that time adds to money. A little bit now is entirely equivalent to more later, and the equalizer is the interest rate that acts over that time.

Now apply this to the question at hand: Your friend is claiming that your $22,000 given to him now is *entirely equivalent* to his giving you $250/month for 4 months, then $400 for 1 month, $0/month for 6 months, and then $25,000, *assuming* an interest rate of 19.175% A.P.R.

Can you prove this equivalence?   Yes—with NPV....

Recall (from pages 89-90) that you can slide cash-flows across a cash-flow diagram (or up and down a T-bar*)—as long as you increase or discount them according to the prevailing interest rate.

What if you were to take each of the cash-flows of this proposal and slide them back to the beginning of the timeline, *discounting* each one of them according to the assumed 19.175% A.P.R.?

Here's the starting situation:

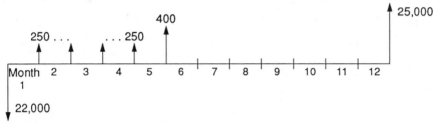

Here it is after you've slid that first $250 back. See how it's reduced? It has been discounted, according to the assumed 19.175% A.P.R.:

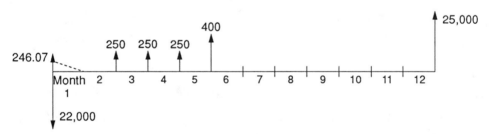

And here it is after the second $250 slides back. It amounts to even less, of course, because it had a longer time to be discounted:

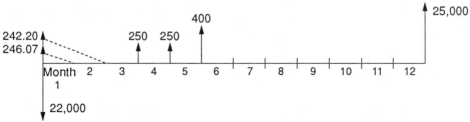

*This particular explanation will use cash-flow diagrams, but you can do it with T-bars, too.

And so on, until the picture looked like this:

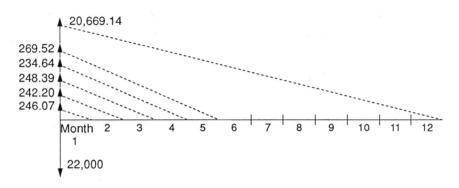

All the cash-flows have been discounted back and stacked up (the zero cash flows would still be zero).

Then, of course, you can add together any simultaneous cash-flows. So one big simplification would be to lump together (sum) all those positive cash-flows:

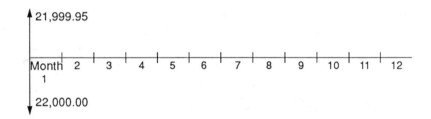

They *balance* the negative cash-flow—to within a nickel! Coincidence? No, this is what your entrepreneur friend, Fred, has said all along: Your $22,000 investment in him *was* equivalent to all his various future repayments, if you discount everything back at 19.175% A.P.R.

That's what NPV is: *A discounting-back-and-summing-up of all cash flows at the beginning of the timeline.*

Of course, the idea here is that your calculator can compute this NPV —do all the discounting and summing—very quickly. And since you've already keyed in the whole picture, you're ready to "crunch," right?

Wrong. Look again at the reminder in your display. You need to tell it what interest rate (I%) to use as the discount rate.

Tell It: Tell your HP 17BII to use a 19.175% A.P.R. as the prevailing discount rate in this cash-flow scenario.

Ahem: Do you just key in 1 9 · 1 7 5 and press I%? Nope.

The CFLO Menu is not like the TVM Menu, where you don't need to worry about converting the A.P.R. to a D.I.R. There the machine does it for you, once you tell it the P/YR. But here in the CFLO Menu, you must *manually* convert any A.P.R. to its correct form (monthly in this case).

So you must press   1 9 · 1 7 5 ÷ 1 2 = (ALGebraic) *or*
1 9 · 1 7 5 INPUT 1 2 ÷ (RPN),
and then I%.

Now you're ready. If your paper analysis has been correct, then the NPV should be about zero, because it nets together everything at the beginning of the timeline, adding your initial –22,000 to that stack of positive cash-flows that were discounted back from the future. Since these amounts are equal and opposite, they *ought* to net out to be zero—within a nickel or so. So press NPV to see: NPV=-0.05

Now, notice the other items on this CALC Menu. Each of them analyzes your CFLO list. For example, press **TOTAL**. You'll get the simple sum of all cash-flows in your list: TOTAL=4,400.00

Silly Question: If you compute an NPV using a discount rate (I%) of zero, what would you get for an answer?

Silly Answer: A zero discount rate means that you're not discounting at all. You're just moving each cash-flow, as is, back to the beginning of the timeline and summing all of them.

So, what should you get? It's the same as taking the TOTAL, which you just did, above: 4,400.00

Make Sure: Do it. Press [0] **I%**, then **NPV**....
Answer: NPV=4,400.00

But what does this 4,400.00 *mean*? And what was the meaning of that leftover nickel (-0.05) from the analysis of Fred's proposal? What *is* the meaning of NPV?

To answer that, look at this simple demonstration....

Problem: If you use a discount rate of 19.175% A.P.R. then the Net Present Value (NPV) of Fred's deal is about zero. That is, after all the discounting and summing, *your investments balance your returns.*

But what would be the NPV of Fred's proposal if you were to use a discount rate of 20% A.P.R. instead?

Solution: Press ②⓪÷①②= (ALG) *or* ②⓪ INPUT ①②÷ (RPN), ▆ I% ▆ NPV ▆.... Answer: NPV=-170.01

Question: What does this number mean?

Answer: It means that *if* the value of your money (i.e. what you could yield with it in some other, similar investment) is really 20% A.P.R., then you would *lose* $170.01 by choosing this deal over that other, similar investment.

That's what you were being told in the 19.175% A.P.R. case also: Under that discount rate, the deal had an NPV of –$0.05, meaning that by helping Fred with his start-up, you were losing just a nickel compared to any other investment that would yield you 19.175% A.P.R..

So NPV is an advisory number that compares the cash-flow scenario you're analyzing with a hypothetical investment that yields exactly the discount rate, I%, that you specify:

- If the resulting NPV is *positive*, this means the cash-flow scenario is earning you *more* than the specified discount rate.

- If the NPV is *negative*, the cash-flow scenario is yielding *less* than the specified discount rate;

- If the NPV is *zero*, then there's no difference—a perfect balance.

Therefore, it's usually wise to use as a discount rate that which you really *could* yield in another investment of similar risk and liquidity. Then the NPV is a very good indicator of any investment's value to you *relative to what else you could reasonably expect to do with that money.*

For another good illustration of the advisory message offered by NPV consider the 4,400.00 NPV value you calculated with a discount rate of 0% (page 193).

$4,400—a *positive* NPV—tells you this: "If the yield on your money in other investments of similar risk and liquidity is *really* 0%, then you come out $4,400 *ahead* by putting your money into Fred's scenario rather than into any of your 0%-yield alternatives."

What Is IRR%?

The other "big" item on your CFLO CALC Menu is IRR%, and now it's time to take a look at what Internal Rate of Return is all about. What exactly does it mean?

In 25 words or less:

"Internal Rate of Return (IRR%) is the discount rate that produces a Net Present Value (NPV) of *zero* for the given cash-flow situation."

Remember your friend Fred's claim about your 19.175% A.P.R. "yield" on his business start-up plan (page 189)? You proved he was right by proving that your returns would *balance* your investment if you were to discount those returns back at a 19.175% discount rate.

This balancing is what IRR% does. It actually performs a set of trial-and-error NPV calculations, varying the discount rate until it finds a rate that gives an NPV of zero.

Indeed, where do you suppose Fred got that 19.175 he quoted to you? Lucky guess, maybe? No, he probably did an IRR calculation.

Prove It: Find the IRR% of Fred's proposal (shown again here):

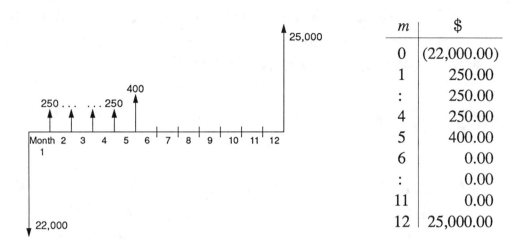

m	$
0	(22,000.00)
1	250.00
:	250.00
4	250.00
5	400.00
6	0.00
:	0.00
11	0.00
12	25,000.00

Solution: This scenario is the list you named FRED, so from the CFLO Menu, GET that list now, by pressing **GET** **FRED**. Then—without any further ado—just go to the CALC Menu and calculate the IRR%: **CALC** **IRR%**....
Answer: IRR%=1.60

Uh... that's not the 19.175 you were expecting, is it? No—remember that all discount rates in the CFLO Menu are *periodic*, not annualized (not true of the I%YR of the TVM Menu). The periods in your friend's scenario are months, so the IRR% is also monthly.

So annualize it: ⊗①②⊜ (ALG) *or* ①②⊗ (RPN)   Result: 19.17
That's better. And if you SHOW its full precision (press ▉ SHOW), you'll see that it *was* just about 19.175—but not exactly, which explains why, when you used *exactly* 19.175, you had a nickel or so of difference.

Thus, in many cash-flow scenarios, IRR% is a very convenient way to compute the discount rate that "balances" the situation—the rate that equates the present value of all your investments with the present value of all your returns. In this respect, you can often think of the IRR% as the "yield" on your investment, and many people do rely heavily upon IRR% to tell them their "yields."

But be careful! There are two traps you can fall into with IRR%:

Trap #1: It's entirely possible to have a cash-flow situation where there is no discount rate that will give a zero NPV. And (even worse), it's also possible to have *more than one* rate that zeros out the NPV—*multiple* IRR%'s.

You can often spot such multiple situations because they tend to flip-flop their cash-flows a lot, maybe with some investments first, then some returns, then some more investments, etc., like this:

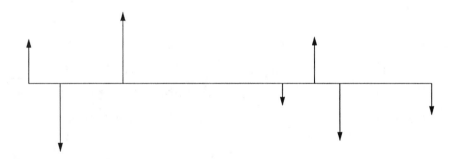

Fortunately, a conventional, one-time investment situation—like FRED—generally has one IRR% at most.

Trap #2: Even when you can find an IRR% that seems reasonable, it's easy to talk yourself right into the land of unreality.

For example, look at this investment:

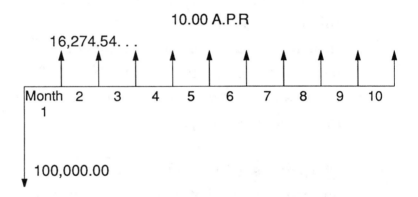

At the beginning, you invested $100,000, and over the next ten years you received steady, even returns on that investment. The IRR% ("yield") for this situation is 10%. So you yielded 10% per year on $100,000 for ten years, right?

Wrong! You actually yielded:

10% for *one* year on $14,795.04, then pocketed $16,274.54
10% for *two* years on $13, 450.03, then pocketed $16,274.54
10% for *three* years on $12,227.30, then pocketed $16, 274.54
...etc. (use TVM to confirm these numbers, if you wish).

In other words, this is the real picture:

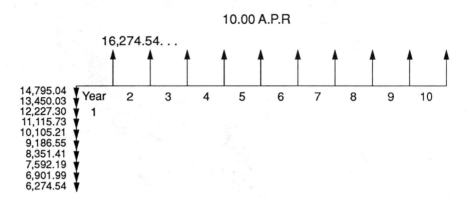

10.00 A.P.R

16,274.54...

14,795.04
13,450.03
12,227.30
11,115.73
10,105.21
9,186.55
8,351.41
7,592.19
6,901.99
6,274.54

Year 1   2   3   4   5   6   7   8   9   10

Every multiple cash-flow situation is really made up of investment/return pairs like this. And—as you've seen—this is exactly how NPV looks at it too: It identifies and transforms each cash-flow into its discounted counterpart back at the beginning of the timeline. The discount rate is used as the *rate of return* on each of these little "internal" investment/return pairs.

The point is, IRR% makes no assumptions about what you do with your "pocketed" returns once you get them. It only claims that the growth rate of each of these little investments was 10% per year *while it was invested*. The minute you get your money back, *the growth stops on that money—* who's to say what you do with it after that?

So you actually yield 10% for *ten years* on only $6,274.54. That's a whole lot different than yielding 10% on $100,000 for ten years.

An easy way to illustrate this is to add up all the pocketed returns of your investment: it comes to $162,745.39. This is what you'd have after the entire ten-year term of your cash-flow scenario—assuming that you did nothing but keep those returns in your pocket.

Now compare that with a simple $100,000 note, invested for 10 years at 10% per year. Its maturity value is $259,374.25.

Those are vastly different numbers. But in both cases your yield is 10% per year. The difference arises in the amount of time you let this yield act. Only in the case of the 10-year note can you say that you yielded 10% on your entire $100,000 for the *entire* term.

Never confuse the term of an investment *analysis* with the term(s) of the actual investment(s) *within* that analysis.

CFLO Quiz

(Draw those T-bars or cash-flow diagrams!)

CFLO Review

1. A loan is written at 12% A.P.R., with $450 monthly payments (in arrears), for 30 years. What is the loan amount? As an exercise, find it with an NPV calculation (don't cheat by using the TVM keys!). Do the same for annuity in advance.

2. How much should you deposit now in a bank account that earns 8% A.P.R. (tax deferred), compounded monthly, so that you can withdraw $10,000 at the beginning of every quarter for 20 years, starting 20 years from now? What about $15,000 withdrawals?

3. Suppose that, for one initial $10,000 investment, you could choose between either of these schedules of income: **(i)** $1000 after Years 1 and 2, $2000 after Year 3, $3000 after Year 4, $5000 after Year 5, $8000 after Year 6; *or* **(ii)** $2800 after each of the six years. Which is better? Comparable investments yield you 16%.

4. What even income stream is *equivalent* to the uneven stream in the previous problem? What would be the first year's income in an equivalent stream that increases annually by 4%?

Residential Real Estate

5. You're transferred to a new city for 4 years. You have $10,000 for a down-payment and are considering a $100,000 home. Property values are growing at 8% annually. The 30-year mortgage rate is 10%, and inflation is 5%. A liquid cash fund earns 8%, but a stock mutual fund could earn 15% annually over 4 years.

    To buy the home, closing costs are $400; the loan fee is 1%. Insurance starts at $30/month, with $180/month in utilities and maintenance. Property taxes are 1.25% per year. Your tax bracket is 28%; capital gains are 100% taxable. You'll pay a 6% commission to resell the home.

    On the other hand, if you rent the home, your security deposit would be $300. Your rent would start at $750, with monthly insurance at $15 and maintenance/utilities at $100.

    "To buy or not to buy—that is the question."

6. You have just made the 84th monthly payment (in arrears) on your 30-year mortgage, whose rate is 11.875%. The balance now stands at $64,750, and current rates are at 10.5%. The refinancing fee is 2.5%. Should you refinance? You may pay off the mortgage on time, or in a balloon after 180th month.

Commercial Investment

7. You're considering the purchase of a double mortgage. The first mortgage was written for $90,000 for 30 years, with end-of-the-month payments at 12% A.P.R. After 15 years, a second mortgage for $30,000 was added, at 13.0% for 20 years, again with monthly payments in arrears. The bank now holding both mortgages is willing to discount them to you so that you can earn 16% on your investment. How much should you pay the bank for the right to "inherit" these contracts (begin to receive their payments) at the end of the third year of the second mortgage (i.e. at the end of the 18th year of the first mortgage)? What if you settle instead on a price that yields you 17.5%?

8. What is the monthly payment amount for a 5-year lease with skipped payments (annual schedule shown below) on a $40,000 computer with a 10% residual buy-out? The lessor is asking for 4 advance payments (other than the first normal payment) and wants an 18% yield.

Month	Payment?	Month	Payment?
1	yes	7	no
2	yes	8	no
3	yes	9	no
4	no	10	yes
5	no	11	yes
6	yes	12	yes

9. A manufacturer is relocating and needs a warehouse until its own facilities are completed (2 years). One suitable building is for sale for $100,000, of which 75% is depreciable. The firm has $30,000 in ready cash. The 20-year mortgage rate is 10%, and inflation is 5%. Cash funds earn 7%; stock funds earn 15%. To buy the building, closing costs are $400; the loan fee is 2%. Insurance starts at $60/month, with $250/month in utilities/maintenance. Property taxes are 1.25% per year. The company's tax bracket is 33%, with capital gains 100% taxable. A broker will charge 6% commission to resell the building. Estimated price: $115,000.

Alternatively, to lease the building from the current owner, rent would start at $750/mo. (including property taxes), with 2 payments (in addition to the first regular payment) due immediately, and with annual adjustments for inflation. Insurance would be $85; maintenance/utilities would be $220.

Should the company buy the building or lease it?

10. A home currently has two mortgages: $100,000 at 10% for 30 years (no balloon); and $50,000 at 11.5% for 10 years, with a $10,000 balloon. The second mortgage began after the 15th year of the first. Now, after the 20th year, the owner wishes to consolidate loans and get financing for more remodelling. You offer to "wrap" his current mortgages (cover all their obligations) and loan him $50,000 in new money, in exchange for 120 monthly payments of $2,200 and a $25,000 balloon. What is your yield? And what is the borrower's overall A.P.R.? He paid 1 point up front on the first mortgage, 2 points up front on the second.

11. You are considering an investment in low-income housing. Your cash-flows will look like this:

Year (end)	Cash-Flow
0 (initial flow)	$ -50,000
1	25,000
2	50,000
3	-25,000
4	50,000
5	-25,000
6	-10,000
7	-10,000

What would be your yield on this investment scenario?

12. Find the FMRR for the following cash-flow scenario, assuming that all cash is taken from, and returned to, an account earning 6%. Compare this FMRR with the IRR% for the same situation.

Year	Cash-Flow
0	$ (75,000)
1	15,000
2	15,000
3	(60,000)
4	75,000
5	(35,000)
6	200,000

13. Using a safe rate of 6% and a risk rate of 15%, find the FMRR, $MIN and $MAX of the scenario in Chapter 5, problem **24** (pages 147 and 170-176).

Personal Finance

14. Recall the comparison of IRA's in Chapter 5 (prob. **9**, pages 142 and 155). The idea was that 7 early years of investment were more valuable after 28 years than similar investments made in each of those later 28 years. Prove this again with a CFLO list.

15. After having invested in three no-load mutual funds as shown in the schedule below, you had a sudden, violent attack of prudence on August 31, 1987, and sold everything—for these net amounts:

A: $34,319
B: $13,526
C: $22,410

Fund	Date	Amount Invested
A	9-30-82	$ 3000
B	3-15-83	1000
C	5-31-83	2500
A	6-30-83	2500
B	11-15-83	1000
C	4-15-84	2500
A	5-31-84	3500
B	8-15-84	1000
C	10-15-84	3000
A	12-31-84	3000
B	4-15-85	1500
C	6-30-85	4000

What was your overall annualized yield?

CFLO Quiz Solutions

1. Here's the situation (as the lender would see it):

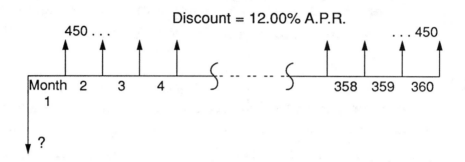

Your unknown is the cash-flow at the beginning of the timeline. Therefore, if you take the NPV of the rest of your list—using the actual rate as the discount rate, the result must exactly balance this unknown flow—equal and opposite (recall Fred's scenario). This makes sense: If the quoted 12% A.P.R. truly represents the interest rate in this mortgage, it *must* be the discount rate for which the entire scenario's NPV is zero. If it produces an NPV either more or less than zero, then the mortgage's yield is either more or less (respectively) than the 12% A.P.R. You use this "incomplete" NPV to deduce what other cash-flow must have happened at the beginning of the timeline to produce a *zero* NPV.

So just key in the cash-flow scenario, ignoring the initial flow: Press **GET** **⊞NEW** at the CFLO Menu. Then:

[0][INPUT]   (no initial cash-flow except the unknown you ignore)
[4][5][0][INPUT][3][6][0][INPUT]   (360 months of $450 payments).
To calculate, press [EXIT] **CALC**, then [1][2][÷][1][2] or [1][2][INPUT][1][2][÷],
then **I%** to specify the monthly discount rate.
Now **NPV**.... Answer: NPV=43,748.25
The amount financed (from the lender's viewpoint) was –$43,748.25

Now redraw the picture for the case of annuity in advance:

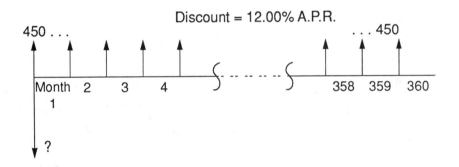

Discount = 12.00% A.P.R.

Again, find the unknown flow at the beginning by ignoring it.
[EXIT] to the CFLO Menu to modify your list now:

■[▲][4][5][0][INPUT]   (in BEGIN Mode, there's a PMT right away)
[▼]   (change only the frequency of FLOW(1))
[3][5][9][INPUT]
[0][INPUT][INPUT]   (the end of month 360 has no cash-flow)
[EXIT] **CALC NPV**   Answer: NPV=44,185.73
The initial cash-flow (from the lender's viewpoint) was –$44,185.73.
Verify these values with the TVM Menu, if you wish.

2. The situation:

q	$
0	(?.??)
1	0.00
:	0.00
79	0.00
80	10,000.00
:	10,000.00
159	10,000.00

Discount = 8.00% (compounded monthly)

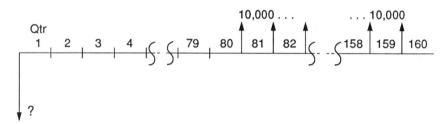

Again, the problem is to find the unknown initial cash-flow. But you have *quarterly* cash-flows with *monthly* interest compounding of interest ("...*sounds like a job for... ICNV!*").

First, draw the picture: At the CFLO Menu: ▮CLEAR DATA ▮YES▮
⓪ INPUT   (nothing happens initially, except for the unknown flow, which you ignore for now.)

⓪ INPUT ⑦⑨ INPUT   (79 quarters of no cash-flows)

①⓪⓪⓪⓪ INPUT ⑧⓪ INPUT   (80 quarters of withdrawals)

Now convert the interest rate: EXIT EXIT ▮ICNV▮ PER▮
⑧ ▮NOM%▮ ①② ▮ P ▮ EFF% ④ ▮ P ▮ NOM%....
Result: NOM%=8.05

Then EXIT EXIT ▮CFLO▮ CALC▮, then ÷④ (ALG) or ④÷ (RPN), then ▮ I% ▮ NPV▮....   Answer: NPV=81,967.88

Change to $15,000 withdrawals: EXIT ▲▲ ①⑤⓪⓪⓪ INPUT EXIT
▮CALC▮ NPV▮....   Answer: NPV=122,951.83

3.   The alternatives:

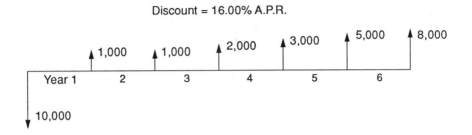

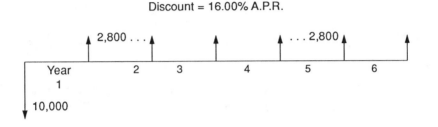

From the CFLO Menu, clear or name the current list, then begin a new list: [1][0][0][0][0][+/−][INPUT][2][8][0][0][INPUT][6][INPUT][EXIT] **CALC** [1][6] **I%** **NPV** .... Answer: NPV=317.26

That's the simple, even cash-flow option. Now [EXIT] to CFLO, and name this list: **NAME** EVEN [INPUT], and **GET** **#NEW**.

Now for the other case:

[1][0][0][0][0][+/−][INPUT]   [1][0][0][0][INPUT][2][INPUT]
[2][0][0][0][INPUT][INPUT]   [3][0][0][0][INPUT][INPUT]
[5][0][0][0][INPUT][INPUT]   [8][0][0][0][INPUT][INPUT]   [EXIT]
CALC **NPV** ....   Answer: NPV=207.52
(NAME this list UNEVEN: [EXIT] **NAME** [U][N][E][V][E][N][INPUT]).

NPV tells you that the EVEN case is worth slightly more to you.

4. This is a question to answer with a NUS ("Net Uniform Series") calculation. NUS takes the NPV of a given set of cash-flows and then computes what uniform series would give that same NPV:

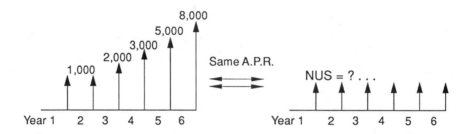

Notice that the initial –$10,000 is not in question; it's assumed in either case. You're analyzing only the positive cash-flows to see what uniform yearly amount could replace each of them.

So just omit the initial investment in your UNEVEN scenario (this should be the current CFLO list if you've just come from the previous problem): ■▲ 0 INPUT EXIT CALC and then NUS ....
Answer: NUS=2,770.22

So (at a discount rate of 16%), your uneven payment scenario has exactly the same value to you as six level payments of $2,770.22. This seems plausible: it's only slightly less than the $2800 EVEN case of problem **3**, and—as the results of that problem showed—there was only a slight difference between those two NPV's.

Prove the equivalency of your NUS, by using it as the cash-flow amount in the EVEN case; the NPV should then be exactly that of the UNEVEN case: EXIT and GET EVEN. Then ■▲▼ and simply INPUT INPUT to replace the $2800 with the NUS (which is still on the Calculator Line). Then EXIT CALC and NPV ....
Answer: NPV=207.52   Sure enough.

The other part of this problem is similar, but it asks you to find a certain *uneven* scenario that satisfies the equivalency:

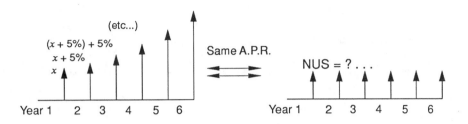

(etc...)

$(x + 5\%) + 5\%$

$x + 5\%$

x

Year 1   2   3   4   5   6

Same A.P.R.

NUS = ? . . .

Year 1   2   3   4   5   6

Each cash-flow in the unknown scenario is 4% more than the previous, *and* its NPV (at 16%) must match that of the UNEVEN scenario. First, find that NPV: (EXIT) **GET UNEV**. Then **CALC NPV**. <u>Answer</u>: NPV=10,207.52

Now, a 4%-increasing scenario that starts with *one dollar* has an NPV that is *x* times less than that of a 4%-increasing scenario that starts with $x. In other words: $NPV_{\$x} = x(NPV_{\$1})$. But you've just calculated that $NPV_{\$x}$ is 10,207.52. So the *x* in the unknown scenario above is given by: $x = 10{,}207.52 \div NPV_{\$1}$

So: (EXIT) and **GET \$NEW**. Then: (0)(INPUT)   (1)(INPUT)(INPUT)

(+)(4)(%) (ALG) *or* (4)(%)(+) (RPN)   (INPUT)(INPUT)(▲)(▲)(RCL)(INPUT)(▼)(▼)

(+)(4)(%) (ALG) *or* (4)(%)(+) (RPN)   (INPUT)(INPUT)(▲)(▲)(RCL)(INPUT)(▼)(▼)

(+)(4)(%) (ALG) *or* (4)(%)(+) (RPN)   (INPUT)(INPUT)(▲)(▲)(RCL)(INPUT)(▼)(▼)

(+)(4)(%) (ALG) *or* (4)(%)(+) (RPN)   (INPUT)(INPUT)(▲)(▲)(RCL)(INPUT)(▼)(▼)

(+)(4)(%) (ALG) *or* (4)(%)(+) (RPN)   (INPUT)(INPUT) (EXIT)

CALC NPV.... (<u>Result</u>: NPV=4.01)   Then (1/x) and

(×)(1)(0)(2)(0)(7)(·)(5)(2)(=) (ALG) *or* (1)(0)(2)(0)(7)(·)(5)(2)(×)(RPN)

<u>Answer</u>: 2,548.38

(If you do a lot of calculations with increasing annuities, you can use a Solver formula—see the note on page 311 in Chapter 9.)

5. **Which NPV is greater?**

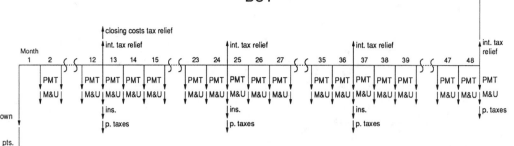

BUY

BUY assumptions: The mortgage payment, utilities and maintenance are due at the END of the month. You pay yearly insurance
(in advance) and property taxes (in arrears), and tax relief from
deductions comes at the end of the year. When you sell the home
and pay off the mortgage, you will owe capital gains tax on your
net gain—after any commission to a broker. The property value
(and thus its tax) increases annually at the given growth rate.

The RENT assumptions: You owe first and last month's rent, plus
a fully-refundable security deposit immediately. Rent is paid at
the beginning of each month, maintenance/utilities at the end.
Your renter's insurance premium is paid annually, in advance.
Also, you pay yearly income tax on the interest accruing on your
investment of the down-payment money.

*In both cases, insurance, utilities / maintenance (and your rent in
the RENT case) increase yearly by the inflation rate.*

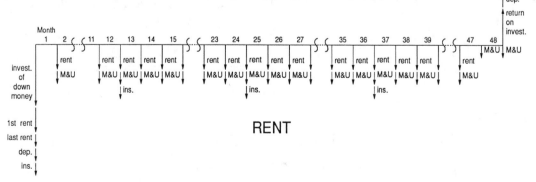

RENT

The <u>ending balance</u> of the down-payment money invested:

⌧EXIT⌧ ⌧EXIT⌧ **TVM** **OTHER** ⌧1⌧ **P/YR** ⌧EXIT⌧, and

⌧4⌧ **N** ⌧1⌧⌧0⌧⌧0⌧⌧0⌧⌧0⌧⌧+/−⌧ **PV** ⌧0⌧ **PMT**

⌧1⌧⌧5⌧⌧−⌧⌧2⌧⌧8⌧⌧%⌧⌧=⌧ (ALG) *or* ⌧1⌧⌧5⌧⌧INPUT⌧⌧2⌧⌧8⌧⌧%⌧⌧−⌧ (RPN) **I/YR**

FV ....   <u>Answer:</u> FV=15,071.59

<u>Monthly rent:</u> ⌧7⌧⌧5⌧⌧0⌧⌧+/−⌧   −750.00 (Year 1)
⌧+⌧⌧5⌧⌧%⌧⌧=⌧ (ALG) *or* ⌧INPUT⌧⌧5⌧⌧%⌧⌧+⌧ (RPN) −787.50 (Year 2)
⌧+⌧⌧5⌧⌧%⌧⌧=⌧ (ALG) *or* ⌧5⌧⌧%⌧⌧+⌧ (RPN)   −826.88 (Year 3)
⌧+⌧⌧5⌧⌧%⌧⌧=⌧ (ALG) *or* ⌧5⌧⌧%⌧⌧+⌧ (RPN)   −868.22 (Year 4)

<u>Yearly insurance</u> (RENT): ⌧1⌧⌧5⌧⌧+/−⌧⌧×⌧⌧1⌧⌧2⌧⌧=⌧ (ALG) *or*
        ⌧1⌧⌧5⌧⌧+/−⌧⌧INPUT⌧⌧1⌧⌧2⌧⌧×⌧ (RPN)   −180.00 (Year 1)
⌧+⌧⌧5⌧⌧%⌧⌧=⌧ (ALG) *or* ⌧5⌧⌧%⌧⌧+⌧ (RPN)   −189.00 (Year 2)
⌧+⌧⌧5⌧⌧%⌧⌧=⌧ (ALG) *or* ⌧5⌧⌧%⌧⌧+⌧ (RPN)   −198.45 (Year 3)
⌧+⌧⌧5⌧⌧%⌧⌧=⌧ (ALG) *or* ⌧5⌧⌧%⌧⌧+⌧ (RPN)   −208.37 (Year 3)

<u>Monthly util./mnt.</u> (RENT): ⌧1⌧⌧0⌧⌧0⌧⌧+/−⌧ −100.00 (Year 1)
⌧+⌧⌧5⌧⌧%⌧⌧=⌧ (ALG) *or* ⌧INPUT⌧⌧5⌧⌧%⌧⌧+⌧ (RPN) −105.00 (Year 2)
⌧+⌧⌧5⌧⌧%⌧⌧=⌧ (ALG) *or* ⌧5⌧⌧%⌧⌧+⌧ (RPN)   −110.25 (Year 3)
⌧+⌧⌧5⌧⌧%⌧⌧=⌧ (ALG) *or* ⌧5⌧⌧%⌧⌧+⌧ (RPN)   −115.76 (Year 4)

<u>Yearly insurance</u> (BUY): ⌧3⌧⌧0⌧⌧+/−⌧⌧×⌧⌧1⌧⌧2⌧⌧=⌧ (ALG) *or*
        ⌧3⌧⌧0⌧⌧+/−⌧⌧INPUT⌧⌧1⌧⌧2⌧⌧×⌧ (RPN)   −360.00 (Year 1)
⌧+⌧⌧5⌧⌧%⌧⌧=⌧ (ALG) *or* ⌧5⌧⌧%⌧⌧+⌧ (RPN)   −378.00 (Year 2)
⌧+⌧⌧5⌧⌧%⌧⌧=⌧ (ALG) *or* ⌧5⌧⌧%⌧⌧+⌧ (RPN)   −396.90 (Year 3)
⌧+⌧⌧5⌧⌧%⌧⌧=⌧ (ALG) *or* ⌧5⌧⌧%⌧⌧+⌧ (RPN)   −416.75 (Year 4)

<u>Monthly util./mnt.</u> (BUY): ⌧1⌧⌧8⌧⌧0⌧⌧+/−⌧   −180.00 (Year 1)
⌧+⌧⌧5⌧⌧%⌧⌧=⌧ (ALG) *or* ⌧INPUT⌧⌧5⌧⌧%⌧⌧+⌧ (RPN) −189.00 (Year 2)
⌧+⌧⌧5⌧⌧%⌧⌧=⌧ (ALG) *or* ⌧5⌧⌧%⌧⌧+⌧ (RPN)   −198.45 (Year 3)
⌧+⌧⌧5⌧⌧%⌧⌧=⌧ (ALG) *or* ⌧5⌧⌧%⌧⌧+⌧ (RPN)   −208.37 (Year 4)

The <u>net (after-tax) yearly property taxes</u>:

[1][0][0][0][0][0][+][8][%][×][1][.][2][5][+/−][%][−][2][8][%][=] (ALG) or

[1][0][0][0][0][0][INPUT][8][%][+][1][.][2][5][+/−][%][2][8][%][−] (RPN)

$$-972.00 \quad \text{(Year 1)}$$

[+][8][%][=] (ALG) or [8][%][+] (RPN) -1,049.76 (Year 2)

[+][8][%][=] (ALG) or [8][%][+] (RPN) -1,133.74 (Year 3)

[+][8][%][=] (ALG) or [8][%][+] (RPN) -1,224.44 (Year 4)

<u>Monthly mortgage pmt</u>: (At TVM—set P/YR to 12) [3][6][0] **N**

[1][0] **I%YR** [9][0][0][0][0] **PV** [0] **FV** **PMT** ....PMT=-789.81

The <u>mortgage balance</u> after 4 years: [4][8] **N** **FV** ....

FV=-87,662.00

The <u>mortgage interest yearly tax relief</u>: **OTHER** **AMRT** ,

[1][2] **#P** **INT** [+/−][×][2][8][%][=] or [+/−][2][8][%] 2,513.70 (Year 1)

NEXT **INT** [+/−][×][2][8][%][=] or [+/−][2][8][%] 2,499.03 (Year 2)

NEXT **INT** [+/−][×][2][8][%][=] or [+/−][2][8][%] 2,482.83 (Year 3)

NEXT **INT** [+/−][×][2][8][%][=] or [+/−][2][8][%] 2,464.93 (Year 4)

The <u>mortgage points tax relief</u>:

[9][0][0][×][2][8][%][=] or [9][0][0][INPUT][2][8][%] 252.00 (Year 1)

The <u>proceeds of re-sale</u>:

[1][0][0][0][0][0][+][8][%][+][8][%][+][8][%][+][8][%][−][6][%][=](ALG) or

[1][0][0][0][0][0][INPUT][8][%][+][8][%][+][8][%][+][8][%][+][6][%][−] (RPN)

(<u>result</u>: 127,885.96). So the gain on the sale is $27,885.96

The <u>net (after-tax) proceeds</u> at resale: [−][8][7][6][6][2]

[−][(][2][7][8][8][5][.][9][6][×][2][8][%][=](ALG) or [8][7][6][6][2][−]

[2][7][8][8][5][.][9][6][INPUT][.][2][8][×][−] (RPN) 32,415.89

The completed RENT diagram:

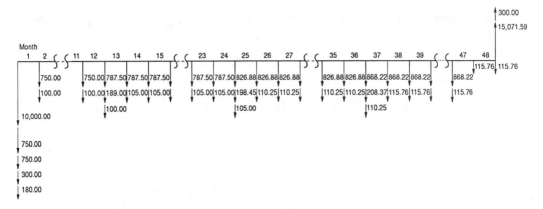

The completed BUY diagram:

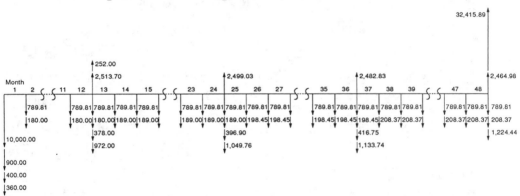

Now find the NPV of each scenario, using your 8% cash fund interest (less taxes) as the discount rate: ⬛MAIN FIN CFLO, etc. (you should now know how to key in the above diagrams). For each scenario, CALC and:

8 − 2 8 % ÷ 1 2 = (ALG) or 8 INPUT 2 8 % − 1 2 ÷ (RPN)

I% NPV....   RENT: NPV=-38,063.48

                   BUY: NPV=-23,912.24

As you can see, either case is a net *expense* to you—your cost of housing—but it will be less if you buy the house.

If you do a lot of rent/buy analyses, use a Solver formula—see the note on p. 311 in Ch. 9.

6. Just find the NPV of the refinanced scenario, *using the original mortgage rate* as your discount rate:

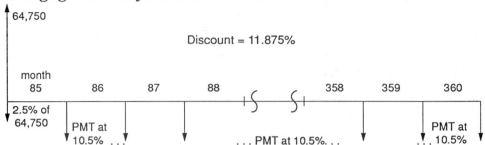

Press ■ MAIN FIN TVM OTHER 1 2 P/YR END . EXIT and:

3 6 0 − 8 4 = (ALG) *or* (RPN) 3 6 0 INPUT 8 4 −

■ N 1 0 • 5 I%YR 6 4 7 5 0 PV 0 FV PMT ....

<u>Result</u>: PMT=-622.81   The refinanced payment.

1 8 0 − 8 4 = ■ N ■ (ALG) *or* (RPN) 1 8 0 INPUT 8 4 − ■ N ■

■ FV ■ <u>Result</u>: FV=-56,342.47   The balloon after 180 months.

EXIT CFLO ■ CLEAR DATA YES , then "draw the picture:" GET #NEW .

First the full-term case: 6 4 7 5 0 − 2 • 5 % = INPUT (ALG) *or*

ENTER 2 • 5 % − INPUT (RPN)

Then 6 2 2 • 8 1 +/− INPUT

3 6 0 − 8 4 = INPUT (ALG) *or* 3 6 0 ENTER 8 4 − INPUT (RPN)

EXIT CALC 1 1 • 8 7 5 ÷ 1 2 = (ALG) *or*

EXIT CALC 1 1 • 8 7 5 INPUT 1 2 ÷ (RPN)

■ I% ■ NPV .... <u>Answer</u>: NPV=4,349.62

If you take the loan to term, you'll save by refinancing now.

If you pay it off in a balloon after the 180th month: EXIT ▲

1 7 9 − 8 4 = INPUT (ALG) *or* 1 7 9 ENTER 8 4 − INPUT (RPN)

5 6 3 4 2 • 4 7 +/− INPUT INPUT EXIT CALC NPV ....

<u>Answer</u>: NPV=2,998.81   You save in this case, too, but *less*; a refinancing fee has a relatively larger effect on a shorter-term scenario (see Ch. 5, prob. **14**, pages 143 and 159).

See p. 311 in Ch. 9 for a note on using a SOLVE formula for this.

7. As the investor, you're the new lender:

Discount = 16.00% A.P.R

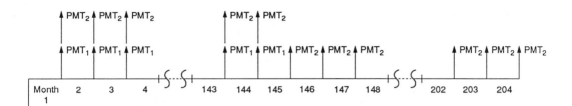

Press ■ MAIN FIN TVM OTHER 1 2 P/YR END . EXIT and:

3 6 0 ■ N 1 2 I%YR 9 0 0 0 0 +/− PV 0 FV PMT ....

Result: PMT=925.75 The payment on the first mortgage.

2 4 0 ■ N 1 3 I%YR 3 0 0 0 0 +/− PV PMT ....

Result: PMT=351.47 The payment on the second.

EXIT CFLO ■ CLEAR DATA YES , and enter the scenario (omitting the unknown initial flow, as in problems 1 and 2): GET #NEW , and:

0 INPUT (no initial cash-flow besides the unknown)

9 2 5 • 7 5 + 3 5 1 • 4 7 (ALG) or

9 2 5 • 7 5 ENTER 3 5 1 • 4 7 + (RPN)

INPUT (your combined payments...) 1 4 4 INPUT (for 12 years...)

3 5 1 • 4 7 INPUT 6 0 INPUT (...and 5 more years of the second)

EXIT CALC , and 1 6 ÷ 1 2 = (ALG) or (RPN) 1 6 INPUT 1 2 ÷

I% NPV .... Answer: NPV=83,714.46

The price of this double mortgage that will yield you 16%.

To yield 17.5%:

1 7 • 5 ÷ 1 2 = (ALG) or (RPN) 1 7 • 5 INPUT 1 2 ÷

I% NPV .... Answer: NPV=78,431.48

See p. 311 in Ch. 9 for a note on using a SOLVE formula for this.

8. Here is the proposed scenario:

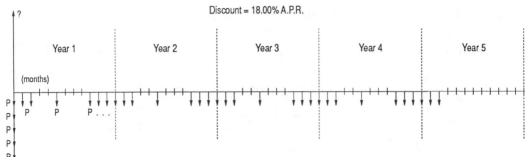

Discount = 18.00% A.P.R.

First, find the NPV which the lease payments must "balance:"
At the CFLO Menu: ■ CLEAR DATA YES 4 0 0 0 0 0 INPUT
0 INPUT 5 9 INPUT 4 0 0 0 +/− INPUT INPUT EXIT CALC
and 1 8 ÷ 1 2 = (ALG) or 1 8 INPUT 1 2 ÷ (RPN) I% NPV ....
NPV=38,362.82   The payments must "balance" this.

Now, as in problem **4**, when you don't know the amount of a given cash-flow—but you do know its NPV—use a $1 cash-flow. That NPV is *proportionally* less than that of the unknown cash-flow, so the *ratio* of the NPV's is the amount of the unknown cash-flow:

EXIT ■ CLEAR DATA YES 5 +/− INPUT (4 in advance, plus the first)

1 +/− INPUT 2 INPUT   0 INPUT 2 INPUT   1 +/− INPUT INPUT
0 INPUT 3 INPUT   1 +/− INPUT 6 INPUT   0 INPUT 2 INPUT
1 +/− INPUT INPUT   0 INPUT 3 INPUT   1 +/− INPUT 6 INPUT
0 INPUT 2 INPUT   1 +/− INPUT INPUT   0 INPUT 3 INPUT
1 +/− INPUT 6 INPUT   0 INPUT 2 INPUT   1 +/− INPUT INPUT
0 INPUT 3 INPUT   1 +/− INPUT 6 INPUT   EXIT

(Remember that the final 4 payments were paid in advance)
CALC NPV ....   NPV=-25.64   Then ■ 1/x and
× 3 8 3 6 2 · 8 2 = (ALG) *or* 3 8 3 6 2 · 8 2 × (RPN)
Result: **-1,496.36**   The monthly lease payment amount.
Note: If you do a lot of leasing calculations, see page 311 in Chapter 9 for a note on using a SOLVE formula.

9. This is like #5 (page 214), but all expenses are tax-deductible. Also, there is depreciation (31.5 years, Straight Line); the capital gain is the difference between the re-sale and *depreciated* values.

<u>Ending balance</u> of the down-payment money invested:
[EXIT][EXIT] **TVM** **OTHER** [1] **P/YR** [EXIT], and
[2] **N** [3][0][0][0][0][+/−] **PV** [0] **PMT**
[1][5][−][3][3][%][=] (ALG) *or* [1][5][INPUT][3][3][%][−] (RPN) **I%YR**
FV ....   <u>Answer:</u> FV=36,333.01

<u>Monthly lease payment:</u>   [7][5][0][+/−]   -750.00 (Year 1)
[+][5][%][=] (ALG) *or* [INPUT][5][%][+] (RPN)   -787.50 (Year 2)

<u>Yearly insurance</u> (LEASE): [8][5][+/−][×][1][2][=] (ALG)
        or [8][5][+/−][INPUT][1][2][×] (RPN) -1,020.00 (Year 1)
[+][5][%][=] (ALG) *or* [5][%][+] (RPN)   -1,071.00 (Year 2)

<u>Monthly util./mnt.</u> (LEASE): [2][2][0][+/−] -220.00 (Year 1)
[+][5][%][=] (ALG) *or* [INPUT][5][%][+] (RPN)   -231.00 (Year 2)

<u>Expenses yearly tax relief (LEASE):</u> [7][5][0][×][1][4][+][1][0][2][0][+]
[(][1][2][×][2][2][0][)][×][3][3][%][=] (ALG) *or* [7][5][0][INPUT][1][4][×]
[1][0][2][0][+][1][2][INPUT][2][2][0][×][+][3][3][%] 4,672.80 (Year 1)
[7][8][7][•][5][×][1][0][+][1][0][7][1][+][(][1][2][×][2][3][1][)][×][3][3][%][=] *or*
[7][8][7][•][5][INPUT][1][0][×][1][0][7][1][+][1][2][INPUT][2][3][1][×][+][3][3][%]
                    3,866.94 (Year 2)

<u>Yearly insurance</u> (BUY): [6][0][+/−][×][1][2][=] (ALG)
        or [6][0][+/−][INPUT][1][2][×] (RPN)   -720.00 (Year 1)
[+][5][%][=] (ALG) *or* [5][%][+] (RPN)   -756.00 (Year 2)

<u>Monthly util./mnt.</u> (BUY): [2][5][0][+/−]   -250.00 (Year 1)
[+][5][%][=] (ALG) *or* [INPUT][5][%][+] (RPN)   -262.50 (Year 2)

Net yearly property taxes: ⑴⓪⓪⓪⓪⓪✕⑴・⑴⑤■ √x̄ ✕
⑴・②⑤+/-%−③③%= (ALG) or ⑴⓪⓪⓪⓪⓪ INPUT ⑴・⑴⑤
■ √x̄ ✕⑴・②⑤+/-%③③%− (RPN) -898.12 (Year 1)
✕⑴・⑴⑤■ √x̄ = (ALG) or
⑴・⑴⑤■ √x̄ ✕ (RPN) -963.13 (Year 2)

Monthly mortgage payment: (At TVM) OTHER ⑴② P/YR
END EXIT ②④⓪ N ⑴⓪ I%YR ⑦⓪⓪⓪⓪ PV ⓪ FV
PMT .... PMT=-675.52

Mortgage balance: ②④ N FV .... FV=-67,562.08

Mortgage interest yearly tax relief: OTHER AMRT ,
⑴② #P INT +/-✕③③%= or +/-③③% 2,292.80 (Year 1)
NEXT INT +/-✕③③%= or +/-③③% 2,252.77 (Year 2)

Mortgage points yearly tax relief: ⑦⓪⓪⓪⓪✕②%✕③③%÷
②= (ALG) or ⑦⓪⓪⓪⓪ INPUT ②%②÷③③% (RPN) 231.00

Depreciation yearly tax relief: ⑦⑤⓪⓪⓪÷③⑴・⑤✕③③%=
(ALG) or ⑦⑤⓪⓪⓪ INPUT ③⑴・⑤÷③③% (RPN) 785.71

Expenses yearly tax relief (BUY): ④⓪⓪+⑦②⓪+
((⑴②✕②⑤⓪)✕③③%= (ALG) or ④⓪⓪ INPUT ⑦②⓪+
⑴② INPUT ②⑤⓪✕+③③% (RPN) 1,359.60 (Year 1)
⑴②✕②⑥②・⑤+⑦⑤⑥✕③③%= (ALG) or ⑴② INPUT
②⑥②・⑤✕⑦⑤⑥+③③% (RPN) 1,288.98 (Year 2)

Proceeds at resale: ⑴⑴⑤⓪⓪⓪−⑥%=(ALG) or ⑴⑴⑤⓪⓪⓪
INPUT ⑥%− (RPN) 108,100.00 (Gross proceeds)
−((⑴⓪⓪⓪⓪⓪−((②✕⑦⑤⓪⓪⓪÷③⑴・⑤=(ALG) or
⑴⓪⓪⓪⓪⓪ INPUT ⑦⑤⓪⓪⓪ INPUT ③⑴・⑤÷②✕−− (RPN)
12,861.90 (Gain)

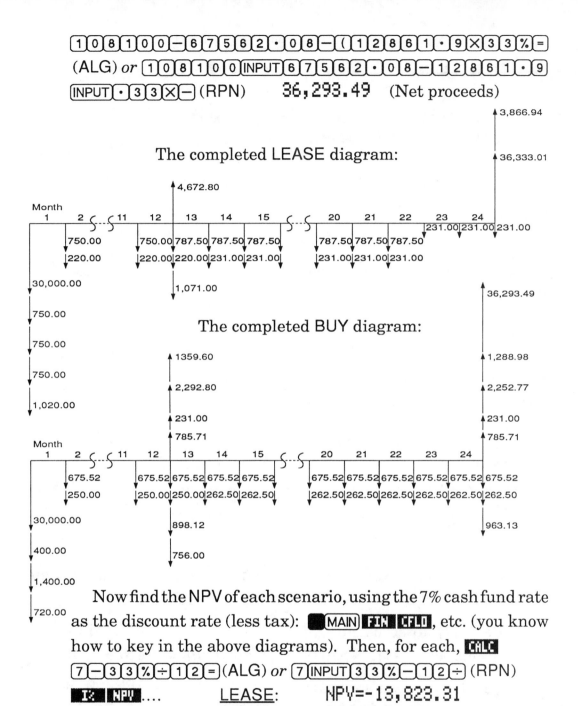

1 0 8 1 0 0 − 6 7 5 6 2 • 0 8 − (1 2 8 6 1 • 9 × 3 3 % =
(ALG) *or* 1 0 8 1 0 0 INPUT 6 7 5 6 2 • 0 8 − 1 2 8 6 1 • 9
INPUT • 3 3 × − (RPN)   36,293.49   (Net proceeds)

The completed LEASE diagram:

The completed BUY diagram:

Now find the NPV of each scenario, using the 7% cash fund rate as the discount rate (less tax): ▮MAIN ▮FIN▮ ▮CFLO▮, etc. (you know how to key in the above diagrams). Then, for each, ▮CALC▮
7 − 3 3 % ÷ 1 2 = (ALG) *or* 7 INPUT 3 3 % − 1 2 ÷ (RPN)
▮I%▮ ▮NPV▮....   LEASE: NPV=-13,823.31
                    BUY: NPV=-14,621.56

The company would be slightly better off leasing the building.

If you do many lease/buy analyses, see p. 311 in Ch. 9 for a note on using a Solver formula.

10. At the TVM Menu: `OTHER` `1` `2` `P/YR` `END` (EXIT). Then:

`3` `6` `0` `N` `1` `0` `I/YR` `1` `0` `0` `0` `0` `0` `PV` `0` `FV` `PMT` ....

PMT=-877.57   (first mortgage payment)

`1` `2` `0` `N` `1` `1` `·` `5` `I/YR` `5` `0` `0` `0` `0` `PV` `1` `0` `0` `0` `0` `+/−`

`FV` `PMT` .... PMT=-658.22   (second mortgage payment)

The complete pictures, from the lender's (your) point of view...

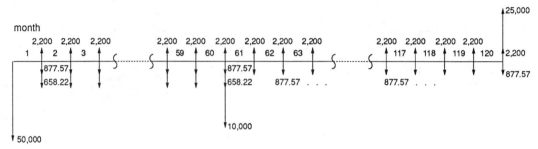

...and from the borrower's point of view:

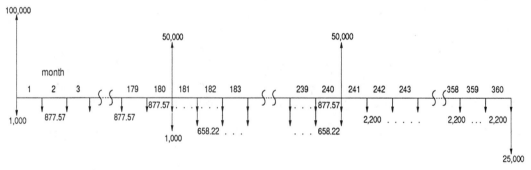

At the CFLO Menu, key in each of these scenarios and calculate their IRR%'s (you should know the keystrokes by now).

Result (your scenario):   IRR%=1.41

Annualize: ×`1``2`= (ALG) *or* `1``2`× (RPN)   16.97

Result (borrower's scenario):   IRR%=0.88

Annualize: ×`1``2`= (ALG) *or* `1``2`× (RPN)   10.51

See page 311 in Ch. 9 for a note on using a SOLVE formula for this kind of calculation.

11. Nothing to it—just GET a new CFLO list and key in the numbers:

5 0 0 0 0 +/- INPUT

2 5 0 0 0 INPUT INPUT   5 0 0 0 0 INPUT INPUT

2 5 0 0 0 +/- INPUT INPUT   5 0 0 0 0 INPUT INPUT

2 5 0 0 0 +/- INPUT INPUT   1 0 0 0 0 +/- INPUT INPUT

1 0 0 0 0 +/- INPUT INPUT   EXIT   CALC IRR% ....What's this?

```
MANY/NO SOLUTIONS; KEY
IN GUESS; [STO] {IRR%}
```

This is one of those cash-flow scenarios that has *more than one IRR%*—more than one discount rate that will give an NPV of zero. The display tells you to key in a guess and press STO IRR%. It will then home in on the *nearest* solution.

What's a good starting guess? Something modest—say, 12%? So press 1 2 STO IRR% .... Result: IRR%=17.77   Not bad.

But you've just been told that there is more than one solution, so try to find another—just for comparison. Try a much more pessimistic guess: 0 STO IRR% .... Result: IRR%=-9.49

Which IRR% is right? Will you be losing or making money on this housing deal?

It's not easy to tell—neither percentage is necessarily "right." Remember that IRR% is simply a number that, when used as the discount rate, happens to make the NPV balance at 0. It *doesn't* always mean that your dollars are actually accruing that much interest—as this example demonstrates.

So this is one of those times when you cannot simply look to IRR% to tell you your "yield." But, fortunately, there's another very logical way to calculate your "yield," the Financial Management Rate of Return (FMRR). Here's how it works:

When you invest money in any one place, you're choosing *not* to invest it somewhere else. Presumably, you do so because this investment best suits your needs—acceptable levels of risk and liquidity and, within those constraints, a good rate of return. But picture how you would actually make the investment(s) in the required schedule....

Question: Where will you get the money at each of the required dates of the investments?

Answer: From a bank account or another *readily liquid* account that is yielding you at least a little interest in the meantime—say, a money market account.

Question: As you receive returns on these housing investments, what will you do with that money?

Answer: If you have more investments (outflows) left on the schedule, you'll certainly use this money to supply those cash-flows. As for any excess, since you're clearly willing to risk that money to the degree of risk of the housing project, you'll probably put these excess returns into some other equally risky investment—a "risk-rate" account—until the end of the housing venture.

To summarize this strategy:

- You start with a certain amount of cash in a liquid account, earning interest at some "safe rate" until you invest it in the housing project.

- You also use interim returns to supply any subsequent investments in the schedule.

- You let all excess returns "ride" in a higher-yielding ("risk-rate") account until the end of whole investment venture.

Keep in mind that this isn't any big secret formula. It's what any competent financial manager does—just common sense, really—which is exactly why it's used for the FMRR.

Question: Under this strategy, what's the very minimum amount of money ($MIN) you'll actually need to commit at the beginning of the housing deal to get the ball rolling?

Answer: *Just enough* so that it—plus any interim returns—will grow sufficiently in that account to supply all your necessary *investments* (outflows).

Question: What's the maximum amount of money ($MAX) you can expect to hold in your hands at the very end of this whole venture?

Answer: It's the ending balance of your risk-rate account, where you have put all excess returns (those not needed for further investments).

What you're doing, then, is reducing your entire investment scenario to this single-investment/single-return model:

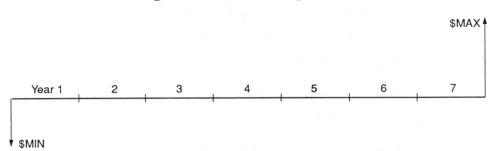

So the only question, really, is how to calculate $MIN and $MAX. The complication is the sharing of returns (positive cash-flows). That is, what portion of these returns must you hold in your safe-rate account to cover investments (outflows) yet to be disbursed; and what portion can you salt away in your risk-rate account? To figure this out, you work *backward* in time—from the last cash-flow to the first—*clearing each flow as you go, by discounting it back or sending it forward:*

- If a cash-flow is *negative*, you discount it back in time—using the *safe rate* as your discount rate—to add to the *previous cash-flow*. Why not just discount this negative flow all the way back to $MIN, just like an NPV calculation? Because it might be covered by a previous positive cash-flow, in which case you don't need to commit any funds for it as part of your minimum up-front commitment, $MIN. Thus, you work back one flow at a time, looking for positive flows to offset negative flows.

- Of course, if a cash-flow is *positive*, you can send it all the way forward—added to $MAX at the end of the scenario—using the *risk rate* as the discount rate. You can salt this flow away, because you don't need any of it to cover future negative cash-flows (working backward, you've already cleared them all).

Watch as you work backward through each of the cash-flows in the housing scenario. Assume a 6% safe rate and a 15% risk rate:

"Discount   –$10,000   *back* 1 period at 6%:"

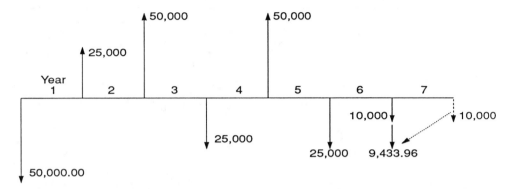

"Discount   –$10,000–$9,433.96   *back* 1 period at 6%:"

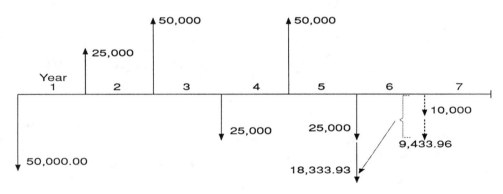

"Discount   –$25,000–$18,333.93   *back* 1 period at 6%:"

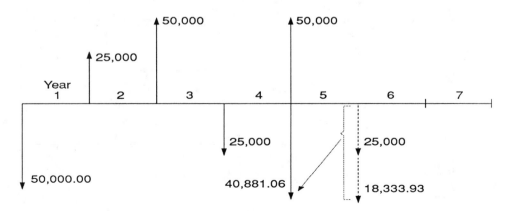

"Send $50,000–$40,881.06   *forward* 3 periods at 15%:"

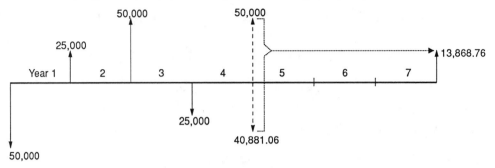

"Discount   –$25,000   *back* 1 period at 6%:"

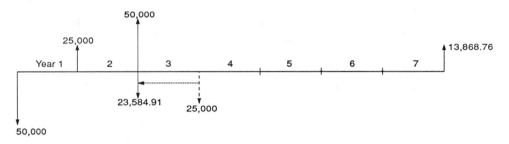

"Send $50,000–$23,584.91   *forward* 5 periods at 15%:"

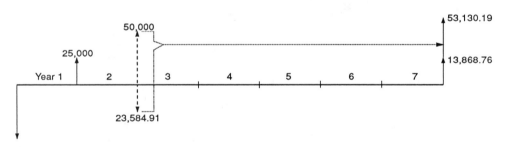

"Send $25,000   *forward* 6 periods at 15%:"

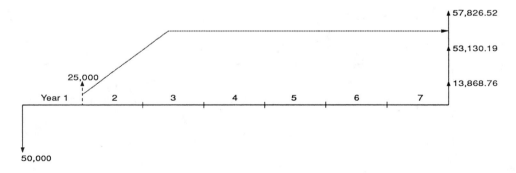

Notice that in this case, $MIN is simply the initial –$50,000. Now here are the keystrokes for the entire solution—all done at the TVM Menu: ■ MAIN FIN TVM OTHER 1 P/YR EXIT. Then:

1 0 0 0 0 FV 0 PMT 1 N 6 I%YR PV ....
PV=-9,433.96

— 1 0 0 0 0 = +/− (ALG) or 1 0 0 0 0 — +/− (RPN) FV
PV ....PV=-18,333.93

— 2 5 0 0 0 = +/− (ALG) or 2 5 0 0 0 — +/− (RPN) FV
PV ....PV=-40,881.06

+ 5 0 0 0 0 = +/− (ALG) or 5 0 0 0 0 + +/− (RPN) PV
3 N 1 5 I%YR FV ....FV=13,868.76

2 5 0 0 0 FV 1 N 6 I%YR PV ....
PV=-23,584.91

+ 5 0 0 0 0 = +/− (ALG) or 5 0 0 0 0 + +/− (RPN) PV
5 N 1 5 I%YR FV ....FV=53,130.19

2 5 0 0 0 +/− (ALG) or 2 5 0 0 0 +/− (RPN) PV
6 N FV ....FV=57,826.52

Now find the growth rate that transforms $MIN into $MAX:
7 N 5 0 0 0 0 +/− PV , then
1 3 8 6 8 • 7 6 + 5 3 1 3 0 • 1 9 + 5 7 8 2 6 • 5 2 = *or*
1 3 8 6 8 • 7 6 INPUT 5 3 1 3 0 • 1 9 + 5 7 8 2 6 • 5 2 +
(Result: 124,825.47 This is $MAX)

Now FV I%YR ....Answer: I%YR=13.96 Your FMRR— a good estimate of your rate of return in this housing scenario.

If you do a lot of FMRR calculations, you may want to use a Solver formula. See the note on page 311 in Chapter 9.

12. At the TVM Menu, press `OTHER` `1` `P/YR` `(EXIT)`. Then:

`3` `5` `0` `0` `0` `FV` `0` `PMT` `1` `N` `6` `I%YR` `PV` ....
`PV=-33,018.87`

`+` `7` `5` `0` `0` `0` `=` `+/-` (ALG) or `7` `5` `0` `0` `0` `+` `+/-` (RPN) `PV`
`2` `N` `FV` ....`FV=47,170.00`

`6` `0` `0` `0` `0` `FV` `1` `N` `PV` ....
`PV=-56,603.77`

`+` `1` `5` `0` `0` `0` `=` `+/-` (ALG) or `1` `5` `0` `0` `0` `+` `+/-` (RPN) `FV`
`PV` ....`PV=-39,248.84`

`+` `1` `5` `0` `0` `0` `=` `+/-` (ALG) or `1` `5` `0` `0` `0` `+` `+/-` (RPN) `FV`
`PV` ....`PV=-22,876.27`

`-` `7` `5` `0` `0` `0` `=` (ALG) or `7` `5` `0` `0` `0` `-` (RPN)
Result: `-97,876.27`   This is $MIN.

Now `PV` `6` `N` , then
`2` `0` `0` `0` `0` `0` `+` `4` `7` `1` `7` `0` `=` *or* `2` `0` `0` `0` `0` `0` `INPUT` `4` `7` `1` `7` `0` `+`
              (Result: `247,170.00` This is $MAX)
`FV` `I%YR` .... Answer: `I%YR=16.70`   The FMRR.

To compare this to the IRR%, key in the scenario as a CFLO list (you know the keystrokes by now, right?), then `CALC` `IRR%`.... Result: `IRR%=20.69`

Which is more accurate? Look at it this way: IRR% is the rate at which your money appears to grow *only while it is invested*, and it doesn't account at all for what happens to the returns—the positive flows—after you receive them (recall pages 199-201). On the other hand, your FMRR assumes that you reinvest excess returns at a rate of 6%. Which is closer to reality?

13. Here's the T-bar of the situation:

y	$\$$
0	(260,250.00)
1	12,896.21
2	14,497.94
3	16,834.26
4	19,244.19
5	414,242.63

Now, you *could* just grind out the FMRR at the TVM Menu, as in problems **11** and **12**. Or, you could observe that all the cash-flows except the initial flow are positive. So $MIN *is* the initial flow.

And notice therefore, that, to find $MAX, you'll just be sending all the positive values forward, using the risk rate, summing the results. That's an NFV (Net *Future* Value) calculation—and it's available on the CFLO Menu. Similar to NPV, NFV sends all cash-flows *forward* (rather than back), summing the results at the *end* of the timeline (instead of the beginning).

So use NFV to find $MAX: At the CFLO Menu, GET a new list (or clear the current one). Then: [0][INPUT] (just the *positive* flows)
[1][2][8][9][6][·][2][1][INPUT][INPUT]   [1][4][4][9][7][·][9][4][INPUT][INPUT]
[1][6][8][3][4][·][2][6][INPUT][INPUT]   [1][9][2][4][4][·][1][9][INPUT][INPUT]
[4][1][4][2][4][2][·][6][3][INPUT][INPUT]   [EXIT]   **CALC** [1][5] **I%** **NFV** ....
Result: NFV=503,241.86   This is $MAX.

Now go to the TVM Menu for the final calculation:
[EXIT][EXIT] **TVM** [STO] **FV** **OTHER** [1] **P/YR** [EXIT]
[2][6][0][2][5][0][+/−] **PV** [5] **N**
I%YR .... Answer: I%YR=14.10   The FMRR.

14. The two alternatives:

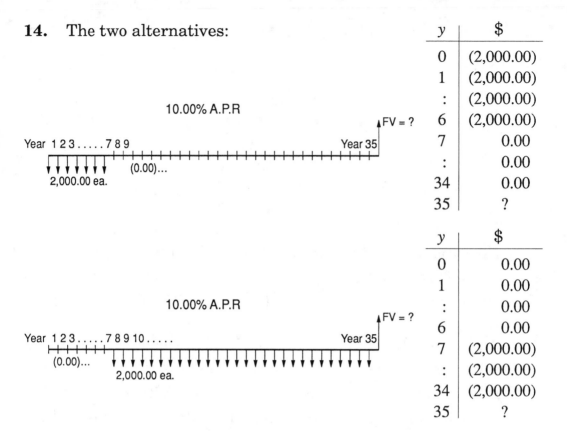

y	$
0	(2,000.00)
1	(2,000.00)
:	(2,000.00)
6	(2,000.00)
7	0.00
:	0.00
34	0.00
35	?

y	$
0	0.00
1	0.00
:	0.00
6	0.00
7	(2,000.00)
:	(2,000.00)
34	(2,000.00)
35	?

Your strategy: Find the Net Future Value (NFV) of each scenario. The save-early plan: At the CFLO Menu, clear the current list ([■ CLEAR DATA]) or NAME it and GET a *NEW list. Then:

[2][0][0][0][INPUT]
[2][0][0][0][INPUT][6][INPUT]
[0][INPUT][2][9][INPUT][EXIT]
[CALC][1][0][I%][NFV].... Answer: NFV=300,991.75

The save-later plan: [EXIT] to the CFLO Menu, [■▲], then:
[0][INPUT]
[0][INPUT]
[▼][2][0][0][0][INPUT][2][8][INPUT]
[0][INPUT][INPUT][EXIT]
[CALC][NFV].... Answer: NFV=295,261.86

15. To find an *overall* rate of return, ignore the fund names (A-B-C). Notice, however, that the time periods between cash-flows are *uneven* (the machine can't handle this). Stymied? Not totally. Look at the dates of those investments. Why not designate the period in the analysis to be a *half-month* (24 per year)? It's a little imprecise, but the error is only a day or two in any given case, and the analysis spans about 5 years, so it's a decent approximation:

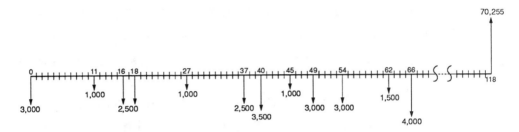

At the CFLO Menu, clear the current list or get a new one. Then:

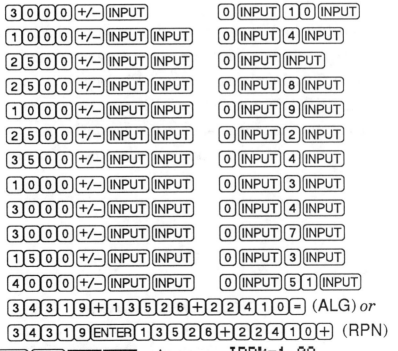

3 0 0 0 +/− INPUT	0 INPUT 1 0 INPUT
1 0 0 0 +/− INPUT INPUT	0 INPUT 4 INPUT
2 5 0 0 +/− INPUT INPUT	0 INPUT INPUT
2 5 0 0 +/− INPUT INPUT	0 INPUT 8 INPUT
1 0 0 0 +/− INPUT INPUT	0 INPUT 9 INPUT
2 5 0 0 +/− INPUT INPUT	0 INPUT 2 INPUT
3 5 0 0 +/− INPUT INPUT	0 INPUT 4 INPUT
1 0 0 0 +/− INPUT INPUT	0 INPUT 3 INPUT
3 0 0 0 +/− INPUT INPUT	0 INPUT 4 INPUT
3 0 0 0 +/− INPUT INPUT	0 INPUT 7 INPUT
1 5 0 0 +/− INPUT INPUT	0 INPUT 3 INPUT
4 0 0 0 +/− INPUT INPUT	0 INPUT 5 1 INPUT

3 4 3 1 9 + 1 3 5 2 6 + 2 2 4 1 0 = (ALG) *or*

3 4 3 1 9 ENTER 1 3 5 2 6 + 2 2 4 1 0 + (RPN)

INPUT INPUT EXIT **CALC** **IRR%**   Answer: IRR%=1.09

Annualize: ×2 4 = (ALG) *or* 2 4 × (RPN)....   26.22

Rest Area

Need a break? It's probably time to stop, stretch your legs, and look at your map.

- In Chapter 5, you saw several variations on amortized loans, including balloon payments, negative amortization, loan fees, differing annuity modes, etc. TVM is the menu to use on such "smooth-road" problems—they all involve a steady PMT amount.

  You also used the ICNV Menu to convert interest rates for these problems, and you also explored depreciation and bonds.

- Here in Chapter 6, you saw how to represent and then build *uneven* cash-flow solutions—the "rougher roads"—with the CFLO Menu. You then learned what NPV does and what it means. Next came IRR%. You saw how IRR% *can* represent your yield in an investment scenario—but not necessarily! So you learned when and how to obtain an alternative investment measure: FMRR.

Next Destination?

Time to check the map again, because here's another junction. Check the signs now and choose your route....

Next Destination?

7. THE DATA YOU COLLECT: SUM LISTS

Saving Numbers

Of course, the whole point of "navigating" through the menus of your HP 17Bɪɪ is to get to places where you can do calculations.

But what about afterwards? What do you do with the results of these calculations? What if you need to use the results from one menu in some other menu—"way across town?"

How do you store your answers for later use? And how do you retrieve this information, edit it, erase it, view it, use it, etc.?

With its continuous memory, the HP 17Bɪɪ doesn't forget numbers, and you should know how to take advantage of this. Up to this point in the Course, although you kept a few results in the Stack while changing menus, that's about the only place you've really stored anything. It's time to learn about other places (the best places) to save numbers—in *registers* and in *lists*.

The Numbered Registers

The simplest way to save the result of any calculation is in a *numbered* storage register, so called because that's how you refer to it—by number—when you want to store into it or recall from it.

Try This: Store the result of 789÷5 into register 4.

Solution: Press ⑦⑧⑨÷⑤=(ALG), or ⑦⑧⑨ENTER⑤÷ (RPN), to get 157.80, then press STO④.... Simple, right?

Now Do This: Clear the History Stack (by pressing ■ CLEAR DATA). Then *recall* the number you just stored.

Nothing To It: Press RCL④.

See how these numbered registers can act as convenient holding bins? And there are ten such registers, numbered 0-9.

Notice that the STO and RCL keys both *copy* values. That is, after you pressed STO④, the value 157.80 was still in the Stack, too; a *copy* was sent to register 4.

Likewise, when you pressed RCL④ to bring that value back, you were bringing back a *copy* of the contents of register 4. Right now, there's still a 157.80 in register 4 (clear the Stack and do another RCL④, if you want to prove this to yourself).

Lists of Numbers

So the ten numbered storage registers give you one option for saving results—the quickest, simplest way. But there's another, far more sophisticated way you may need, too.

For example, what if you have a set of numbers that represent, say, your income levels for the past 11 years? You can't store these in the numbered registers because there are only ten registers. Besides, it would be very handy to keep all of these figures in one list, so you can compare them and analyze them.

Well, you *can* do this—and here's how: Suppose that you're an income property owner, and that the numbers below show the gross annual rental incomes for 11 different buildings:

Building	Gross Rental Income
1	17,000.00
2	22,000.00
3	21,500.00
4	24,000.00
5	14,500.00
6	19,000.00
7	23,000.00
8	24,000.00
9	24,500.00
10	18,000.00
11	27,000.00

Starting from the MAIN Menu, press the ▉SUM▉ key. You'll see something like this:

The SUM Menu is for *lists*—and you're about to start building one.

Question: How do you start a new list?

Answer: First you GET a *NEW (blank) list—so press ▉GET▉.

The machine then asks you which list you want to get, and it gives you a choice of list names on the Menu Line. If you had already saved some lists of your own, their names would now appear alongside ▉*NEW▉.

But right now, ▉*NEW▉ is probably the only game in town, so choose it. (Actually, therefore, you didn't need to GET it at all, since a *NEW list was already in your display, above. But now you know how to GET any list, new or named.)

That takes you back to the SUM Menu display (above)— and you're ready to enter numbers.

Fill in the Numbers: Put all eleven items of your rental income data into this list.

Solution: (Watch your display as you do these keystrokes. That will tell you a lot about how to lists work in the HP 17BII.):

1 7 0 0 0 INPUT
2 2 0 0 0 INPUT
2 1 5 0 0 INPUT
2 4 0 0 0 INPUT
1 4 5 0 0 INPUT
1 9 0 0 0 INPUT
2 3 0 0 0 INPUT
2 4 0 0 0 INPUT
2 4 5 0 0 INPUT
1 8 0 0 0 INPUT
2 7 0 0 0 INPUT

Did you notice how the running total of the items in your list is displayed below?

But here are some important things to notice:

1. List items are *numbered*. In this particular list, each building is identified by its number, **1-11**.

2. You tell to the calculator to "accept" a number by pressing INPUT (just as with a CFLO list).

3. Each time you press INPUT, the machine accepts the number *and* recomputes the **TOTAL** of all items.

4. After you've keyed in all eleven of your numbers, the machine still sits there and waits for the twelfth item....

Now what? How do you say, *"I'm finished!"* ?

(Read on)

Editing Your List

First of all, just ignore your machine's prompting for another item. It's *always* going to allow you to add one more to the bottom of your list.

But are you sure all your numbers are keyed in correctly? How about a quick review?

Do It: Jump to the beginning of your list and step down through it to check each entry.

How?   First, you must move the pointer back up to the top. Remember the ▲ and ▼ keys that roll your History Stack around? Those keys are good for all sorts of lists and stacks—including this kind of storage list.

So you could press ▲ eleven times to move the pointer back to item 1. *Or* you could press ■▲. That's a quick way to jump to the beginning of the list, all in one motion (and no prizes for guessing how to jump to the end of the list again).

So "go first class"—use the ■▲ method. Then use ▼ to "walk" down the list and check your numbers.... If you find a mistake, simply position the pointer to the erroneous number, key in the correct value and press [INPUT].

A good indicator that your numbers are all right is that your TOTAL is 234,500.00.

Problem: Suppose that you've numbered your income properties according to the time you have owned them—oldest to newest. But now you sell building 1, which you've held longer than any of the others—and buy a new building, which produces $34,000 in rental income. How do you change the list?

Solution: You delete the first building's income and then tack on the new building's income at the end of the list:

First, press ■▲ to jump to the top of the list, if you're not there now. Then (EXIT) (to get the menu) and press the ▮DELET▮ selection. This deletes the item the pointer is currently indicating—**17,000.00**—the first value in the list. Remember: the item displayed is the item affected when you do anything to one item in your list.

So now the new first item in your list is **22,000.00**, and there should be ten items altogether. Jump to the end of the list (press ■▼), to check this.... Sure enough, you see **ITEM(11)=?**. So key in ③④⓪⓪⓪ and press (INPUT) to store it there.

Voilá. You've just updated your 11-building income list. And notice that your running **TOTAL=251,500.00** is now up-to-date, too.

Notice that this same method works for any fixed-length list intended to keep a chronological record (for moving averages, etc.): Delete the oldest value (at the top) and add the newest value to the bottom.

Analyzing Your List

Of course, you can do much more analysis on your list data than simply to sum the TOTAL. Press [EXIT] and notice the CALC item on the menu. Press CALC now and try some of the calculations available:

TOTAL...(you've already seen this).... TOTAL=251,500.00

MEAN...the *average* data item value.... MEAN=22,863.64

MEDN...the *median* value, the value that is less than half the values but greater than the other half.... MEDIAN=23,000.00

STDEV...the *standard deviation* is a measure of how consistent (closely grouped around the mean) your data is.... STDEV=5,074.89

RANG...the difference between the greatest item value and the least... RANGE=19,500.00

(press MORE)

MIN...the least value in your data set...   MIN=14,500.00

MAX...the greatest value in your data set... MAX=34,000.00

(Don't press SORT or FRST right now.)

Naming Your List

Before you go any farther into analyzing the data in your rental income list, you should (EXIT) back to the SUM Menu and *name* it—so that you can build other lists, do other calculations, and yet be able to GET this list back again whenever you need it.

Problem: Name your list INCOME.

Solution: Press ▮NAME▮; then type INCOME. (You type each alphabetical character via two consecutive menu selections: ▮FGHI▮ ▮ I ▮NOPQ▮ N ▮, etc.) Then press (INPUT). Your list is now named, and you can (EXIT) to the MAIN Menu.

Later: First, GET a *NEW list (press ▮SUM▮GET▮*NEW▮), to pretend that you've been working with other lists.

Now go GET your INCOme list (▮GET▮INCO▮).... As you see, all *named* lists appear on the GET Menu, too. But notice that not all the letters of INCOME will fit into a menu box. There's room only for four or five letters, so choose short names.

FoReCaSTing with Your List

One of the most common kinds of analysis you'll probably want to do with a list of data is to use it to forecast—to *predict*—something.

Example: Suppose you're considering the construction of another income property—a twelfth building in your list—similar to the other eleven in quality and location. How can you predict the annual rental income it might generate?

Answer: Use the pattern of rents from the existing buildings to help you forecast this.

Problem: Your existing buildings all have different rents because they are of different sizes (floor square footage). So a simple average of those rents won't tell you very much—especially for your new building, which will have quite a bit more space (5000 ft²).

Solution: Create a second list, composed of each building's rental floor area, to *correlate* with its rental income. Use that correlation (rental income per square foot), to predict the rental income for your new building.

Take it step-by-step....

Here are the rental floor areas of your current 11 buildings, alongside their annual rents (which you've already built into your INCOme list):

Building	Rental Floor Area (ft²)	Gross Rental Income
1	2,650	$ 22,000.00
2	2,500	21,500.00
3	2,700	24,000.00
4	1,500	14,500.00
5	2,100	19,000.00
6	2,600	23,000.00
7	2,650	24,000.00
8	2,700	24,500.00
9	2,000	18,000.00
10	2,900	27,000.00
11	3,750	34,000.00

So: GET and NAME a new list: `GET` `#NEW` `NAME` AREAS (INPUT)

Then fill in the data:

2 6 5 0 (INPUT)   2 5 0 0 (INPUT)   2 7 0 0 (INPUT)
1 5 0 0 (INPUT)   2 1 0 0 (INPUT)   2 6 0 0 (INPUT)
2 6 5 0 (INPUT)   2 7 0 0 (INPUT)   2 0 0 0 (INPUT)
2 9 0 0 (INPUT)   3 7 5 0 (INPUT)

(Quick accuracy check: Your TOTAL should be 28,050.00)

Now you can use this list of floor areas to forecast the income of your new building. To do so, you must GET the list of the income data.

Do It: Press (EXIT) `GET` `INCO`, then `CALC` `MORE`, then `FRCST`...

Question: What does SELECT X VARIABLE mean?

Answer: To forecast, you need to decide "what to graph against what." So the question your machine is really asking you is, "Which list is your X-variable data—your *area* list (AREAS) or your *income* list (INCOme)?"

Think about it like this: You're looking for a trend that shows that the income level *depends* on the floor area. So your income must be the *dependent* variable (along the Y-axis), and therefore area must be the *independent* variable (along the X-axis) on your graph:

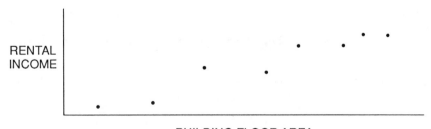

So, answer the calculator's prompts by pressing `AREAS` for the X-variable list and `INCO` for the Y-variable list.

Question: What does the display mean now?

Answer: Your machine is telling you which mathematical model—i.e. what shape curve—it will be using to fit to your data unless you change it. Press **MORE** and then **MODL**. Your choices are LINear, LOGarithmic, EXPonential or POWer. You're looking for the linear relationship between floor area and rent per square foot. So press **LIN**.

Now, what you want is a number—a prediction based upon given floor area. You want to be able to key in any floor area and have the machine tell you corresponding income expected.

Easy: Key in the area of your new building: ⑤⓪⓪⓪, then **AREAS**. Now press **INCO** to find the corresponding income:
INCOME=44,433.47

And now you can play "What-If?" all day like this—with any building size you wish: Just enter the floor space, and press **AREAS**, then **INCO**. What could be simpler?

Quiz

1. Fill up the Stack with 1.00, 2.00, 3.00, and 4.00. Now use the numbered storage registers to reverse their order.

2. Is there a strong *non*-linear correlation between your building rents and floor areas? Is it stronger than the linear correlation?

3. Use the following values of your current eleven properties to estimate the expected value of your 5000 ft² building now under construction:

1.	$ 160,000
2.	$ 162,500
3.	$ 180,000
4.	$ 105,000
5.	$ 144,000
6.	$ 175,000
7.	$ 175,000
8.	$ 190,000
9.	$ 140,000
10.	$ 210,000
11.	$ 250,000

Quiz Solutions

1.   First, fill up the History Stack: Press $\boxed{1}\boxed{\text{INPUT}}$, $\boxed{2}\boxed{\text{INPUT}}$, $\boxed{3}\boxed{\text{INPUT}}$, $\boxed{4}$. Then extract its four values, storing the numbers into four cor-responding storage registers: $\boxed{\text{STO}}\boxed{1}$ $\boxed{\blacktriangledown}$ $\boxed{\text{STO}}\boxed{2}$ $\boxed{\blacktriangledown}$ $\boxed{\text{STO}}\boxed{3}$ $\boxed{\blacktriangledown}$ $\boxed{\text{STO}}\boxed{4}$. Now recall them back to the Stack: $\boxed{\text{RCL}}\boxed{1}$ $\boxed{\text{RCL}}\boxed{2}$ $\boxed{\text{RCL}}\boxed{3}$ $\boxed{\text{RCL}}\boxed{4}$.... Voilá! And notice that you don't need to $\boxed{\blacksquare\text{CLEAR DATA}}$ the previous History Stack before beginning your recall process. Those previous values simply "pop off the top" as you recall more.

2.   When you use the FoReCaSTing feature in the SUM Menu, it asks you to SELECT A MODEL. To estimate the income likely from your new building, you selected LIN to find the best *straight-line* correlation between floor space and rent. But what about the other three types of correlations the HP 17Bɪɪ can compute— LOGarithmic, EXPonential and POWer curves? How do you know which curve type best fits your data? You don't—not without trying each type. So on the FoReCaSTing Menu, there's an item called ▐CORR▌, that finds the *CORRelation coefficient* (r) for the current curve type. This r is a measure of the "goodness" of the fit of the curve to the data points. The better the fit, the closer r approaches 1 or -1. A poorer fit gives an r nearer to 0. So, to find the best-fitting curve, just compute r for each type:

▐MORE▌ ▐MODL▌ ▐LIN▌ ▐CORR▌	Result:	CORR=0.99	(.987475213604)
▐MORE▌ ▐MODL▌ ▐LOG▌ ▐CORR▌	Result:	CORR=0.96	(.959580918724)
▐MORE▌ ▐MODL▌ ▐EXP▌ ▐CORR▌	Result:	CORR=0.99	(.988251144624)
▐MORE▌ ▐MODL▌ ▐PWR▌ ▐CORR▌	Result:	CORR=0.99	(.986513832084)

All the fits are quite good (close to 1), but the EXPonential fit is the best of the four. So, what does it predict for the income of your 5000 ft² building? Press `MORE` `MODL` `EXP` `5` `0` `0` `0` `AREAS` `INCO` ....

Result: `INCOME=57,517.50`. That's a bit higher than the LINear estimate, so the more conservative amount to count on for income from your new building is still the linear estimate (about $44,500).

3. It's another forecasting problem.* At the SUM menu, GET and NAME a new list: `GET` `#NEW` `NAME` `VALS` `INPUT`. Now key in the data:
`1` `6` `0` `0` `0` `0` `INPUT` `1` `6` `2` `5` `0` `0` `INPUT` `1` `8` `0` `0` `0` `0` `INPUT`
`1` `0` `5` `0` `0` `0` `INPUT` `1` `4` `4` `0` `0` `0` `INPUT` `1` `7` `5` `0` `0` `0` `INPUT`
`1` `7` `5` `0` `0` `0` `INPUT` `1` `9` `0` `0` `0` `0` `INPUT` `1` `4` `0` `0` `0` `0` `INPUT`
`2` `1` `0` `0` `0` `0` `INPUT` `2` `5` `0` `0` `0` `0` `INPUT` (`TOTAL=1,891,500.00`)
Press `EXIT` `CALC` `MORE`, then `FRCST`. To forecast the value of your new building based upon its floor area, use `AREAS` as your X-variable and `VALS` as your Y-variable. Try a linear correlation: Press `MORE` `MODL` `LIN` `5` `0` `0` `0` `AREAS`, then `VALS` to find the predicted value:

`VALS=331,563.73` But is linear the best fit?

Find out: `CORR` Result: `CORR=0.97` (.974993369088)

`MORE` `MODL` `LOG` `CORR` Result: `CORR=0.96` (.956276883471)

`MORE` `MODL` `EXP` `CORR` Result: `CORR=0.97` (.970082365602)

`MORE` `MODL` `PWR` `CORR` Result: `CORR=0.98` (.97768675078)

All the fits are quite good (close to 1), but the POWer fit is the best of the four. And what does it predict for the income of your 5000 ft² building? Find out: `5` `0` `0` `0` `AREAS` `VALS` ....`VALS=325,030.20`. That's lower than the LINear estimate, and the fit *is* slightly better, so it's the safer value to assume for the new building.

*If you find yourself needing to do a lot of these comparisons—trying to find the best correlation coefficient (r)—you might consider using a SOLVE equation. See the note on page 311.

Which Way Now?

Here's another fork in the road.

As you've heard, the best choice is probably to keep going straight on through the book. Each topic will teach you a lot about the calculator. But if you want to, you can "skip around."

So read the sign now, and make another choice....

8. TIME TRAVELLING

Using the Clock

Hold your place here and flip back for a minute to page 56.... Remember that big diagram of the TIME Menu "highway and suburbs?" You didn't get to explore those then, so now here's your chance.

Basics First: What time is it? What's today's date? Is it Friday yet?

One Key: To find out all of this from your HP 17BII, go to the MAIN Menu (■ MAIN) and press **TIME**. You'll see a display similar to this (but of course, yours will probably show a different date and time):

```
┌─────────────────────────────────────┐
│ MON 02/22/93 02:57:12P               │
│ CALC APPT ADJST SET                  │
└─────────────────────────────────────┘
```

One key tells you all that; anytime you want to check the clock or the calendar, press ■ MAIN **TIME**.

But what if your HP 17BII clock/calendar is wrong? How do you set it or adjust it?*

---

*You've had one quiz problem (Chapter 4, problem **2**, page 70) that showed you briefly how to set the time and date, but there's a lot more to that story.

SETting the TIME

Suppose that today is actually March 29, 1990, and that it's about 1:30:36 in the afternoon. To set your HP 17Bɪɪ to show this, from the TIME Menu, press **SET**. You'll see a display similar to this:

```
┌─────────────────────────────────┐
│ MON 02/22/93 02:57:12P          │
│ DATE TIME A/PM M/D 12/24 HELP   │
└─────────────────────────────────┘
```

The idea is to key in a number that represents the date or the time, then press **DATE** or **TIME**.

Like So: Press ③ ⦁ ② ⑨ ① ⑨ ⑨ ⓪ **DATE** ; ① ⦁ ③ ⓪ ③ ⑥ **TIME** ....

See how this works? You mimic the order of the time and date numbers as you see them in the display, using the ⦁ to separate the months from the days and the hours from the minutes.

And if you ever forget how this works, you can press **HELP** for a reminder (do it now, just to see)....

The other selections on this menu (**A/PM**, **M/D** and **12/24**) are all *format* options for the time and date. Try them now and observe how your display changes....

And simply press them again to undo the changes.

ADJuSTing the TIME

When the time and date are just plain wrong as they were on the previous page, the easiest thing to do is to use **SET**, as you did.

But what if the time is only slightly off—and you want to improve the accuracy? Use **ADJST**...

Ah, Spring: On the first Sunday in April, most parts of the U.S. go to Daylight Savings Time, setting all clocks ahead by an hour. So before you step out to get the Sunday paper, you open your HP 17BII and...

Do This: (EXIT) the SET Menu (if you're still there), then press **ADJST**. Now, with one keystroke, you can advance or delay the clock by exactly one hour, one minute, or one second. So just press **+HR**, and voilá!—you've Saved some Daylight.

Anytime you want, you can adjust the clock for more accuracy. As another example, suppose you notice that your HP 17BII is, say, 4 seconds fast, according to The Official Time. No problem: Just press **-SEC** **-SEC** **-SEC** **-SEC**, and that's all there is to it.

CALCulating with Dates

How do you calculate the number of days between two given dates? For example, how would you calculate how many days in 1990 will be on Daylight Savings Time, which runs from April 1 to October 28 (the first Sunday in April to the last Sunday in October)?

Easy: (EXIT) the ADJuST Menu, if necessary, and press **CALC**. Now, the idea here is to key in any two dates (using the current date format, as the display reminds you now), then press **DAYS** to calculate the actual number of calendar days between those two dates. Try it:

(4)(·)(0)(1)(1)(9)(9)(0) **DATE1** (1)(0)(·)(2)(8)(1)(9)(9)(0) **DATE2**
DAYS .... Result: $ACTUAL\ DAYS=210.00$

And you can go the other way, too: if you know the number of days and just one of the dates, you can calculate the other date.

Like So: What date was 45 days after March 22, 1988? How about 45 days *before* March 22, 1988?

(3)(·)(2)(2)(1)(9)(8)(8) **DATE1** (4)(5) **DAYS** **DATE2**....
Result: $DATE2=05/06/1988$ FRI

(4)(5)(+/−) **DAYS** **DATE2**....
Result: $DATE2=02/06/1988$ SAT

As you can see, a negative number of DAYS means simply that you go backward into the past—instead of ahead into the future. Notice that the calculator assumes that DATE1 is earlier than DATE2: if you give a DATE1 later than a DATE2, the number of DAYS will be negative.

Now, what about those other three items on the CALC Menu: **3600**, **3650** and **TODAY**? What do they do?

TODAY is easy—it's just a convenient way to see and/or key in the current date. Try it.... As for the other two items,...

Find Out: How many days are there from February 1st to March 1st, in the year 1992?

(2)(•)(0)(1)(1)(9)(9)(2)**DATE1**(3)(•)(0)(1)(1)(9)(9)(2)**DATE2**
DAYS.... Result: ACTUAL DAYS=29.00

Ah, but what if you ignore leap-year considerations and simply assume that every year has 365 days?
Press **3650**.... Result: 365 DAYS=28.00

And what if you assume that every month has 30 days— a nice, tidy 360-day year?
Press **3600**.... Result: 360 DAYS=30.00

These alternative calendar assumptions help you calculate days between dates on the "simplified calendars" commonly used for interest calculations with bonds and other financial instruments.

Making APPoinTments

Probably the best thing about the TIME Menu in your HP 17Bɪɪ is that it can store appointments for you (up to ten of them, in fact)—and then beep to remind you at the right times.

(EXIT) from the CALC Menu, if you're still there now. Then press ▐APPT▌. You'll probably see one of the following messages in the display:

SELECT AN APPOINTMENT   (currently, you have no appointments set for any time in the future.)

DUE: 1,2...   SET: 1,2...   (some appointments are currently set or past due)*

Fine. Now, to set up a demonstration appointment, choose one of the appointments from the menu (say, ▐APT1▌). Then press ▐ (CLEAR DATA) to clear everything so that you're ready to begin.

To set an appointment, the idea is to key in (in any order):

- the **date** and **time** you want to be reminded of the appointment;
- the **message** you want to see at that time;
- the **repeat** interval (if any), so that the machine will automatically reset itself to go off again after that interval (handy for daily or weekly schedules.

*Don't worry if your machine has one or more appointments showing as set or past due. These won't interfere.

OK, suppose you want to set an appointment that repeats every 2 minutes, starting about 2 minutes from now, with a message that says, `THIS IS ONLY A TEST.`

Easy: Press `MSG`, then follow the display's instructions, typing a message and pressing `INPUT` when you finish:*

`THIS IS ONLY A TEST.` `INPUT`....The display will then return to the APPT Menu.

Now set the repeat interval: Press `RPT`, then key in `2` and press `MIN`....Again, the display returns to the APPT Menu.

Next, key in a time that reflects *your* current time, plus about two minutes, then press `TIME` (the date should automatically default to your current date). Be sure that the am/pm setting is correct (adjust it with `A/PM` if necessary).

Now `EXIT` the APPT Menu. You should see:

`SET: 1`   (appointment #1 is now pending.)

So, press `■`MAIN), then turn the page and wait for your appointment to come due....

---

*Reminder about alphabetic characters: You type these via two-keystroke combinations from the menu (`RSTUV` `T` `FGHI` `H` `FGHI` `I` `RSTUV` `S` `WXYZ` `FGHI` `I`... etc.).

When Your Appointment Comes Due

Even if your calculator is off, an appointment that comes due will cause it to turn on, beep at you, and show the message for about 20 seconds. Here are your options:

- If you press any key ((ON) is a good one) *during* that time, this automatically acknowledges the appointment, and allows the machine to reset it for the next repeat interval, if there is one.

- If you don't press any key until after the beeping stops, the ((•)) annunciator will stay on, to tell you—no matter where you are in the machine's menu system—that you have a past due appointment. To acknowledge it, you must simply go into that appointment's menu (press **APT1** or **APT2**, etc.—whichever one it was). *Only after you acknowledge it* will it reset itself for any repeat.

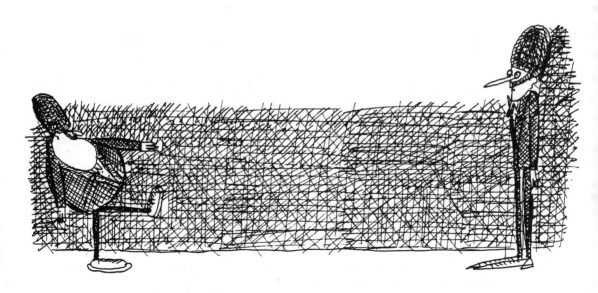

Quiz TIME

1. When it's 2:00 p.m. in Arch Cape, Oregon, it's 7:00 a.m. *the following day* in Okinawa. How do you cure your calculator's "jet lag" when travelling back and forth across the International Date Line like this?

2. According to your HP 17BɪɪI, how many (actual) days are in the years 2000 and 2100?

3. Set the following appointments in your HP 17BɪɪI:

    APPT1:   Today, 15 minutes from now
             TAKE A BREAK (repeat: 2 hours)

    APPT2:   September 9, 1999   9:09 a.m.
             CATCH PLANE (repeat: 10 days)

    APPT3:   February 29, 2040   10:30 a.m.
             SEE DENTIST (no repeat)

4. How do you stop an appointment from repeating? How do you clear any given appointment? How about *all* appointments?

5. Can an appointment come due without beeping at you?

Answers TIME

1.   Okinawa is 17 hours ahead of Oregon. Or, you can think about this as being 7 hours less than one *day* ahead. So, when going west (to Okinawa), and assuming your HP 17BII is set to Oregon time, you could do one of the following:

   Starting from the MAIN Menu (■ MAIN), press TIME ADJST, then press +HR *seventeen* times (just don't lose count);

   Or, starting from the MAIN Menu (■ MAIN), press TIME ADJST. Then press -HR *seven* times, then EXIT SET and set the date to tomorrow (whatever your current date happens to be, just key in the date for the next day).

   Of course, when going east (to Oregon), you'd do the reverse of one of those two procedures: Use -HR seventeen times in a row; or use +HR seven times in a row and SET the date to yesterday.

2.   From the MAIN Menu (press ■ MAIN), press TIME CALC.
   Then 1 · 0 1 2 0 0 0 DATE1 1 · 0 1 2 0 0 1 DATE2 DAYS....
   <u>Answer:</u> ACTUAL DAYS=366.00

   1 · 0 1 2 1 0 0 DATE1 1 · 0 1 2 1 0 1 DATE2 DAYS....
   <u>Answer:</u> ACTUAL DAYS=365.00

   The year 2000 is a leap year, but the year 2100 is not (you might want to read up on the rules of leap years to find out why this is the case).

3. Starting from the MAIN Menu (■MAIN), press **TIME** **APPT**, then select **APT1**. Now key in some time about 15 minutes from now (using the format HH.MM), then press **TIME** (the current date will automatically be entered at this point).

Then: **MSG** TAKE A BREAK (INPUT);
then **RPT** (2) **HOUR** and (EXIT).

Next: Press **APT2**, and (9)(•)(0)(9)(1)(9)(9)(9) **DATE**, (9)(•)(0)(9) **TIME**;
then **MSG** CATCH PLANE (INPUT);
then **RPT** (1)(0) **DAY** and (EXIT).

Next: **APT3**, then (2)(•)(2)(9)(2)(0)(4)(0) **DATE** * (1)(0)(•)(3) **TIME**;
then **MSG** SEE DENTIST (INPUT), then **RPT** **NONE**, and (EXIT).

4. To stop an appointment from repeating, from the MAIN Menu (■MAIN) press **TIME** **APPT**, then select the appointment you're interested in—say, APT1 (press **APT1**), for example. Then select **RPT** **NONE**, to specify no repeat.

To clear an appointment altogether, from the MAIN Menu (■MAIN) press **TIME** **APPT**, then select the appointment you want to clear — say, APT1 (press **APT1**). Then ■(CLEAR DATA).

To clear all appointments at once, from the MAIN Menu (■MAIN) press **TIME** **APPT**, then ■(CLEAR DATA) and respond with **YES** to the machine's request for confirmation of this "sweeping purge."

---

*"Whoops—say! That's a Wednesday! Guess we'll have to reschedule! How about...next year...?"

5.   Well, the machine will always *try* to beep when an appointment comes due, but you won't hear it if the beeper is turned off. Press ■ MODES and notice the menu item called **BEEP**. Press it *once*.... The beeper message changes: BEEPER ON: APPTS ONLY

This is just like having the beeper turned off—i.e. anytime the beeper would normally sound, it will be silenced—*except* for appointments, so that you won't miss them.

Now press **BEEP** once more.... BEEPER OFF
In this mode, you *never* hear a beep, not even for appointments.

Now press **BEEP** again to set the beeper to ON again.... As you can see, **BEEP** is a three-way switch that controls the beeper.

Whither Now?

Time to check the map again, because here's another junction.

As usual, it's best to simply keep on going, straight through the book. But check the signs now and choose your route....

9. BUILDING YOUR OWN ROADS:
THE SOLVE MENU

Memory Space: The Final Frontier

So much for civilization. Now you're on your own.

Now you need to learn how to solve problems for which there are no calculations already built into your HP 17BII. You need to learn how to go places that just aren't on the map.

"How?"

You literally add to your calculator's "map"—invent your own solutions. And once you've invented these formulas, you *store* them in a list in the machine, where they reside until you need them again.   Of course, you can erase them, too, when you don't need them anymore.

But since your customized formulas will take up space in the memory of your HP 17BII, you need to know a little more about that memory before you start building your formulas....

First of all, recall (from Chapter 7) what the numbered registers are all about: There are ten of them, called 0-9, and each stores just one number at a time—usually some value you want to keep "on the side" for awhile.

But you've discovered other registers, too: As you recall (from Chapter 4), the names that appear on a calculations menu are really names of built-in registers used by that menu. You vary their values when playing "What-If," so these are called "variable registers," or just "variables."

The point is, every variable uses space in your calculator's memory. Sometimes, the same variable is used in more than one formula. For example, you saw how the variables COST and PRICE are actually shared between the MU%C and MU%P formulas. When you stored a value into the variable PRICE at the MU%C Menu, that value was still there when you moved over to the MU%P Menu and pressed [RCL] PRICE.

A Picture of Memory

The variable registers used by the built-in formulas are indeed built into the machine. You can reset their values to zero, but you can't erase their formulas. But that's not the case for your "user memory." There you can create (and delete) new lists, formulas and registers of your own.

For example, here's a picture of how your HP 17BII's memory probably looks right now:

Numbered Registers

0
1
2
3
4
5
6
7
8
9

Built-In Variables

OLD	NEW	%CH	COST	PRICE	M%	M%P

(APT1)

DATE	TIME	MIN	HR	DAY	WEEK

:

DATE	TIME	MIN	HR	DAY	WEEK

(APT2)

:

(APT3)

:

(APT10)

DATE	TIME	MIN	HR	DAY	WEEK

N	I%YR	PV	PMT	FV

.
.
.

(And so on, for all the variables of the built-in menus)

CFLO Lists

FRED
EVEN
UNEVEN

SUM Lists

INCOME
AREAS
VALS

Appointment Messages

(APPT1:) TAKE A BREAK
(APPT2:) CATCH PLANE
(APPT3:) SEE DENTIST

SOLVE Formulas   ## SOLVE Variables

◄———————————— (Nothing here so far) ————————————►

Of course, you haven't created any formulas or formula variables yet—which is what this chapter is all about:

Full Speed Ahead: From the MAIN Menu, press the ▒▒▒▒ key, and enter the world of HP SOLVE:

```
{NEW} FOR NEW EQUATION
CALC EDIT DELET NEW
```

This is the SOLVE Menu, where you go to create or use a formula of your own. The machine is now expecting you to calculate with, edit or delete an existing formula, or begin to type in a new one.

Creating Formulas

For openers, since you're "driving" through this Easy Course, how about a simple little formula to help you figure your gas mileage?

Do It: Create an equation for gas mileage. Then compute your mileage for a trip of 350 miles that used 12 gallons of gasoline. If the car has a 15 gallon tank, how far could you have gone before the last "fumes" ran out?

Solution: At the SOLVE Menu, press **NEW** and type MPG=MILE÷GAL (in other words, press **JKLM** **M** **NOPQ** **P** **FGHI** **G** =)..., etc.). Then press INPUT, then **CALC**. The machine will verify your formula to make sure that it understands everything you typed, and this is what you'll see:

```
┌──────────────────────────────────┐
│                                  │
│  (some number is here)           │
│  MPG MILE GAL                    │
└──────────────────────────────────┘
```

And now you know what to do:
3 5 0 **MILE** 1 2 **GAL**
MPG Answer: MPG=29.17

Now for that old familiar "What-Iffing:" Change the number of gallons to the maximum: 1 5 **GAL**.

And calculate how many miles you could have gone:
MILE.... Answer: MILE=437.50

All right, you're happy with the way your formula works, but suppose you'd like to rename the variables in it. What do you do?

Edit It: Instead of **MILE**, you want **MILS**; and instead of **GAL**, you want **GALS**.

Solution: EXIT to the SOLVE Menu an press **EDIT**. You will see this display:

The blinking cursor shows you where your editing will occur, but of course you can move it around: Press **-->**. It goes one space over. Press **■ -->**. It goes all the way to the end of the formula (just as **■ ▼** goes all the way to the bottom of a list).* And now, since you're there, type **ALPHA RSTUV S** to change GAL to GALS.

Next press EXIT, then **<-- | <-- | <-- | <-- | <-- | <--**, then **ALPHA RSTUV S** again. Notice how the cursor *inserts* in front of the character currently under it. So press EXIT and **DEL** and you're done—press INPUT.

Now press **CALC** to let the machine verify the formula again, and then you'll see your modified variable names come up on the menu.

---

*The other pair of selections on the menu, **<<--** and **-->>**, move the cursor one screenful at a time—very handy for quickly proofreading long formulas, as you may discover later.

Problem: Some service stations sell gasoline by the liter. Write yourself an equation to help you convert between liters and gallons so that you can still use your mileage formula (there are about 3.785 liters in a U.S. gallon).

Solution: [EXIT] to the SOLVE Menu, then press **NEW** and type this formula:

$$LTRS=GALS \times 3.785$$

Press [INPUT] and then **CALC**.... Your conversion formula.

Try It: On another trip, you used 40.7 liters to cover 306 miles. What was your mileage?

Solution: Press [4][0][·][7] **LTRS**, then **GALS**.
Answer: GALS=10.75

Now [EXIT] to the SOLVE Menu, move up to the mileage equation (press [▲]), and press **CALC**.

Then press [RCL] **GALS**, and notice that GALS is already set to 10.75. Simply by spelling its name the same in each equation, you have created a *shared variable*.

Now key in what you need to finish the calculation:
[3][0][6] **MILS** and **MPG**.... Answer: MPG=28.46

Take a look at the memory diagram of your machine now:

| Numbered Registers | Built-In Variables |

Numbered Registers

0
1
2
3
4
5
6
7
8
9

Built-In Variables

| OLD | NEW | %CH | COST | PRICE | M% | M%P |
| DATE | TIME | MIN | HR | DAY | WEEK | (APT1) |

| DATE | TIME | MIN | HR | DAY | WEEK |

:

(APT2)

:

(APT3)

:

(APT10)

| DATE | TIME | MIN | HR | DAY | WEEK |

| N | I%YR | PV | PMT | FV |

.
.
.

(And so on, for all the variables of the built-in menus)

CFLO Lists	SUM Lists	Appointment Messages
FRED	INCOME	(APPT1:) TAKE A BREAK
EVEN	AREAS	(APPT2:) CATCH PLANE
UNEVEN	VALS	(APPT3:) SEE DENTIST

SOLVE Formulas	SOLVE Variables
MPG = MILS ÷ GALS	MPG
LTRS = GALS x 3.785	MILS
	GALS
	LTRS

How much more room do you have? If you're curious, just press ■ MEM to see the percentage of the total memory still available.... Now try another problem, to become more familiar with the rules of SOLVE....

A contractor often quotes the square-footage area of the rectangular concrete slabs he lays and then figures the cubic yards of mixed concrete necessary for the job. He knows the length and width (in feet) of the slab, and its depth in inches—and he orders ready-to-pour concrete only in whole cubic yards (no extra fractions of yards).

First: Devise a SOLVE formula to help him compute the area of a slab, in square feet.

Easy: You get area by multiplying length by width. So an area formula isn't too much of a problem:

$$\texttt{AREA=LONG}\times\texttt{WIDE}$$

Next: Devise a SOLVE formula to help the contractor find the volume of concrete required for a given slab.

OK: You get volume when you multiply length by width by depth—or, multiply *area* by depth. So here's a formula:

$$\texttt{VOL=AREA}\times\texttt{DEEP}$$

That's about all there is to the logic of the formulas—but you must take care to keep your units consistent! You can't expect to get a volume in cubic yards by multiplying a length and width in feet and a depth in inches. After all, what kind of unit is a "foot·foot·inch?" It's neither a cubic foot, nor a cubic inch, nor a cubic yard.

To use your formulas meaningfully, therefore, you must key in all your dimensions in the same unit. Things work fine as is for your area formula, but as you just observed, your *input* units aren't consistent with one another, nor do they match the *output* units you need in your volume formula. To get the right result, you would have to convert the inputs to other units at the time you key them in—not too convenient.

Suggestion: Let the calculator do these conversions for you. That is, build the conversions into the formulas, thus allowing the inputs to be in the conventional-but-inconsistent units that the contractor would be likely to use—depth in inches; length and width in feet.

How?   How do you modify your formulas to do this?

Hmm: The area formula doesn't need to change at all; multiplying feet × feet gives area in square feet. But the *names* of the variables should probably be improved, though, to tell you which units they assume:

$$\mathtt{FTAR=FTLG \times FTWD}$$

This is a good habit—making the name of a variable tell you as much as possible about it.

The volume formula needs some work: First, you convert the depth in inches to depth in feet by dividing the number of inches by 12: $\mathtt{VOL=FTLG \times FTWD \times (INDP \div 12)}$

But that's cubic *feet*, so now divide by 27 (because 27 cu. ft = 1 cu. yd.): $\mathtt{VLYD=(FTLG \times FTWD \times (INDP \div 12)) \div 27}$

About those parentheses: You don't really need them here. They're included simply to remind you of the reasons for the 12 and the 27. If you omit them, the result will be the same, because ✕ and ÷ have the same *priority of evaluation* in a formula.

The HP 17Bɪɪ doesn't evaluate a SOLVE formula in quite the same way as it evaluates an ALGebraic* arithmetic problem. For instance, to compute 2+(3×5) via ALGebraic arithmetic, you press ⟨2⟩⟨+⟩⟨(⟩⟨3⟩⟨×⟩⟨5⟩⟨=⟩, because the machine just works left-to-right if you don't use parentheses. But the SOLVE formula A=2+3x5 will produce the same result *without* parentheses, because the ✕ has a higher *priority of evaluation* than does the +.

So keep in mind that the HP 17Bɪɪ does not simply proceed left-to-right when evaluating a SOLVE formula; it evaluates according to the following list of different operations:

- First are the *functions*, such as SQRT(A+B), which is "the square root of A+B."

- Next comes *exponentiation*, such as A^5, i.e. "A raised to the fifth power."

- Next in line are multiplication (✕) and division (÷).

- Last of all come addition (+) and subtraction (-).

- When evaluating two or more operations of the same priority, then the calculator works left-to-right.

*With SOLVE formulas, you don't have the choice of arithmetic methods: The syntax for SOLVE formulas is only algebraic—parentheses and all—no RPN.

Those are the rules that tell you if you need parentheses in your formulas. Of course, if it's too much to remember, you can just go ahead and use parentheses anyway—to be on the safe side.

Back to the problem of those concrete slabs. Here are the two formulas you've developed—without unnecessary parentheses:

$$FTAR=FTLGxFTWD$$

$$VLYD=FTLGxFTWDxINDP÷12÷27$$

Notice: Dividing by 12 and then by 27 is really dividing by 324:

$$FTAR=FTLGxFTWD$$

$$VLYD=FTLGxFTWDxINDP÷324$$

And notice that you could *share* the variable FTAR between the two formulas:

$$FTAR=FTLGxFTWD$$

$$VLYD=FTARxINDP÷324$$

Now you can use the first equation to compute the area of a slab, then use the second equation to compute the yards of concrete necessary—simply by keying in the inches of depth—since the area (FTAR) will already be calculated and sitting there!

So that's it then....except...the problem stated that the contractor could order concrete loads only in whole cubic yards.

Oh: You need to round your volume calculation *up* to the next whole cubic yard. How do you adjust the equation for this?

Ah: Suppose you take your actual cubic yards requirement, add 1 yard, and then keep just the whole-yards portion of the result. Thus, if your real concrete needs were 3.4 yards, you'd calculate it to be IP(3.4+1), where IP stands for the *Integer Portion*. The IP of (3.4+1) is just 4. So the formula would correctly recommend an order of 4 cubic yards when a slab needs 3.4.

How about 1.9 yards?   IP(1.9+1) = 2.   That checks, too.

How about 2.0 yards?   IP(2.0 +1) = 3.

Hmmm... if a slab needs exactly 2 yards, then you *don't* want to order and waste an entire extra yard—the formula isn't perfect yet. To fix it, just use some common sense: If the real needs were 2.01 yards, would you order 3? Probably not. But if the requirement were 2.1 yards? Probably so.

So change your formula to reflect this judgement—adding a tenth *less* than a whole yard, like this: IP(2.0+.9). Therefore:

$$FTAR=FTLG{\times}FTWD$$

$$VLYD=IP(FTAR{\times}INDP{\div}324+.9)$$

Ready: Key in those versions of the formulas and test them.

Solution: From the SOLVE Menu, press **NEW** and type:

FTAR=FTLGxFTWD (INPUT) **CALC** ....Looks OK on the menu.
Try it: (4)(0) **FTLG** (3)(0) **FTWD** **FTAR**
Answer: FTAR=1,200.00   OK.

Now (EXIT) and **NEW** and do the other one:

VLYD=IP(FTARxINDP÷324+.9) (INPUT), and **CALC**.
Now press (RCL) **FTAR**, to see if your shared FTAR variable
works correctly: FTAR=1,200.00   Yep.

So this slab is 30 feet × 40 feet. If it's 6 inches deep, how
many cubic yards of concrete should you order?

Press (6) **INDP** and **VLYD**....
Answer: VLYD=23.00   Right on.

Combining Formulas

So there you have it— a set of equations to help the contractor. What could be more convenient?

Well…actually, it would be more convenient to have just a single equation—one menu with both calculations, no? Could you put both of the calculations into the same formula?

Stop and think for a minute: Isn't every formula an *equation* (i.e. "something *equals* something else")? Right now, for example, you've developed these two separate equations:

$$FTAR=FTLG{\times}FTWD$$

$$VLYD=IP(FTAR{\times}INDP{\div}324+.9)$$

And when you CALCulate with either of these, it builds its own separate menu, of course. But, more importantly, notice that you always solve for one of the variables by using the given values of *all* the others.

It seems, therefore, that you can have only one "unknown;" the rest must all be "knowns." So it seems that you cannot have a single formula for both FTAR or VLYD— because that would be two unknowns in the same equation.

But this is where the HP 17BII "cheats" a bit—to make such things possible. There *is* a way to write two separate, unrelated formulas into one, so that all the variables of both formulas appear on one menu….

To use this method, first you must hearken back to those happy, golden days of algebra class, and *rewrite* both formulas so that everything is on one side of the $=$ and a $\emptyset$ is on the other (you "add the negative to both sides of the equation"):

$$\text{FTAR-FTLGxFTWD=}\emptyset$$

$$\text{VLYD-IP(FTARxINDP}\div\text{324+.9)=}\emptyset$$

Now, notice that if you keep FTAR as a shared variable, it would be the *unknown* in the first equation but a *known* in the second one. There's nothing wrong with this, but it would mean that you would always have to solve for the FTAR before solving for the VLYD. That would defeat your purpose here—to use a single menu to solve for either unknown *in any order you want*.

Therefore, you should probably use FTLGxFTWD in the VLYD formula, since FTLG and FTWD are always *knowns* that you key in anyway.*

Thus, here is your set of equations, properly written in ...=$\emptyset$ form, so that they're ready to be combined:

$$\text{FTAR-FTLGxFTWD=}\emptyset$$

$$\text{VLYD-IP(FTLGxFTWDxINDP}\div\text{324+.9)=}\emptyset$$

---

*This is a good point in general: If a set of equations uses a shared variable that is treated as the *unknown* in one equation but as a known in another, then combining them will limit the order of your calculation.

Now to do the combining itself, you need to use the proper "phrase" in the SOLVE language, which is IF(S)....* Here's how:

```
IF(S(FTAR)
  :FTAR-FTLGxFTWD
  :VLYD-IP(FTLGxFTWDxINDP÷324+.9))=0
```

Note: The line breaks and indentations shown above appear for the sake of clarity only. When the time comes for you to key this in (don't do it yet) you would simply ignore this visual formatting; the result will appear in your display all packed together, without the line breaks.

Here's what that formula says:

"IF you're Solving for FTAR
  then [the first **:** means *"then"*] *solve* FTAR-FTLGxFTWD=0
  otherwise [the second **:** means *"otherwise,"* i.e., IF you're
                Solving for something *other* than FTAR], *solve*
VLYD-IP(FTLGxFTWDxINDP÷324+.9)=0"

You rewrote the two separate equations set equal to 0 so that you could also implicitly equate them with the 0 at the end of the IF(S... combined-equation structure.

---

*In fact, for the rest of this chapter, keep your Owner's Manual opened to Table 11-2, to get an idea of the various handy "phrases" in your HP 17BII's SOLVE "vocabulary."

Test It: Key in and use this combined, two-in-one formula.

Solution: First, delete your FTAR equation: At the SOLVE Menu, use the ▲ key to move up to your FTAR formula. Then press `DEL`. You then have the option to delete both the formula and its variables or just the variables. If you delete just the variables, the formula will remain in your list, but none of its variables will exist in the machine's memory until the next time you CALCulate with it (an option to save memory). But you want to delete both the formula and its variables, so press `YES` `YES`.

Now, since your new combined formula is rather long, why not create it by EDITing VLYD? Press `EDIT`, `ALPHA`, and type*: IF(S(FTAR):FTAR-FTLGxFTWD:

Now EXIT and move four places: `-->` `-->` `-->` `-->` and replace = with - (press ⊖ `DEL`). Then replace the FTAR with FTLGxFTWD: `-->` `-->` `-->` `-->` `-->` `DEL` `DEL` `ALPHA` LGxFTWD EXIT, and finish: `■ -->`)=0 INPUT.

Now `CALC` and check this with your 30×40 slab:
③⓪ `FTWD` ④⓪ `FTLG` ⑥ `INDP` and `VLYD`....
Answer: VLYD=23.00

Now find the `FTAR`.... Answer: FTAR=1,200.00
Voilá!

Notice that you get the : character (and most other miscellaneous characters) via the `OTHER` selection that appears along with each set of five individual alphabetic characters.

Take a moment now to review the steps you take to use the IF(S... syntax to combine separate formulas onto a single menu:

1. Rewrite the separate formulas so that nothing but 0 appears to the right of the =. For example, you would rewrite

$$25x(A+B)=11\div C+D$$

as
$$(25x(A+B)-D)xC-11=0$$

and
$$E=MxC^2$$

as
$$E-MxC^2=0$$

2. To avoid being forced to solve in a certain order for the unknowns in the combined formula, be sure that any variable shared between the equations will always be a *known* value. Thus, the above formulas will best combine as long as the shared variable C is always a known. If C is an unknown in one formula, you'll always be forced to solve for C before you can use it in the other part of the combined formula.

3. Use the IF(S... syntax to tell the HP 17BII when to use each part* of the combined formula:

```
IF(S(E)                        ("IF you're Solving for E
 :E-MxC^2                          ...then solve this
 :(25x(A+B)-D)xC-11)=0    ...otherwise solve this")
```

*You're not limited to just two parts. You can combine many formulas with a *nested* arrangement of IF(S...:

```
IF(S(A)                     ("IF you're Solving for A
 :...                           ...then solve this
 :IF(S(B)                   ...otherwise, IF you're Solving for B
  :...                          ...then solve this
  :IF(S(C)                  ...otherwise, IF you're Solving for C
   :...                         ...then solve this"), etc.
```

To see if you're getting the hang of IF(S), try one more...

For the Road: Remember your gas mileage and your liters-gallons conversion formulas (pages 277-279)? Combine them now into a single formula that will allow you to compute your mileage (in miles per gallon) no matter whether you buy fuel in liters or gallons.

A Good Route: Here are the two formulas as they exist now in your HP 17BII's memory:

$$MPG=MILS \div GALS$$

$$LTRS=GALS \times 3.785$$

Of course, you could re-write the latter as

$$GALS=LTRS \div 3.785$$

And so your two formulas for mileage would be:

$$MPG=MILS \div GALS$$

$$MPGL=MILS \div (LTRS \div 3.785)$$

Now you have two formulas with two separate unknowns. So you're ready to rearrange them to get zero on the right sides and then scoop them both into a single formula with IF(S....

Rearranging to isolate 0 on the right:

MPG-MILS÷GALS=0

MPGL-MILS÷LTRSx3.785=0

Now combine these, using the IF(S... structure:

```
IF(S(MPG)
   :MPG-MILS÷GALS
   :MPGL-MILS÷LTRSx3.785)=0
```

Or, in the compacted format you'll see when entering and editing:

```
IF(S(MPG):MPG-MILS÷GA
LS:MPGL-MILS÷LTRSx3.
785)=0
```

Key this in: At the SOLVE Menu, delete the two separate gas mileage formulas (recall from page 290 how to delete formulas). Then press **NEW** to begin a new formula. Now type the above combined formula and press (INPUT) and **CALC** to test it— try that first mileage problem you did on page 277:

(3)(5)(0) **MILS** (1)(2) **GALS** **MPG**
Answer: MPG=29.17

And if you went the same distance on 50 liters?
(5)(0) **LTRS** **MPGL**   Answer: MPGL=26.50

Naming Formulas

Question: As you begin to build your list of SOLVE formulas, what with the IF(S...and all that), how will you remember which formula does what, as you move up and down the formula list?

Answer: Just put a *name* in front of any formula whose purpose you might otherwise forget. A name is separated from the start of the formula itself by a colon (:).

Thus, you could give your combined gas mileage formula the name GAS, like this:*

```
GAS: IF(S(MPG):MPG-MILS÷GALS:MPGL
     -MILS÷LTRSx3.785)=0
```

Or, give your combined concrete slab formula the name SLAB, like this:

```
SLAB: IF(S(FTAR):FTAR-FTLGxFTWD
      :VLYD-IP(FTLGxFTWDxINDP÷324
      +.9))=0
```

Exercise: Do it—name your two formulas as shown: Just **EDIT** each and insert the name and a colon at the beginning of each formula. Now they're stored in your HP 17Bɪɪ.

---

*Again, remember that the line breaks and indents are shown here simply to emphasize the parts of the formula under discussion. Such formatting will never appear in your calculator's display.

Question: How many formulas can you store in your HP 17BⅡ?

Answer: That depends on how long or complex they are and how many variables they use. Of course, it takes memory to store the typed formula itself, but each *variable* created by the formula needs space when you use the formula.

Prove It: Select your GAS formula and press **CALC** as if you were going to use it.... Now (EXIT) (as if you've finished using it) and check the available free memory (press ■(MEM)). Make a note of the result.

Now press **DELET** and delete only the *variables* of the GAS formula—without deleting the formula itself (i.e. your keystrokes would be **YES** **NO**). The idea here is that since you've finished using GAS for now, why take up memory space for its variables (MPG, MILS, GALS, MPGL and LTRS)? After all, you'll just create them again anyway, whenever you next **CALC** with GAS.

Press ■(MEM) again.... Result: There's more memory available, now that you've deleted the GAS variables. Moral of the Story: To maximize the amount of memory available to you, delete the *variables* of SOLVE formulas that you're not currently using.

Of course, you can do a lot more with SOLVE than just gas mileage. As Table 11-2 of the HP Owner's Manual shows, you have many "formula-building-blocks," including sophisticated financial calculations....

Optimizing Formulas

Problem: How would you devise a SOLVE formula to compute the true A.P.R. of a loan with loan fees ("points up front"), as you computed manually back on pages 116-117?

Solution: You would build a *simulated TVM* solution, using the TVM equation shown in Appendix B (page 235) of your HP Owner's Manual.

In Appendix B, HP lists most of the mathematical formulas it has used for the built-in menus, including these two TVM formulas:

$$i\% = \frac{I\%YR}{P/YR}$$

and

$$0 = PV + \left(1 + \frac{i\% \times S}{100}\right) \times PMT \times \text{USPV}(i\%{:}n) + FV \times \text{SPPV}(i\%{:}n)$$

Now, if you substitute the smaller, top expression for $i\%$ into the longer, main formula, here's how that main formula would look:

$$0 = PV + \left(1 + \frac{\frac{I\%YR}{P/YR} \times S}{100}\right) \times PMT \times \text{USPV}\left(\frac{I\%YR}{P/YR}{:}n\right) + FV \times \text{SPPV}\left(\frac{I\%YR}{P/YR}{:}n\right)$$

Or, in SOLVE notation, it would look like this:

```
0=PV+(1+I%YR÷P/YRxS÷100)xPMT
            xUSPV(I%YR÷P/YR:N)+FVxSPPV(I%YR÷P/YR:N)
```

This is the one equation that correctly relates all seven TVM variables.

"But aren't there just five TVM variables?"

Don't forget about the OTHER Menu, where you establish the values of two other variables: the number of payments per year (P/YR) and the annuity mode (BEGIN or END—represented in the formula by the value of the variable, S). Even if you don't usually vary these when playing "What-If?", they are still used—and essential—for TVM computations. And there's no OTHER Menu for SOLVE formulas, so you must include all relevant values in one equation like that.

Question: What are those two SOLVE functions, USPV and SPPV?

Answer: They are "Uniform-Stream Present Value" and "Single-Payment Present Value."

USPV($i\%$: n) is the Present Value of a Uniform Stream of n periodic $1 cash-flows, discounted at $i\%$ per period.

SPPV($i\%$: n) is the Present Value of a *single* $1 cash-flow discounted n periods at $i\%$ per period.

These are useful for all sorts of TVM calculations; indeed, HP even used them in their built-in formulas.

Here again is the "TVM-mimicking" formula you've developed so far:

```
0=PV+(1+I%YR÷P/YRxS÷100)xPMT
                xUSPV(I%YR÷P/YR:N)+FVxSPPV(I%YR÷P/YR:N)
```

Question: If they're named the same, are SOLVE variables then *shared* with those of the built-in TVM Menu?

Answer: No. A SOLVE variable may be shared only with another SOLVE variable. And variables for the built-in menus are shared only with those of other built-in menus. So you can give your SOLVE variables names such as the PV, PMT, FV, etc., as above, and they will have absolutely no connection to the built-in TVM variables of the same names. The SOLVE variable names may *mean* similar things to you (that's why you use similar names*). But the actual, built-in TVM Menus (and BUS Menus, etc.) are in a separate world from your SOLVE formulas.

*After all, you could use other, less meaningful names in your formula, like this:

```
0=A+(1+B÷CxD÷100)xExUSPV(B÷C:F)+GxSPPV(B÷C:N)
```

But then, how would you remember that A is the variable name for your Present Value, and F is the name for the number of periods, etc.? A SOLVE formula without meaningful variable names is almost worse than useless.

Now, back to the problem: to develop a formula that mimics TVM *and* accounts for a loan's prepaid finance charge ("points up front"). Right now you have just a simple TVM simulator: If you were to **CALC** with it now, you'd key the number of payments into **N**, the amount financed (using the sign convention) into **PV**, etc.* It would look and feel much like the built-in TVM—but it wouldn't be any more convenient for handling a finance charge—so what would be the point?

Problem: Modify your formula to account for "points up front."

Solution: Looking back at your keystroked solution for a mortgage with loan fees (pages 116-117), you'll see that there's no difference in the way you treated any TVM quantity except PV. So there's no need to change the way you're using the N, PMT, FV, P/YR and S variables in your formula here. But in calculating the true A.P.R. on page 117, the idea was to *reduce* the actual amount financed (i.e. the original PV) by the amount of the finance charges, then put *that* into the PV register and recompute I%YR. So use PV+FC** instead of PV (thus FC becomes another variable on the menu):

0=PV+FC+(1+I%YR÷P/YRxS÷100)xPMT
    xUSPV(I%YR÷P/YR:N)+FVxSPPV(I%YR÷P/YR:N)

---

*For the **S** variable, you would key in a 1 for BEGIN mode or a 0 for END mode.

**You might think this would increase PV, but remember that the TVM equation you're mimicking assumes the cash-flow sign conventions: FC will always be of the *opposite sign* from PV.

Test It: Try a 30-year, 10.3935% mortgage for $100,000, monthly payments (in arrears) of $906.79 and a 2% loan fee.

Solution: At the SOLVE Menu, press `NEW` and type: `0=PV+FC+ (1+I%YR÷P/YRxS÷100)xPMTxUSPV(I%YR÷P/YR:N) +FVxSPPV(I%YR÷P/YR:N)` `INPUT`. Then `CALC` and test:
`1` `0` `0` `0` `0` `0` `PV`
`2` `0` `0` `0` `+/-` `FC` (remember the sign convention!)
`1` `2` `P/YR` `0` `S` (for END mode)
`MORE` `9` `0` `6` `·` `7` `9` `+/-` `PMT` `3` `6` `0` `N` `0` `FV`
`MORE` `I%YR`.... Result: `I%YR=10.64` Correct!

Question: Wouldn't it be more convenient to key in the loan fee as percentage points rather than as a dollar amount?

Answer: Probably. So instead of `PV+FC`, you could use

$$PVx(1-PTS÷100)$$

Your formula would then become:

`0=PVx(1-PTS÷100)+(1+I%YR÷P/YRxS÷ 100)xPMTxUSPV(I%YR÷P/YR:N)+FVx SPPV(I%YR÷P/YR:N)`

So `EXIT` and `EDIT` your formula, then `CALC` to test it:
`1` `0` `0` `0` `0` `0` `PV` `2` `PTS` `1` `2` `P/YR` `0` `S`
`MORE` `9` `0` `6` `·` `7` `9` `+/-` `PMT` `3` `6` `0` `N` `0` `FV`
`MORE` `I%YR`.... Result: `I%YR=10.64` Still OK.

Hm: The order of menu items in your formula doesn't really match the order on the built-in TVM Menu—disconcerting if you're used to finding things in certain places. Can you somehow adjust your formula to get its menu to more closely match the built-in TVM Menu? **N** **I%YR** **PV** **PMT** **FV** **MORE**

Yes: The order of menu items is the order in which each variable first appears in the formula. To rig this order, just use a phony set of "first appearances"—in the order you want—multiplying them by zero so as not to affect the math:

```
0x(N+I%YR+PV+PMT+FV+P/YR+S+PTS)
+PVx(1-PTS÷100)
+(1+I%YR÷P/YRxS÷100)xPMTxUSPV(I%YR÷P/YR:N)
+FVxSPPV(I%YR÷P/YR:N)=0
```

This is a good, simple trick to remember. Re-edit your formula into the above version and **CALC** to test this as before:

3 **6** **0** **N** **1** **0** **0** **0** **0** **0** **PV**
9 **0** **6** **.** **7** **9** **+/−** **PMT** **0** **FV**
MORE **1** **2** **P/YR** **0** **S** **2** **PTS**
MORE **I%YR** .... Result: I%YR=10.64

That's an easier menu to use, don't you think?

Problem: Your formula now computes the true A.P.R. of a mortgage with "points up front"—as long as you've already used the real, built-in TVM Menu to compute the PMT and/or FV and then copied all values to the corresponding variables on the formula's menu. But wouldn't it be nice to be able to do all the computation in one place?

You Can: Use your formula to perform the other calculations first, using the original mortgage rate as your I%YR and ignoring the finance charge. Watch:

③⑥⓪ N ①⓪·③⑨③⑤ I%YR
①⓪⓪⓪⓪⓪ PV ⓪ FV
MORE ①② P/YR ⓪ S ⓪ PTS
MORE PMT .... Result: PMT=-906.79
Then MORE ② PTS
and MORE I%YR .... Result: I%YR=10.64

Comment: This can still be confusing: Sometimes I%YR will contain the mortgage rate; sometimes the true A.P.R. Isn't there some way to further simplify things?

Idea: Create two formulas and combine them with IF(S...: In one formula, use the loan amount less points to allow you to solve for the true A.P.R. In the other formula, use the nominal mortgage rate and the real loan amount in a true "TVM-mimicking" manner to allow you to solve for (and play "What-If?" with) *any* of the TVM parameters.

Do It: First—to solve for the true A.P.R. (this should look familiar, except for the name of the interest rate, APR)—this formula:

```
PVx(1-PTS÷100)+(1+APR÷P/YRxS÷100)xPMT
xUSPV(APR÷P/YR:N)+FVxSPPV(APR÷P/YR:N)
=0
```

And the second formula—the simple "TVM-mimicker"—is this:

```
PV+(1+I%YR÷P/YRxS÷100)xPMTxUSPV
(I%YR÷P/YR:N)+FVxSPPV(I%YR÷P/YR:N)=0
```

Notice that both are already conveniently arranged into the proper "=0" format required by $IF(S$.... So, combine them:

```
IF(S(APR)
:PVx(1-PTS÷100)+(1+APR÷P/YRxS÷100)xPMT
        xUSPV(APR÷P/YR:N)+FVxSPPV(APR÷P/YR:N)
:PV+(1+I%YR÷P/YRxS÷100)xPMTxUSPV
        (I%YR÷P/YR:N)+FVxSPPV(I%YR÷P/YR:N))=0
```

Add "opening appearances"—for the menu order—and a name:

```
PTS:0x(N+I%YR+PV+PMT+FV+P/YR+S+PTS)
+IF(S(APR)
:PVx(1-PTS÷100)+(1+APR÷P/YRxS÷100)xPMT
        xUSPV(APR÷P/YR:N)+FVxSPPV(APR÷P/YR:N)
:PV+(1+I%YR÷P/YRxS÷100)xPMTxUSPV
        (I%YR÷P/YR:N)+FVxSPPV(I%YR÷P/YR:N))=0
```

Now key in and test this.... The menu will behave like the built-in TVM Menu except for the last items, **PTS** and **APR**.

Using L( ) and G( )

Question: Can you imitate the built-in TVM Menu's ▊BEG▊ and ▊END▊ items on your menu—instead of using ▊S▊?

Answer: Yes, to a great extent, you can.

Consider how the ▊BEG▊ and ▊END▊ items operate on the built-in TVM Menu: They are always *knowns* (you never solve for the annuity mode as your unknown). But you don't key in any values before pressing them, either; they're just "yes-or-no" *mode* items. You simply select one item or the other and that selects the annuity mode.

But in a SOLVE formula, whenever you press a variable's menu key without first keying in a value, the HP 17Bɪɪ will solve for that variable. You can't stop it from doing this solving, but you can tell it to do something else—*set another value*—in the process.

Look: These simple formulas will always give you the same result for the variable BEG: 1=BEG   *or*   1+0=BEG

So will this: 1+L(END:0)=BEG Indeed, you are still saying "BEG=0+1," but *at the same time* ("in passing,") you are also saying "Let END be set to: 0."

Does this give you any ideas on the ▊BEG▊ and ▊END▊ problem?

??: Write three formulas that, respectively: set BEG to 1 and END to 0; set BEG to 0 and END to 1 ; and use BEG as the annuity mode variable in a "TVM-mimicking" formula. Then use IF(S... to combine the three formulas into one.

!!: To set BEG to 1 and END to 0:   1+L(END:0)=BEG

To set BEG to 0 and END to 1:   1+L(BEG:0)=END

To use BEG as the annuity mode in a "TVM-mimicker":

```
PV+(1+I%YR÷P/YRxBEG÷100)xPMTxUSPV
   (I%YR÷P/YR:N)+FVxSPPV(I%YR÷P/YR:N)=0
```

Now two of them need to be rearranged into ...=0 format:

$$1+L(END:0)-BEG=0$$
$$1+L(BEG:0)-END=0$$

Then combine them all:*

```
IF(S(BEG)
  :1+L(END:0)-BEG
  :IF(S(END)
    :1+L(BEG:0)-END
    :PV+(1+I%YR÷P/YRxBEG÷100)xPMTxUSPV
     (I%YR÷P/YR:N)+FVxSPPV(I%YR÷P/YR:N)
))=0
```

---

*This is an example of a combination of *more* than two formulas—as in the footnote on page 291. The parentheses that end the two *nested* IF(S... statements are isolated here for clarity (as always, line breaks and indents are for clarity only; the calculator doesn't display this way).

OK: Using what you've just learned, see if you can modify the formula from page 303 to include BEG and END items that behave a little more like their TVM counterparts.

Go: It's going to be a nested set of IF(S...'s, for sure. Your existing formula already has one IF(S..., and now you're going to add a couple more.... Here goes nothing:

```
PTS:                                    (The formula's name)
0x(N+I%YR+PV+PMT+FV                      (Set up
   +P/YR+BEG+END+PTS+APR)+                 the menu order)
IF(S(BEG)                               ("IF you're Solving for BEG
  :1+L(END:0)-BEG                          ...then solve this formula
  :IF(S(END)               ...otherwise, IF you're Solving for END
    :1+L(BEG:0)-END                       ...then solve this formula
    :IF(S(APR)             ...otherwise, IF you're Solving for APR
      :PVx(1-PTS÷100)+(1+APR÷P/YRxBEG
      ÷100)xPMTxUSPV(APR÷P/YR:N)+FVx
      SPPV(APR÷P/YR:N)             ...then solve this formula
      :PV+(1+I%YR÷P/YRxBEG÷100)xPMT
      xUSPV(I%YR÷P/YR:N)+FVx
      SPPV(I%YR÷P/YR:N)        ...otherwise solve this")
)))=0
```

Notice how you work through each *specific* case first—where you tell the machine what to do when solving for one specific variable. That leaves the final *"otherwise"* formula to include all the other possible variables you might solve for.

Exercise: Key in and test this formula (EDIT the previous version).

Solution: Press **EDIT** and modify the formula. Then **CALC** to test it:
③⑥⓪ **N** ①⓪·③⑨③⑤ **I%YR** ①⓪⓪⓪⓪ **PV**
⓪ **FV** **MORE**①② **P/YR** **END** (display: END=1.00)
MORE **PMT** .... Result: PMT=-906.79
Then **MORE**② **PTS** **APR** Result: APR=10.64

Question: The formula uses I%YR÷P/YR and APR÷P/YR three times each. Could you avoid this repetition?

Answer: Yes. The first time you need to use I%YR÷P/YR, just use L(I: I%YR÷P/YR) to simultaneously assign that value to the variable, I. From that point on, you can just use G(I), which means: "Get the value of I without showing I on the menu." The same goes for A. Thus:

PTS:0x(N+I%YR+PV+PMT+
FV+P/YR+BEG+END+PTS+
APR)+IF(S(BEG):1+L(E
ND:0)-BEG:IF(S(END):
1+L(BEG:0)-END:IF(S(
APR):PVx(1-PTS÷100)+

(defining A) (1+L(A:APR÷P/YR)xBEG

(using A) ÷100)xPMTxUSPV(G(A):
N)+FVxSPPV(G(A):N):P

(defining I) V+(1+L(I:I%YR÷P/YR)x

(using I) BEG÷100)xPMTxUSPV(G(
I):N)+FVxSPPV(G(I):N
))))=0

Question: Using L(:) and G(), you saved yourself some typing—but did you save the machine any memory space?

Find Out: A formula uses more memory when you use it (when its menu is in the display). So, with your current version of PTS, run the test calculations on page 307. Then press ■ MEM to see how much memory is available.... Note this number. Now edit your formula back to the "longer" form shown below (i.e. as it was on page 306) and repeat the above calculations and memory test....

```
PTS:0x(N+I%YR+PV+PMT+
FV+P/YR+BEG+END+PTS+
APR)+IF(S(BEG):1+L(E
ND:0)-BEG:IF(S(END):
1+L(BEG:0)-END:IF(S(
APR):PVx(1-PTS÷100)+
(1+APR÷P/YRxBEG÷100)
xPMTxUSPV(APR÷P/YR:N
)+FVxSPPV(APR÷P/YR:N
):PV+(1+I%YR÷P/YRxBE
G÷100)xPMTxUSPV(I%YR
÷P/YR:N)+FVxSPPV(I%Y
R÷P/YR:N))))=0
```

This "longer" formula uses about 28 *fewer* bytes during calculation—*because it uses fewer variables*. Recall (from page 274) that each variable uses memory space. With the additional variables A and I, you bought some typing convenience by using a little more memory.

One other comment: Notice that in your PTS formula, you must always solve for PMT first—so that the APR portion of the formula has that value to use when solving for APR. In the PTS formula, that assumption isn't a big problem; you're probably in the habit of solving for the PMT first, anyway. But you *can* make these unknowns entirely independent—just as you did with your SLAB formula (page 288). As usual, you trade memory for convenience. Here's the modification:*

```
PTS:0x(N+I%YR+PV+PMT+
FV+IF(P/YR=0:L(P/YR:
12):0)+BEG+END+PTS)+
IF(S(BEG):1+L(END:0)
-BEG:IF(S(END):1+L(B
EG:0)-END:IF(S(APR):
PVx(1-PTS÷100)+(1+AP
R÷P/YRxBEG÷100)x(-PV
-FVxSPPV(I%YR÷P/YR:N
))÷USPV(I%YR÷P/YR:N)
÷(1+BEG÷100xI%YR÷P/Y
R)xUSPV(APR÷P/YR:N)+
FVxSPPV(APR÷P/YR:N):
PV+(1+I%YR÷P/YRxBEG÷
100)xPMTxUSPV(I%YR÷P
/YR:N)+FVxSPPV(I%YR÷
P/YR:N))))
```

Is this capability worth the extra typing and/or memory, just to be able to solve for APR first, if you wish? Maybe not. But you'll see formulas where such *unknown independence* is indeed advisable—where, instead of just two unknowns, you may have nine or ten. Then it's *really* inconvenient to dictate the order in which you must solve for them.

*Notice some other modifications, too: It sets the value of P/YR to 12 as a *default*, if you neglect to give it a value (i.e. leave it at 0). Also, in the menu-ordering portion (0x(…)), there's no need to include APR. And notice that there's no =0 at the end. If a formula ends in =0, you may omit it.

SOLVE Review

"Set the brake and idle" for a moment, and review all the things you now know about the SOLVE Menu of your HP 17Bɪɪ:

- You know how to use the SOLVE Menu to select or type a formula, and how to EDIT a formula with ⬛➤⬛, ⬛⬅⬛ and ⬛DEL⬛;

- You know that ⬛ MEM shows the memory remaining, and you can maximize this by deleting the *variables* of formulas not in use;

- You know that a SOLVE formula is basically just an algebraic equation—variables and numbers equated by an = and evaluated according to *operator priorities* (not just right-to-left).

- You know how the machine creates the menu of variables that appear in a formula—in the order of the first appearance of each variable. So you choose a short but *meaningful* name for each variable, to describe it and its units or other assumptions;

- You know that SOLVE formulas may share variables (i.e. use the same variable name and value) with other SOLVE formulas, and built-in menus may share with other built-in menus—but a SOLVE variable is never shared with a built-in variable;

- You've worked through the logic of some practical calculations, including unit conversions and rounding (recall the IP function); you've worked quite a lot with the IF(S... notation, which allows you to combine two or more separate formulas (so long as each formula has been written into the form "*something* =0");

- You've seen how to use L(:) to assign a value to a variable "in passing;" and you've seen how to use G( ) to get the *value* of a variable without causing its name appear on the menu.

For More Formulas

If you do a lot of repetitive calculations, some SOLVER formulas can make life a lot easier. However, you may not wish to try writing large or complex formulas on your own. Good news: Grapevine has done it for you—a collection of 25 useful and powerful formulas in these areas:

Commercial Investment:
- Income property analysis (NOI, GRM, cap rate, equity/cash returns)
- FMRR (Financial Management Rate of Return)
- Lease payment, value and residual, w/skipped and advanced payments
- Lease vs. buy analysis   • Property valuation
- Wraparound and second mortgages
- After-tax/commission bond price and yield

Residential Real Estate:
- Mortgage qualifying
- Rent vs. buy analysis   • Adjustable Rate Mortgages (ARM's)
- Accelerated mortgage payment schedule

Personal:
- Inflation/tax analysis   • Savings goals
- Retirement planning (inflation, taxes, IRA's and Social Security)
- Obstetric calendar

TVM Variations:
- Time to specified principal balance
- Constant payment to principal
- Increasing/decreasing annuities

Business Management:
- Depreciation, including MACRS
- Inventory optimization   • Manufacturer return on investment
- Mileage reimbursement   • Advertising yield
- Weekly payroll   • Tax structure analysis

If any formulas here could save you hours of keystroking, then use the form at the back of this book to order *Business Solutions on Your HP Financial Calculator*.

Where To Now?

Time to come back down to Earth now. This is the last chapter in the Course. Now you can go back and read/review any chapter you wish.....

Where To Now?

A. APPENDIX

Here are some Solver formulas and related explanations to help your calculations with Canadian mortgages. Be sure to read and digest Chapter 9, to familiarize yourself with the Solver before trying to use these formulas:

Canadian Mortgage Interest Conversions

Use the following formula to compute the equivalent U.S. A.P.R. (that's the I%YR) for Canadian mortgages with *monthly* payments and *semi-annual* compounding interest (most Canadian mortgages carry these terms).

Formula: `C%~US%:((1+CI%YR÷200)`
`^(1÷6)-1)x1200=I%YR`

Approx. Memory Required: 3% to use, 1% to store.
Required Knowns: None.

Example: A Canadian mortgage with monthly payments is written at 12% A.P.R., compounded semi-annually. What is the equivalent U.S. A.P.R.?

Solution: Key in the above Solver formula.

Then press `CALC` `1` `2` `CI%YR` `I%YR`....

Result: `I%YR=11.71`

Use the following formula for Canadian mortgages with *monthly* payments and *annual* compounding of interest (not common).*

Formula: C%~US%:((1+CI%YR÷100)
 ^(1÷12)-1)×1200=I%YR

Approx. Memory Required: 3% to use, 1% to store.
Required Knowns: None.

Example: A Canadian mortgage with monthly payments is written at 12% A.P.R., compounded annually. What is the equivalent U.S. A.P.R.?

Solution: Key in the above Solver formula.

Then press CALC ①② CI%YR I%YR....

Result: I%YR=11.39

---

*The rate specified on a Canadian mortgage document may compound no more than twice per year. Most such mortgages use semi-annual compounding (in which case you should use the formulas on pages 315 or 317); the only alternative is annual compounding, given here for completeness.

Use the following formula for Canadian mortgages *in general* (you specify the payment and compounding periods during calculation). Canadian rules allow no more than 2 compounding periods per year.

Formula:
```
C%~US%:(((1+CI%YR÷C/Y
R÷100)^(C/YR÷P/YR))-
1)×P/YRx100=I%YR
```

<u>Approx. Memory Required</u>: 5% to use, 1% to store.
<u>Required Knowns</u>:   None.

Example: A Canadian mortgage is written at 12% A.P.R.. Find the equivalent U.S. A.P.R. if:

    a. compounding is semi-annual, payments monthly;
    b. compounding is annual, payments monthly;
    c. compounding is semi-annual, payments quarterly;
    d. compounding is annual, payments annual;

Solution: Key in the above Solver formula. Then:

    a. (1)(2) CI%YR (2) C/YR (1)(2) P/YR I%YR ....
    <u>Result</u>: I%YR=11.71

    b. (1) C/YR I%YR ....
    <u>Result</u>: I%YR=11.39

    c. (2) C/YR (4) P/YR I%YR ....
    <u>Result</u>: I%YR=11.83

    d. (1) C/YR (1) P/YR I%YR ....
    <u>Result</u>: I%YR=12.00

Canadian TVM

Use the following formula to do any general TVM calculation (except AMRT) for Canadian mortgages.

Formula:

```
CTVM:0x(N+CI%YR+PV+PM
T+FV+IF(P/YR=0:L(P/Y
R:12):0))+IF(S(BEG):
1+L(END:0)-BEG:IF(S(
END):1+L(BEG:0)-END:
PV+(1+BEG÷100xL(I:((
1+CI%YR÷100÷IF(C/YR=
0:L(C/YR:2):C/YR))^(
C/YR÷P/YR)-1)x100))x
PMTxUSPV(G(I):N)+FVx
SPPV(G(I):N)))
```

Approx. Memory Required: 15% to use, 3% to store.
Required Knowns: None.

Example: A 30-year, $150,000 Canadian mortgage is written at 10.5%, compounded semi-annually.

   a. Find the monthly payment (in arrears).

   b. Find the balloon due in 10 years.

   c-d. Repeat **a** and **b** for a 20-year amortization.

Solution: Key in the above Solver formula. Then:

a. [3][0][×][1][2][=] (for ALGebraic arithmetic); *or*
[3][0][INPUT][1][2][×] (for RPN arithmetic)
N̲ [1][0][.][5] C̲I̲/̲Y̲R̲ [1][5][0][0][0][0] P̲V̲ [0] F̲V̲ ,
M̲O̲R̲E̲ [2] C̲/̲Y̲R̲ [1][2] P̲/̲Y̲R̲ E̲N̲D̲ (END=1.00).
M̲O̲R̲E̲ P̲M̲T̲.... Result: PMT=-1,347.21

b. Continuing from the previous solution:
[1][0][×][1][2][=] (for ALGebraic arithmetic); *or*
[1][0][INPUT][1][2][×] (for RPN arithmetic)
N̲ . Then F̲V̲ ....
Result: FV=-136,984.93

c. Continuing from the previous solution:
[2][0][×][1][2][=] (for ALGebraic arithmetic); *or*
[2][0][INPUT][1][2][×] (for RPN arithmetic)
N̲ . Then [0] F̲V̲ and P̲M̲T̲ ....
Result: PMT=-1,475.21

d. Continuing from the previous solution:
[1][0][×][1][2][=] (for ALGebraic arithmetic); *or*
[1][0][INPUT][1][2][×] (for RPN arithmetic)
N̲ . Then F̲V̲ ....
Result: FV=-110,344.15

As you can see, this substitute TVM formula can allow you to do the same sorts of "What-If?" calculations as you could do with the built-in TVM—but this one uses the compounding assumptions required for Canadian mortgages.

Use the following formula to do any general TVM calculation, *including* AMRT, for Canadian mortgages. This works the same in all respects as the previous formula, plus it offers an AMRT capability similar to that built into the HP 17BII. However, there are some keystroke differences to this version of AMRT, as illustrated here.

Formula:

```
CTVM~AMRT:0x(N+CI%YR+
PV+PMT+FV+IF(P/YR=0:
L(P/YR:12):0)+BEG+EN
D+IF(C/YR=0:L(C/YR:2
):0)+AMRT+#P)+IF(S(B
EG):1+L(END:0)-BEG:I
F(S(END):1+L(BEG:0)-
END:IF(S(AMRT):L(Z:B
EG)xL(BAL:RND(PV:2))
xL(NEXT:L(INT:L(PRIN
:0)))-AMRT:IF(S(NEXT
):NEXT-1E3-#P-1001E3
xFP(G(NEXT)÷1E3)+0xL
(B:BAL):IF(S(BAL):RN
D((RND(PMT:2)xUSPV(G
(I):#P-G(Z))+G(B)+G(
Z)xRND(PMT:2))÷SPPV(
G(I):#P-G(Z)):2)-BAL
:IF(S(PRIN):PRIN+G(B
)-BAL:IF(S(INT):#PxR
ND(PMT:2)-PRIN-INT+L
(Z:0):PV+(1+BEG÷100x
L(I:((1+CI%YR÷100÷C/
YR)^(C/YR÷P/YR)-1)x1
00))xPMTxUSPV(G(I):N
)+FVxSPPV(G(I):N))))
))))
```

Memory Required:	32% to use, 8% to store.	
Required Knowns:	Before using AMRT, solve for PMT.	

Example: A 30-year, $150,000 Canadian mortgage is written at 10.5%, compounded semi-annually. Find the balance, interest and principal paid in each of the first two years.

Solution: Key in the above Solver formula opposite.

First, find the payment: `3` `0` `×` `1` `2` `=` (ALG) *or*
`3` `0` `INPUT` `1` `2` `×` (RPN)

`N` `1` `0` `.` `5` `CI%YR` `1` `5` `0` `0` `0` `0` `PV` `0` `FV` `,MORE`
`2` `C/YR` `1` `2` `P/YR` `END` (END=1.00) `MORE` `MORE`
`PMT` .... Result: PMT=-1,347.21

Press `MORE` `AMRT` (display: AMRT=0.00) to start the amortization. Then `MORE` to go to the next menu page. Press `1` `2` `#P` to amortize 12 payments at once.

Now, *in this order*, press:
`NEXT` to identify the payments in the group. You'll see:
   NEXT=1,012.00 (that is, payments 1-12)
`BAL` to see the new balance: BAL=149,213.23
`PRIN` to see the principal paid: PRIN=-786.77
`INT` to see the interest paid: INT=-15,379.75

`NEXT` NEXT=13,024.00 (payments 13-24)
`BAL` BAL=148,341.68
`PRIN` PRIN=-871.55
`INT` INT=-15,294.97

As with the built-in AMRT, you may change #P between groups or use `AMRT` to start over completely.

Discussion

Here's a little more detail about the calculations in these formulas.

A mortgage rate, as used in the U.S., is the nominal annualized rate that you must divide by the number of payments per year (PMTS/YR) to get the actual Defined Interest Rate (D.I.R.). Thus, a U.S. mortgage rate and the HP 17Bɪɪ's I%YR are directly equivalent.

Not so for Canada. On most* Canadian mortgages, the rate actually used (the D.I.R.) is the rate which, when compounded over a year's worth of payment periods (D.I.P.'s), produces the same *effective* yield as the rate appearing on the mortgage document would produce when compounded *not more than twice per year.*

That calls for a little thought....

As you saw in the interest conversion (ICNV) discussion on pages 118-119, an effective yield is higher than a nominal annualized rate whenever the interest compounds more often than once per year. And the more often it compounds, the bigger this difference becomes.

But when competing for borrowers, a lender wants to put his rates in the best possible light. So, for example, if he's allowed to quote a 10.5% nominal rate alongside the effective yield of 11.02%, he'll probably want to emphasize the nominal rate. The lower number is simply more attractive to the loan shopper.

---

*If the mortgage payments are for interest only or if the mortgage is placed outside of Canadian territory, a Canadian lender may not be required to use the Canadian convention.

Well, the Canadian law simply puts a limit on how "approximate" the quoted nominal rate can be. The rule says that the quoted rate may not be converted into an effective yield by compounding any more than twice a year. Thus, for a 10.5% quoted nominal rate, the *effective* rate may not be any higher than 10.78%—*no matter how often the actual D.I.R. is compounded.* 10.78% is the limit on the effective yield.

But the HP 17BII needs a *nominal* rate (I%YR) to work with, since it then converts this to a D.I.R. according to U.S. assumptions. So the idea is to translate the known effective yield limit of the Canadian mortgage back into its nominal-rate equivalent under the U.S. convention. That's what these formulas do with the value of CI%YR—and you can do it "manually" with the ICNV Menu:

Canadian rate = **NOM%**

Key in ① or ②* ---> **P**

Solve for **EFF%**

Key in payments/year in actual loan ---> **P**

NOM% = U.S. rate (I%YR for TVM)

And remember that this works both ways: You can also start at the bottom—with a known U.S. mortgage rate (I%YR)—and work back up to the top to find the comparable rate for Canada.

---

*Most Canadian mortgage documents will specify semi-annual compounding for computing the effective yield, in which case the value to use here is 2. But if a Canadian mortgage happens to use annual compounding, you would use 1 for this value.

Index

"The Book Stops Here"

That's about it—the end of the Easy Course.

Of course, it doesn't mean you've seen it all. As we said at the start, this Course doesn't even pretend to cover all of the many possible uses of your machine. But now that you know the basics, learning new uses should be fairly straightforward. So explore and enjoy: get the most out of your HP 17Bɪɪ!

So, how did you like this book? Do you find yourself wishing we had covered other things? More of the same things? Or did you find any mistakes, typos, or other little mysteries we ought to know about (we usually have a few innocent-looking little errors—did any leap out and grab you by the lapels)?

Please let us know. Your comments are our only way of knowing if these books help or not. Besides, we like to receive mail, so drop us a note.

Grapevine Publications, Inc.
P.O. Box 2449
Corvallis, Oregon   97339-0118   U.S.A.

Anyway, thanks for going along for the ride. When all is said and done, we hope this book has said and done a lot for you—helping you and your HP 17Bɪɪ to become good business partners.

By the way, if you liked this book, there are many others that you—or someone you know—will certainly enjoy also. Here are descriptions of a couple of them:

The HP 17B Pocket Guide: Just In Case

For the Easy Course graduate, here's the perfect "carry-on" companion. Take this handy little book wherever you go. It's a ready reminder of keystrokes for common financial calculations—fast reference and convenient reminders whenever and wherever you need them. Just check the index on its back cover and flip right to the help you need *now*.

Business Solutions on Your HP Financial Calculator

This is a collection of 25 powerful and useful SOLVE formulas (see page 311 for more details on the subjects covered). Each formula applies to both the HP 17BII and HP 19BII and has a complete description of all variables, options/limitations, and a solved sample problem. So if you spend hours doing tedious, repetitive calculations, here's a real time-saver.

For more details on these books or any of our titles, check with your local bookseller or calculator/computer dealer.

For a full Grapevine catalog, write, call or fax:

Grapevine Publications, Inc.
626 N.W. 4th Street   P.O. Box 2449
Corvallis, Oregon   97339-2449   U.S.A.
Phone: 1-800-338-4331 *or* 503-754-0583
Fax: 503-754-6508

Reader Comments

We here at Grapevine like to hear feedback about our books. It helps us produce books tailored to your needs. If you have any specific comments or advice for our authors after reading this book, we'd appreciate hearing from you!

Which of our books do you have?

Comments, Advice and Suggestions:

May we use your comments as testimonials?

Your Name: Profession:

City, State:

How long have you had your calculator?

Please send Grapevine Catalogues to these persons:

Name _____

Address _____

City _____ State _____ Zip _____

Name _____

Address _____

City _____ State _____ Zip _____

ISBN		Price*
	Books for personal computers	
0-931011-28-0	**Lotus** Be Brief	$ 9.95
0-931011-29-9	A Little **DOS** Will Do You	9.95
0-931011-32-9	Concise and **WordPerfect**	9.95
0-931011-37-X	An Easy Course in Using **WordPerfect**	19.95
0-931011-38-8	An Easy Course in Using **LOTUS 1-2-3**	19.95
0-931011-40-X	An Easy Course in Using **DOS**	19.95
	Books for home electronics	
0-931011-39-6	**House-Training Your VCR:** A Help Manual for Humans	9.95
	Books for Hewlett-Packard Scientific Calculators	
0-931011-04-3	**HP-41 Statics** For Students	9.95
0-931011-15-9	Computer Science Using the **HP-41**	9.95
0-931011-16-7	An Easy Course in Using the **HP-16C**	9.95
0-931011-18-3	An Easy Course in Using the **HP-28S**	9.95
0-931011-21-3	An Easy Course in Using the **HP-27S**	9.95
0-931011-24-8	An Easy Course in Using the **HP-22S**	9.95
0-931011-25-6	**HP-28S** Software Power Tools: **Electrical Circuits**	9.95
0-931011-26-4	An Easy Course in Using the **HP-42S**	19.95
0-931011-27-2	**HP-28S** Software Power Tools: **Utilities**	9.95
0-931011-31-0	An Easy Course in Using the **HP 48**	19.95
0-931011-33-7	**HP 48** Graphics	19.95
0-931011-TBA	**HP 48** Machine Language	19.95
	Books for Hewlett-Packard financial calculators	
0-931011-08-6	An Easy Course in Using the **HP-12C**	19.95
0-931011-12-4	The **HP-12C Pocket Guide:** Just In Case	6.95
0-931011-13-2	The **HP Business Consultant (HP-18C)** Training Guide	9.95
0-931011-19-1	An Easy Course in Using the **HP 19B**II	19.95
0-931011-20-5	An Easy Course In Using the **HP 17B**II	19.95
0-931011-22-1	The **HP-19B Pocket Guide:** Just In Case	6.95
0-931011-23-X	The **HP-17B Pocket Guide:** Just In Case	6.95
0-931011-41-8	**Business Solutions** on Your HP Financial Calculator	9.95
	Books for Hewlett-Packard computers	
0-931011-34-5	**Lotus in Minutes** on the **HP 95LX**	9.95
0-931011-35-3	**The Answers You Need** for the **HP 95LX**	9.95
0-931011-42-6	**Making Connections**: Data Communications w/the **HP Palmtop**	9.95
	Books for teachers	
0-931011-14-0	**Problem-Solving Situations:** A Teacher's Resource Book	9.95

For order information, contact: **Grapevine Publications, Inc.**
626 N.W. 4th Street   P.O. Box 2449
Corvallis, Oregon   97339-2449   U.S.A.
800-338-4331 (503-754-0583)   *Fax:* 503-754-6508

*Prices shown are as of 2/6/93 and are subject to change without notice. Check with your local bookseller or electronics/computer dealer—or contact Grapevine Publications, Inc.